N. E. Davis

A History of Southern Africa

This edition prepared with the advice and assistance of Atieno Odhiambo

Longman

Longman Group Ltd
London and Harlow

Longman Kenya Ltd, PO Box 18033
Kenya Commercial Bank Building (6th Floor)
Enterprise Road, Nairobi

Longman Tanzania Ltd
PO Box 3164, Dar es Salaam

Longman Uganda Ltd
PO Box 3409, Kampala

Associated companies, branches and
representatives throughout the world

First published 1972
New edition 1978

ISBN 0 582 60349 8

Printed in Hong Kong by
Sing Cheong Printing Co Ltd

Contents

Acknowledgements

I wish to convey my thanks to Mr Eric Wyatt, former principal of Adams College and principal of the Friends' Bible Institute, Kaimosi, Kenya for making available his collection of the *Africa Digest*, numerous press cuttings and books dealing with South Africa.

I am also grateful to the headmistress of Kaimosi Girls' High School, Miss E. Mary Hooper, for her encouragement and to Mrs Theo Dearing for her careful typing of the manuscript. Lastly, I would like to thank Longman representatives in both Nairobi and Harlow for their sympathetic and valuable help in the preparation of this book.

The publishers are indebted to the following for their help and permission to reproduce photographs: Africana Museum, Johannesburg for pages 8, 9, 16, 22, 23, 24, 32 left, 32 right, 35, 39, 40, 42, 49, 58, 59, 71, 83, 87, 112, 117 bottom, 119 top and 127; Anglo-American Corporation of South Africa for page 134; The Argus, Cape Town for page 55; Associated Press Photo for page 158 left; Camera Press Ltd for pages 6 top (Ian Berry), 125 (John Bulmer), 132 (Tom Blau), 137, 141 (T. R. Sharpe), 142 top (John Seymour), 142 bottom (Anthony Howarth), 143 (Marion Kaplan), 144, 150 (William Raynor), 159 (A. Bailey), 161, 168 (Geoff Dalglish), 171 (Geoff Dalglish), 172 (Jane Bown), 173 (D. A. Sawa) and 190; Cape Archives for pages 119 bottom and 120; Gerald Cubitt for pages 2, 4, 133 and 153; Mary Evans Picture Library for pages 11, 37, 51 top, 73, 84 and 95; William Fehr Collection, Cape Town for page 34; Geoslides for page 148; John Hillelson Agency for pages 160 and 162; International Defence and Aid Fund for page 184; Keystone Press Agency Ltd for page 129; Mansell Collection for pages 5, 6 bottom, 20, 26, 36, 38, 46, 51 bottom, 66, 70, 77, 81 and 116; Popperfoto for pages 158 right, 163 and 191; Radio Times Hulton Picture Library for pages 14, 21, 27, 61, 85, 86, 88, 89, 90, 98, 100, 124, 128 and 139; SWAPO for pages 181 and 183; United Press International (UK) Ltd for page 164; USPG for page 147.

The publishers regret that they have been unable to trace the copyright owners of the following photographs, and would like to apologise for any infringement of copyright caused: 99, 103, 106, 117 top, 136 and 189.

The cover photograph was kindly supplied by Hamlyn Group Ltd.

List of maps and diagrams

1 Geographical introduction

Boundaries of the area

Southern Africa, as far as this book is concerned, includes the Republic of South Africa; the former High Commission Territories of Botswana, Lesotho and Swaziland; and Namibia (South-West Africa). Reference will also be made to areas north of the Limpopo such as Zimbabwe (Rhodesia),

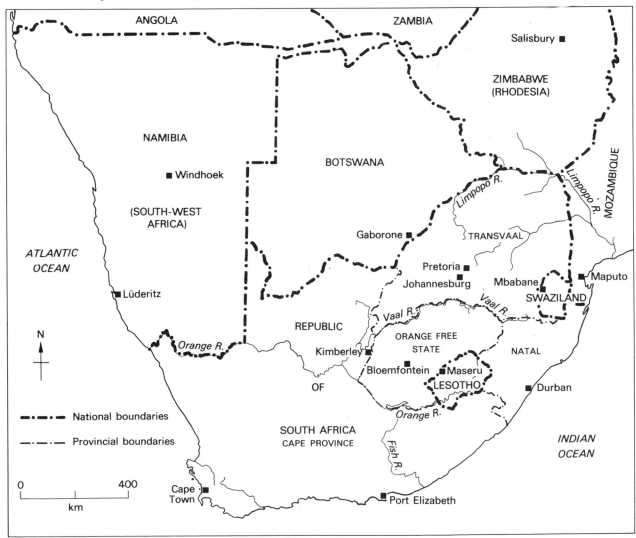

Fig. 1 Southern Africa: National boundaries and provinces (adapted from Atlas for Botswana, *2nd ed., Collins Longman Atlases, 1974)*

Zambia and the former Portuguese territories of Angola and Mozambique whose history is closely related to events and developments further south.

The geography behind the history

It is important to have some understanding of the geography of Southern Africa to appreciate fully the history of the area. The history of Southern Africa is largely concerned with the movements, meetings, rivalries and conflicts between the various peoples who have settled in the region. The physical factors of landscape, climate, soils, and the presence of valuable minerals decide to a large extent where man will settle, what food can be hunted, gathered or grown, where livestock can be grazed, and where industrial development can take place.

Two of the more important physical factors are firstly the high plateau or 'veld', reaching 4,000 metres in the Drakensberg Mountains in the east and dipping gradually to the west coast, and

secondly, the prevailing south-easterly winds blowing off the Indian Ocean. The high plateau provides a barrier to the passage of the south-easterlies. Rainfall brought on by the forced rising of the moist winds over the plateau occurs throughout the summer months near the south-east coast and the Drakensberg and Lesotho Highlands, but decreases the further west the winds travel until the parched conditions of the Kalahari and the Namib Desert are reached.

Fig. 2 indicates the close connection between the amount of rainfall and the density of population. The south-eastern part of the region (the Eastern Cape and Natal) receives a high rainfall and supports a high density of population; this means a large number of people to each square kilometre of land. This was the area which attracted the Bantu people who were practised pastoralists (sheep or cattle farmers) and cultivators. In fact before the eighteenth century this was the traditional grazing land of the Bantu. It will be seen later that it was this same area which also attracted large numbers of European settlers. There was great competition for land, which led inevitably to conflict near the Great Fish River. Today the area is mostly a mixture of

The Drakensberg Mountains, which form a barrier to the moist south-east winds and to movement eastwards from the Cape

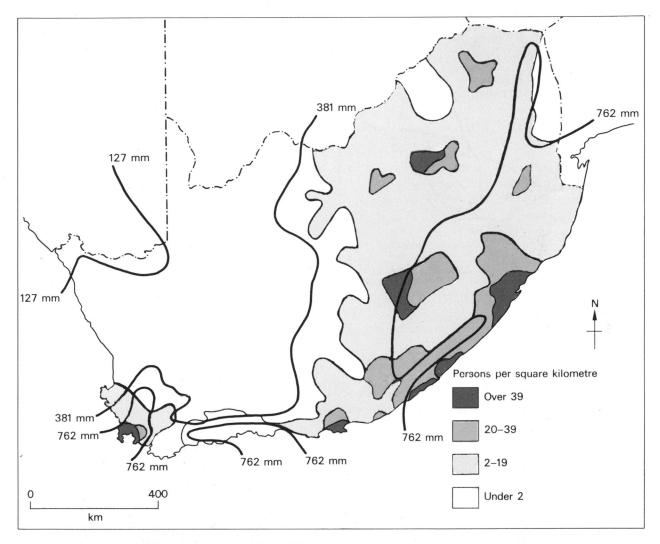

Fig. 2 *Southern Africa: Density of population and rainfall*

white-owned land and Bantu homelands such as the Transkei and Kwazulu.

The western half of Southern Africa includes the plateau areas of the Middle Veld and Windhoek as well as the deserts. The unreliable and very low rainfall of the whole area has discouraged cultivation on a large scale and has been incapable of supporting a closely settled rural population. Instead the main occupation has been pastoral farming, and it was no accident that the early Boers (farmers of Dutch descent) followed the example of the already established African people in pursuing a semi-nomadic or wandering pastoral existence.

Much of the Transvaal and the Orange Free State (two of the four modern South African provinces) is made up of the 'veld'; a series of

grassy plateaux ranging from the High Veld at 1,450 metres, through the dry Bush Veld of northern Transvaal to the well-watered foothills of the Low Veld in the east. The High Veld was an established area of Bantu settlement before the coming of the European and it became a focal point of European settlement in the mid-nineteenth century. A settlement pattern based on a pastoral economy remained largely unchanged until the second half of the nineteenth century when valuable diamond and gold fields were discovered. These discoveries heralded the beginning of large permanent town settlements such as Kimberley and Johannesberg. Although accepted as one of the country's leading agricultural areas only 12 per cent of the land is cultivated because of the problems of

3

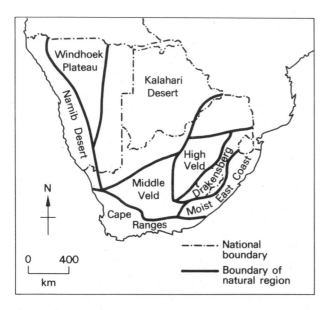

Fig. 3 Southern Africa: Natural regions

periences a climate typical of Mediterranean areas with warm, wet winters and hot, dry summers. It falls under the influence of the moist westerly winds which bring rain in winter. Cape Town is the site of one of the few good harbours in the country. The area around Cape Town (from being formerly inhabited by nomadic pastoralists) has become well-known for its fruit, wheat and merino sheep. It is no coincidence that the Cape encouraged the earliest European settlement since the climate of the Cape was not too unlike the climate which the settlers had left behind in Europe.

unreliable rainfall, soil erosion and destructive thunderstorms.

The Western Cape is the one remaining area of high population density. The Cape region ex-

The people of South Africa

One of the features of South Africa which makes it an immensely interesting and rewarding region to study is the great variety of people leading very different kinds of lives. South Africa has been a point of contact between people of at least three different racial groups, African, European and Asian. A closer look at the racial proportions of

Spring Bok in the Kalahari Desert

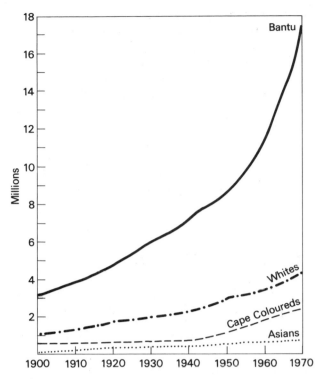

Fig. 4.1 South Africa: Graph illustrating the growth of population by racial groups, 1900–70

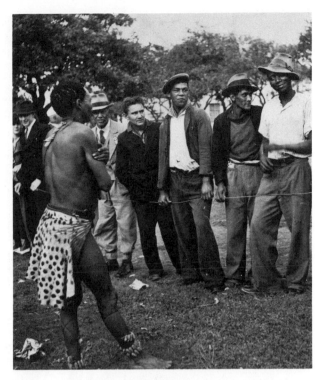

Cape Coloureds, men of mixed blood, identify with Black South Africa today

South Africa's population as shown in Fig. 4.1 indicates still further the great difference between South Africa and the rest of the African continent.

By far the largest group is the Bantu which provides about 70 per cent of the total population. As time goes on, it is predicted that the Bantu share of the total population will increase still further. From being mainly mixed farmers until the end of the nineteenth century, more and more Bantu have moved into the towns, and about half of the Bantu people live and work in the industrial urban areas today.

The second largest group is the European. They number some four million and are the largest concentration of European people in Africa. The group is divided into two: 60 per cent of them are Afrikaners, people of Dutch descent, who first settled in the Cape in 1652. Another name used to describe the Afrikaner is 'Boer' which should be used more strictly to refer to an Afrikaner farmer. The other major European group is English-speaking and has been associated with South Africa since the beginning of the nineteenth century.

Thirdly, there are about one and a half million people of mixed racial origin living in the Republic

today. They are called Cape Coloureds. Nearly all of them live in Cape Province and they are descended from Europeans, Bantu, slaves, sailors and Khoisan people.

The Asian population, although numbering less than a million, is important since nearly all of them live in Natal. They came to South Africa in the

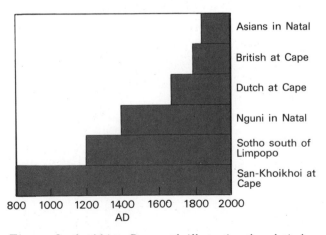

Fig. 4.2 South Africa: Bar graph illustrating the relatively recent occupation by Europeans, compared with the non-white population

The Asian population began to arrive in the late nineteenth century and is mainly concentrated in the Durban area

second half of the nineteenth century in response to a demand for plantation labour in Natal. Today a small proportion are traders but many live at a level no better than the poorer Africans in the towns.

A San hunter

Remnants of two other African peoples can be found in and near the western deserts. They are the San (Bushmen) and the Khoikhoi (Hottentot). The Khoisan people settled the Cape area before the Europeans came but suffered from contact with both Bantu and European until they were driven towards arid and semi-arid areas to the north-west. The San still live in the Kalahari in much reduced numbers but there are few pure-blooded Khoikhoi left.

Underlying themes in South African history

The history of Southern Africa is a history of the movements of various groups of people, the reaction of one community upon another and the story of how the different groups either accepted or were forced to accept change. In almost every case the group tried to maintain its traditional way of life. The San fought desperately for the survival of their nomadic existence; Moshesh, leader of the Basuto exemplifies the struggle of the Bantu to keep their land, and the Boers in their trek away from the Cape demonstrated their burning desire to retain a way of life established over a period of two hundred years. Despite this fight for the retention of traditional practices and territory, there has always been a mixing between the different racial groups and from this exchange of **cultures*** has developed a growth of civilisation. Different ways of living, ideas of government and administration and modern scientific and technical knowledge have crossed barriers of colour and have shown that people can adopt a culture different from the one into which they are born.

The main themes of this book will be concerned with the movement of people and the effect they had on each other; the setting up of African states in the nineteenth century, and how, after the discovery of precious minerals in the interior, this African power was eclipsed by the increased power of the European communities. The different methods of African resistance to European control will be discussed against a background of European rivalries at the end of the nineteenth century. When the Act of Union was passed in 1910, South Africa entered a period of white domination reinforced in the policy of apartheid. African reactions to the policies of apartheid are given prominence through the careers of major African leaders such as Luthuli, Mandela and Sobukwe. South Africa is gradually being isolated in the modern world, especially with the emergence of an independent Black Africa. The big questions which will have to remain unanswered for the present are how long South Africa can maintain its present position of minority rule and what the effect will be for Africa if the white minority government is not overthrown in the next generation or so.

*The words in the text in bold type are explained in the Glossary at the end of the book.

Short questions on Chapter 1

(Answer, and if necessary complete, the Short and Long questions at the end of every Chapter in your exercise book.)

1 Which countries are included in Southern Africa?
2 The Cape region is famous for its .... and wheat as well as its .... Complete the sentence.
3 Find out what you can about merino sheep from other parts of the book.
4 Which two European groups settled in South Africa and when?
5 Name the four other main non-white people of South Africa apart from the Bantu.
6 Name three important African leaders against white domination in modern South Africa.

Longer questions and exercises on Chapter 1

1 Describe how geographical conditions (landscape, climate, minerals) have influenced where people live in Southern Africa.
2 Using the figures provided below, produce a bar graph to illustrate the population of South Africa by races:

African	18,000,000
Europeans	4,000,000
Coloureds	2,300,000
Asians	700,000

3 Using the graph that you have drawn for question 2 and the 'growth of population' graph shown on page 5 (Fig. 4.2), answer the following questions.
  a) What fraction of the total population is:
    i) the European population;
    ii) the African population.
  b) What is the most significant trend to be seen in the graph showing the growth of population in South Africa?

2 The early history of the region

Early evidence of life

The full history of Southern Africa, before the Europeans came is not yet known. Digging into the earth, at the few **archaeological sites** in the region, has revealed that during the Later Stone Age there were separate groups of people who had different ways of life. This theory seems to be true because there are at least four different kinds of languages amongst the San.

We can learn a lot from the rock paintings in the caves in Southern Africa. There are many rock paintings and many engravings (these are drawings scratched onto the walls of the caves). But there are not many domestic animals in the drawings, animals such as cows or sheep. This sort of art was at its height in the fourteenth century. This may mean that domestic animals were only kept from the fifteenth century by the Khoikhoi, who by that time had made contact with the cattle-owning Bantu. There are more sheep than cows in the rock paintings so they may have been domesticated first. We know that sheep existed in a village to the north of the Limpopo by the end of the second century.

Radio-carbon methods can help to tell us the age of some of the things found at these archaeological sites. Dating of the Mapungubwe and Bambandyanalo and Uitkomst sites in the Transvaal show that there were widespread Iron Age settlements by the eleventh century. The exact development and progression in time – the chronological history – of the Bantu-speaking people of Southern Africa before the seventeenth and eighteenth centuries is not completely known. But we can piece together the histories of the major groups such as the Nguni and the Sotho. We know this history from oral traditions, records kept at the time, studies of how their language developed and from archaeological research.

Rock paintings such as this one, 'the Rising Eland', provide evidence of early settlement and culture among the Khoisan

The San – the hunters

Distribution

The earliest inhabitants of South Africa were most likely the ancestors of the modern San. These are short, yellow or brown-skinned people with a distinctive 'click' sound in their language. The San now lead a hunting life in and around the Kalahari Desert. It would be a mistake to think of the San as having lived only in these difficult desert areas. Remains of their settlements as shown in rock paintings and engravings have been found in many parts of South Africa. They occupied the highland areas of the Brakenstein, Camdeboo, Winterberg and Drakensberg Ranges. They were found along the Orange River and to the north of it. They had settled the Vaal, Kei and Tugela River Valleys to the east.

Ways of life

The hunters used bows and poisoned arrows for small game. They dug pits to trap the large game (eland and springbok), who were driven into them by a series of carefully built fences. The San were, and are, accomplished trackers. They had to be, to find the path made by a wounded animal, which they followed until the poison took effect. Other sources of food included the gathering of wild berries, roots, wild honey and small creatures such as caterpillars and termites and catching fish from the rivers. The hunters did not and could not cultivate the land. They kept only dogs as domesticated animals.

These early San lived a hunting and gathering existence. They relied on the plentiful wild game in Southern Africa. They lived, as they still live, in small groups. They were nomadic by necessity. The size of most groups was about fifty but there were larger groups of about three to five hundred. If the San settled, then they lived in caves. Here important rock paintings have been found.

Initiation, marriage and the family among the hunters

It was quite common for girls of seven or eight to be married to boys of fourteen or fifteen years. Generally the boys underwent initiation, which included a test of their skill as hunters. They learnt about the application of medicines to assist them in the hunt, as well as initiation dances. After the marriage ceremony, the boy would join his wife's family for whom he was obliged to hunt. Despite the early marrying age it is doubtful if women had more than three or four children, since more children would have been too great a burden, because of the hunter's wandering life. Polygamy (one man with more than one wife) was widely practised, perhaps as a result of the big difference in the marrying ages of boys and girls.

A group of San hunters. These early inhabitants of the Cape now live in or near the Kalahari Desert

Dancing, painting and religious belief

Dancing has always been important to the hunter. The importance of the hunted animal was shown in all types of dance. The dancers imitated the hunting of eland, the scavenging of vultures and hyenas and the chasing of ostrich.

Animals were also represented in paintings on rocks, stones and ostrich egg-shells. Where caves were used as the main dwellings of a group, the name of the group was taken from the name of the animal shown on the walls of the cave. Rock paintings showed the hunted game – eland, springbok and wildebeeste – and occasionally scenes of fights between the small San armed with bows and arrows and the larger Bantu with their shields and assegais. Later pictures found in the Drakensberg Mountains showing white men and horses must have been done in the nineteenth century. It is amazing that such a people whose life was so difficult found the time to compose such intricate dances, draw such lively rock paintings and develop such important mythical stories about their lives. It does indicate how closely related their religious belief was to their various art forms. It is not possible to generalise about their religious belief but the Cape hunters spoke of a creator God (Kaggen) and the insect 'praying mantis', who represented Kaggen. The mantis was a symbol of wealth and good fortune. The new and full moons in particular, were celebrated in dance, and the hunters prayed for good fortune in the hunt.

Contact with other people

This simple hunting culture was quite satisfactory so long as there was no competition for the hunting lands. But the San were forced to retreat to the limits of their old areas by the advance of the Bantu. The Bantu came from the north and north-east during the last thousand years. The Boers came from the south-west from the seventeenth century. The San could not compete with these more advanced cultures. They were either absorbed, or they retreated. Or they were destroyed by the white settlers or the Khoikhoi from whom they were forced to steal cattle.

The white farmers held the San in contempt. They called them Bushmen and thought of them as animals. They even hunted them like animals. The San hunters were now the hunted, and despite a desperate defence of their traditional areas, thousands were killed, and many children were forced to work on the farms. Today it is only in the desert areas that the traditional way of life can survive, and even here there are no examples of recent rock paintings. The number of hunters is declining as fresh demands are made on their hunting lands. Many have been prepared to settle on farms to avoid the terrible periods of drought in the desert. Only a handful of the San live in the Republic of South Africa today. The rest, about 10–15,000, live in Botswana or Namibia.

The Khoikhoi – the herders

Distribution

Portuguese accounts of the early inhabitants of the Cape did not draw any distinction between the hunters (San) and the herders (Khoikhoi). They were both yellow-skinned and physically similar, although it is thought that the herders were somewhat taller than the hunters. The herders settled the land from the Atlantic Coast to the Buffalo Coast on the Indian Ocean and some little way inland if the coast was without fresh water. They were not found on the interior plateaux south of the Orange River. The differences between the hunters and the herders came about because of the way of life followed by the Khoikhoi.

Ways of life

The herders kept large flocks of fat-tailed sheep and herds of long-horned cattle. They were nomadic, like the hunters, as they moved in search of fresh pasture for their animals. They also relied on hunting, fishing and gathering to supplement the food supplied by their animals. Milk from their cows and ewes was very important. They usually only killed livestock for a particular celebration.

The Khoikhoi reared both sheep and cattle, but since sheep are more common in the various Khoikhoi ceremonies it is likely that they were herders of sheep before cattle. Over the years the herders trained oxen as pack animals. They were used as shields in time of war and were ridden by the herders.

A Khoikhoi village. The Khoikhoi were early nomadic herders at the Cape

A regular supply of milk provided better and more secure nourishment than the San could rely on. Consequently, the Khoikhoi lived in much larger communities than the San. A group was composed of a number of camps, each of which would be occupied by the men of one clan, descended from a common ancestor in the male line. Frequently these clans would operate independently, but it is thought that representatives of the clan would stay with the central camp of the group. The size of a group varied from 600 to 2,000, but the Saldanhars, one of the groups, were reported to number 16,000 in 1695.

Because of the much larger numbers involved, social and political organisation was more complicated amongst the Khoikhoi than amongst the San. Disputes were settled by the chief of the group together with the leaders of the clans in front of all the men of the group. There were limitations placed on the chief's authority, but it is at this point that the idea of a 'chief' begins to emerge. Amongst the Bantu people the importance of a chief was to be critical, but undoubtedly it had developed more amongst the Khoikhoi than the San. The Khoikhoi, more than the San, remembered their history and thought it was important.

The Khoikhoi, with a society based on kinship, identified much more with the large family. Many of their celebrations related to founders of the clan rather than more recent ancestors. However, the graves of the recent dead were important to them, especially in times of great trouble.

Rituals, marriage and religious beliefs

Important moments in Khoikhoi life – birth, puberty, marriage and death – were celebrated by sprinkling the person with the gall of a sacrificial animal and an aromatic herb, and the wearing of the dead animal's entrails. These rituals are similar to those practised by the Bantu-speakers.

Marriage usually took place after the initiation ceremonies performed at puberty, generally at a later date than among the San. The marriage pair stayed with the bride's parents until the birth of the first child, after which they were free to return to the man's family. Sheep were presented to the bride's parents before their return and the bride brought her own animals as presents from her family, which remained her property in the new home. She would also provide poles and mats for her new hut.

Like the San, the Khoikhoi danced at the new

and full moon and treated the mantis, the symbol of wealth and good fortune, with respect, but it is not absolutely certain that they believed in a Supreme Being. If anything, they thought of God as part of the mystery of the skies, which brought rain. Tsuigoab was worshipped as the provider of rain. He was called 'Father of our Fathers' and considered as the giver of good health. Although he was almost a Supreme Being, he was thought of as a hero and rain god only. In a predominantly dry area, it is not surprising that ritual and sacrifice to the rain was the most crucial ceremony among any Khoikhoi group.

Contact with other people

Although the San and the Khoikhoi were closely related in racial terms, they developed differently, and it was the San who frequently attached themselves to the Khoikhoi for food and protection. A Swedish traveller, Wikar, noted in 1779 that 'Every tribe that owns cattle also has a number of Bushmen (San) under its protection.'[1] Thus the Khoikhoi, because of their more secure way of life, were able to 'own' San, who assisted them in their hunting and herding. The Khoikhoi were not as successful in absorbing the white settlers when they came to the Cape in 1652. By the eighteenth century they were retreating northwards before the advancing Boers. Van Riebeeck estimated that there were about 200,000 Khoikhoi in the Cape area in 1652, but through smallpox epidemics, outbreaks of other diseases and withdrawal to the north there were scarcely 20,000 left in the Cape by 1805.

The San and Khoikhoi only prospered as long as their traditional lands were not invaded by people with better weapons. The bows, arrows and slings were no match for European guns. Superior killing power decided the issues. In the face of such an invasion the hunters and herders had the choice either to resist, to withdraw, or to be absorbed by a new group of people.

The Bantu speakers

Both the hunters and the herders suffered at the hands of the immigrant white settlers from the

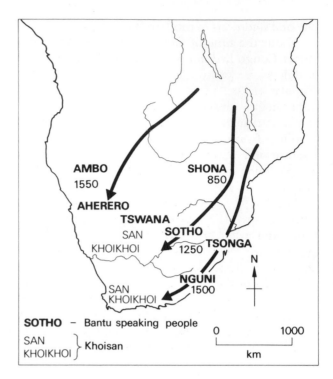

Fig. 5 The origins and expansion of the Bantu

seventeenth century onwards. But before the Europeans appeared in Southern Africa another people, the Bantu, was extending its influence over the northern and eastern parts of the region. The Bantu were more numerous and more advanced than either the San or the Khoikhoi. They were cultivators as well as herders and were well-practised in iron-making. The hunters and herders had not advanced beyond using stone implements, and the presence of Iron Age settlements in Swaziland and the Transvaal indicate that the Bantu were in those areas about a thousand years ago.

The dispersal of the Bantu people

The Bantu people are linked by a basic similarity of language, and it is thought that they originated in the western Sudanic areas of West Africa before moving to the other regions of Central, Eastern and Southern Africa. Perhaps a movement to these areas began about two thousand years ago. There is little scientific evidence at present as to how Bantu groups moved into Southern Africa, and theories rely heavily on the records of early travellers and the oral traditions of modern Bantu people.

About the time of Christ, people living in the upper Congo had improved farming methods and had developed a more stable political organisation. Population began to increase and, as a result of this expansion, there was greater pressure on the land which eventually contributed to a reduction in the fertility of the soil. Also drought, the withering of pasture and famine provided other reasons for people living in an overcrowded area to move off in search of new land.

The Bantu of Southern Africa can be divided into four major groups based on where they came from and where they eventually settled. These groups are: *the Shona*, who settled in what is now Zimbabwe (Rhodesia) and founded the Zimbabwe culture from the ninth century; *the Sotho-Tswana*, who moved from the plateau area between Lakes Tanganyika and Nyasa, and settled to the north of the point at which the Orange and Vaal Rivers meet. It is thought that the Sotho were in the eastern part of their present areas as early as the thirteenth century. *The Nguni-Tsonga* people took a more easterly route south of the Great Lakes, travelling from the Low Veld into Natal and the Eastern Cape. By the sixteenth century they were living along the Natal coastal plain, and by the eighteenth century there were distinct ethnic associations formed from parent groups; examples of such peoples being Xhosa, Thembu, Pondo, Zulu, Mthethwa, Ngwane and Swazi. Separate language development among the Nguni, the Sotho and the lesser groups – the Tsonga and the Venda – could only have occurred if each group was separated from the others for some considerable time. There has been a great deal of interaction between the language groups over the last two or three hundred years. This suggests that for the Nguni to develop their separate cultural identity they must have been established in their present areas by the fifteenth century. The last group is *the Aherero-Ambo*. These people left the south-eastern part of the Congo Basin in about the sixteenth century, and moved into Namibia (South-West Africa). The Ambo reached what is now Amboland, where an average rainfall of 500 millimetres allowed a precarious existence based on subsistence agriculture and pastoralism. The Herero moved west of Amboland, through the Kaokoveld, and southwards into the dry grasslands of the Namibian Plateau. Today the Bantu are the most widespread of all people in Southern Africa and by far the most numerous. To understand why this is so it is necessary to look more closely at their traditional way of life.

Ways of life

We have seen how the Khoikhoi had a more secure food supply than the San because of their herding of cattle. This led eventually to a growth in population and a more complicated social order. The Bantu not only herded cattle but also grew cultivated crops such as millet, beans and yams. This mixed economy of agriculture and pastoralism provided a more stable, a richer and more varied diet, which enabled the Bantu population to grow more rapidly than that of the San or the Khoikhoi.

This growth in the Bantu population led to a demand for more land, and eventually territorial expansion had to be at the expense of the hunters and herders. The Bantu had another big advantage over the San and the Khoikhoi when it came to competition for land. They were iron-workers, and

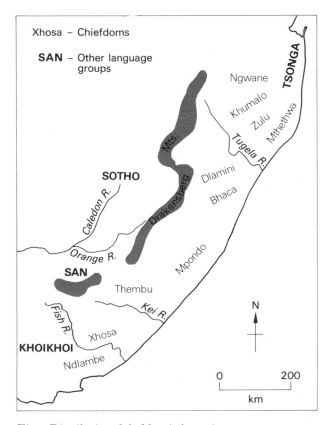

Fig. 6 Distribution of the Nguni about 1800

Zulu women outside a kraal

their iron weapons and tools gave them a strong advantage in any struggle with the San and Khoikhoi, who had to rely on stone weapons and bows and arrows.

At this point it is necessary to consider the political and social development among two of the Bantu groups: *the Nguni*, living in the fertile lands between the Drakensberg and the Indian Ocean, and *the Sotho-Tswana*, living on the drier, interior plateaux stretching from the Drakensberg to the Kalahari.

The Nguni

The Nguni are a group who speak the same language and settled the land from the Fish River in the south to Kosi Bay in the north. There are many dialects of this language, which change from one end of the territory to the other. In 1965 there were more than 7 million Nguni in Southern Africa, mostly in the Republic, but a sizeable number in Swaziland and Zimbabwe, as follows:

Xhosa in the Republic	3,044,000
Zulu in the Republic	2,867,000
Swazi in the Republic	334,000
Ndebele in the Republic	294,000
Swazi in Swaziland	229,000
Ndebele in Zimbabwe	400,000

Distribution

The early Portuguese voyages at the end of the fifteenth century contributed little to our knowledge of the inhabitants of south-eastern Africa. The first valuable recorded account of the country was made in 1552 by the survivors of the shipwrecked *Sao Joao*. Travelling about 800 kilometres from Pondoland to Delagoa Bay, they found that the coastal area was only thinly populated, but that much further inland there were more villages. A fuller account was provided by the survivors of the *Santo Alberto* in 1593, when they moved inland rather than risk the unhealthy climate of the coast. The sailors of the *Nossa Sanhore de Belem*, wrecked in 1635 on the coast near the Mthatha River, found Xhosa living in much the same conditions as they were two hundred years later. In 1593 it was observed that the Transkei was already occupied by cattle-owning people speaking a language which did not have the clicks of the Khoikhoi. So we can see that by then, the Nguni people were living in an area from Zululand in the north to at least as far south as the Mthatha River in Xhosa territory.

Contacts with other groups

There are distinct cultural links between the Sotho, the Venda and the Tsonga. But (except where Nguni groups have withdrawn from south of the Drakensberg) there has been little cultural mixing between the Nguni and the groups to the north. Two bands of Ndebele established themselves in the northern Transvaal but they were able to maintain their own language, which is more typical of Xhosa or Zulu than the neighbouring Sotho dialects. The first migration probably took place in the seventeenth century and must not be confused with the exodus of Mzilikazi's Ndebele from Zululand in 1823.

Connections of language and custom between the Nguni and the Khoikhoi were much greater. The Xhosa language includes the 'click' sound of the Khoikhoi: religious customs crossed the ethnic barriers without any difficulty; the Xhosa dressed like the Khoikhoi and Xhosa chiefs often took Khoikhoi women as their principal wives. On the western margins of Nguni territory there was also mixing with the San who frequently lived side by side with the Xhosa and Thembu. In the eighteenth century there was a deterioration in the relatively friendly relationship between the San and Nguni. This was because the drier, higher savanna inhabited by the San became more attractive to the Nguni who had been driven from the well-watered forests and grasslands behind the coast.

Nguni economy

The Nguni were pastoralists and cultivators and their basic food crop until the early nineteenth century was sorghum (millet). Other important crops were beans, yams, pumpkins and calabashes, while the Dutch later introduced crops such as wheat, potatoes and peas. Metal-working was not so common among the Nguni as the Sotho, but the Zulu did smelt iron ore, and the Xhosa were able to obtain iron from their neighbours, the Thembu. The Nguni were not well known for their trading activities and little occurred on a large scale until the chieftaincy of Dingiswayo in 1795, when trade was opened up with the Portuguese at Delagoa Bay.

The Sotho

Early history

Early Sotho settlement was probably determined by the incidence of the tsetse fly and may have been limited to the area between the Limpopo, Molopo and Hart Rivers. In 1965 there were about five million Sotho-speakers, distributed as shown in the following table.[3]

Bapedi in the Republic	1,000,000
Basuto in the Republic	1,282,000
Tswana in the Republic	1,048,000
Basuto in Lesotho	638,000
Tswana in Botswana	440,000
Sotho in Barotseland	378,000

Distribution

Undoubtedly the Sotho speakers came from the north and may have been occupying Botswana by about the thirteenth or fourteenth centuries. As these people were some distance inland, contemporary records for the sixteenth and seventeenth centuries do not tell us much. The earliest useful records are those of the European missionaries of the early nineteenth century, who recorded much valuable material about the customs and traditions of the Sotho people.

Sotho economy

As with the Nguni, the Sotho were hunters, herders and cultivators. Unlike the Nguni, the Sotho were very skilled metal-workers in iron, copper and tin. In his travels through the country in 1843, David Livingstone reported a thriving

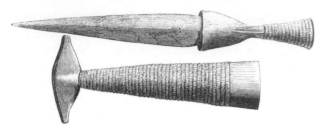

An iron dagger smelted by the Sotho

metal industry near Mabotsa, which was obviously well-established. The Sotho learnt the art from the Zisi of Lesotho. Although smelting was practised from the eighth century it was not distributed throughout the Sotho areas until the sixteenth. Most of the early Sotho settlements, such as Dithakong and Kuruman, developed along the geological outcrop of iron ore at about this time. The rock would have provided the Sotho with iron ore sufficient for their iron-making needs, both in quality and quantity. There was some trading from the Sotho areas, but there is little evidence of markets growing up, despite the amount of metal-working, carving and weaving which the Sotho practised.

Political and social systems among the Southern Bantu

The economic stability of life among the Southern Bantu led to the growth of complicated social and political systems. Society was based first of all on family relations. The smallest social unit among the Nguni was the homestead, in which a man lived with his wife and children. Kinsmen would live close at hand and the neighbouring homesteads would form a local group which recognised the leadership of the senior man. A number of local groups made up a chiefdom. Chiefdoms were generally small in size before the late eighteenth century because of the repeated breaking away from the parent body by younger princes.

Chiefdoms among the Xhosa numbered between 1,000 and 35,000. The largest Nguni grouping based entirely on common ancestors on the male side was the lineage. A number of lineages constituted a clan. Each clan claimed a common ancestor. In time, and through marriage, there

would be a group of clans with one more powerful than the others. The chief of the central clan would be recognised as chief of all the clans.

The chief and the rule of law

The chief was the recognised leader of all civil, military, judicial and religious matters affecting his people. It was important that the chief governed with the agreement of the senior members of the clan, and it was usual for the chief to consult with a small council of advisors. In matters of great importance an assembly of all the regional chiefs was called. Justice was carried out in courts presided over by the chief or the sub-chief. The chief usually employed permanent officials or indunas to assist in the governing of his people. They were expected to keep the chief informed of affairs in the clans, and at times would deputise for him. The indunas, who became very powerful, were often selected from families outside the ruling family so that they were very loyal to the ruling family and did not interfere in the royal succession.

Ownership of land

The Southern Bantu as a whole regarded the land as the property of the community. The chief decided how it was to be used. He had the power to give other people the right to use the land on a temporary basis, provided that he could recover the land at any time for his own people. This attitude to land use and ownership was to lead to great problems when the Boers began to move into Bantu areas at the end of the eighteenth century.

If separated homesteads were typical of the Nguni, larger settlements were characteristic of the Sotho people. Dithakong is recorded as having a population of between 10,000 and 15,000 people in 1801. Many settlements were founded on hilltops, like Thaba Bosiu, and many were near metal-working areas. Trade in skins, ivory and metal was less important than the normal practice of mixed farming, that is farming with both crops and livestock. The reasons for this type of settlement are not known with any certainty, but undoubtedly the defensive qualities of a hilltop site must have been of considerable importance.

The basic Sotho political unit was the chiefdom

which included a major settlement, cattle grazing areas, neighbouring villages and groups of hunters. The chieftaincy was hereditary, the title being passed from father to senior son. The different lineages occupied separate zones in the large settlement and were equivalent to the Nguni homesteads and local groups.

Initiation and age group regiments

The most important cultural ceremony among the Southern Bantu was the initiation or admittance of the young men into full membership of the clan. It was particularly important for the Sotho since the age-groups established by the circumcision ceremonies were formed into regiments with military and civil responsibilities. Normally a ceremony occurred every four to seven years and usually coincided with the son of a chief reaching puberty. All boys initiated at the same time as the son of the chief were bound to him and fought in his regiment in times of war. In this way all sons of chiefs were provided with a loyal group which eventually became his advisers, representatives, messengers as well as warriors. The age-group system cut across loyalties of kinship because brothers could not belong to the same age-group and therefore the loyalties of kinsmen would be centred on different groups. Dingiswayo, chief of the Mthethwa, adopted the Sotho method of age-group regiments when he decided that a permanent army was necessary in the unsettled conditions of the early nineteenth century.

Common ideas among the Southern Bantu

Although there were differences in language, culture and distribution between the various groups of Southern Bantu, there were ideas and practices common to all. They all recognised the social importance of kinship, the interdependence of the living and the dead, the need for a peaceful community protected by the rule of law. Pitsos, or general assemblies of the male clan members, were more typical of the Sotho than the Nguni because of the more closely-knit pattern of Sotho settle-ment. Frequently held meetings of the pitso provided a valuable check on the power of the chief and tended to prevent the possibility of despotic government.

The seeds of modern statehood can be seen in the political organisation of the Southern Bantu. It is as well to recognise them as they were largely absent in the cultures of the San and Khoikhoi. A feeling of belonging politically was not based entirely on kinship, but was related to possession of a particular piece of land, and loyalty to a particular group as symbolised by the chief. In the nineteenth century these attitudes were to be reinforced in such a way that new African nations were formed.

Summary of Chapter 2

The San
Early locations: highland areas; Orange River and north; Vaal, Kei and Tugela Rivers.
Way of life: hunters and gatherers; early polyga-mous marriage; dancing and rock painting; Kaggen and the mantis.
Contact with others: absorbed, destroyed or retreated into desert areas before the Bantu and European.

The Khoikhoi
Early locations: coastal areas from Atlantic to Buffalo Coast on Indian Ocean.
Way of life: nomadic herders; marriage after initiation; Rain God.
Structure of society: clans and groups; importance of chief.
Contact with others: San as their 'clients' or dependents; absorption by and retreat from Bantu and Boers.

The Bantu-speakers
Early distribution: Nguni: Fish River to Kosi Bay. *Sotho:* between Limpopo, Molopo and Hart Rivers.
Way of life: Nguni: herders and cultivators (cattle and millet); little iron-making. *Sotho:* herders and cultivators: skilled metal-workers.
Structure of society: Nguni: individual homesteads; the clan all claiming common ancestor; chief from central clan. *Sotho:* larger settlements; number of lineages made up a chiefdom centred on single settlement.

Rule of law: Nguni: chief – leader in all military, religious and judicial matters; consultation with small advisory council; use of indunas. *Sotho:* rule of chief limited by pitsos (council of all male members of the clan).

Short questions on Chapter 2

1. What four methods have been used to write the social history of Southern Africa before the colonial period?
2. Which parts were occupied by the San?
3. The San are ....; the Bantu are ....; the Khoikhoi are ....
4. Which animals did the Khoikhoi keep?
5. How did the political organisation of the Khoikhoi differ from that of the San?
6. What was the estimated Khoikhoi population in 1652?
7. Which crops did the Bantu grow?
8. The Sotho were skilled craftsmen in ...., ..., and ....
9. The chief of all the clans was the leader in ...., ..., and .... matters.
10. What were indunas?
11. What was the attitude of the Bantu to land ownership?
12. What were the age-group regiments?
13. What was a pitso?

Longer questions on Chapter 2

1. Describe the contrasts in their respective ways of life between the Khoisan and the Bantu people.
2. Describe and account for the distribution of African people in Southern Africa before 1800.
3. In what ways did the political and economic organisation of the Sotho differ from the Nguni?

Notes to Chapter 2

1. M. Wilson and L. Thompson, (ed.), *Oxford History of South Africa*, Vol. 1, Oxford University Press, 1969. p. 63.
2. *ibid*, p. 76.
3. *ibid*, p. 132.

3 Beginning of European interest in South Africa

There has been European settlement in Southern Africa for over 300 years. The Portuguese had started to settle parts of modern Angola and Mozambique from the fifteenth century but most European colonies dated from the 1880s, the period of the 'Scramble for Africa'. The exceptions were Algeria, Sierra Leone and the Gold Coast, which were colonised in the first half of the nineteenth century.

The growth of the Portuguese Empire

The first European to visit the southernmost part of Africa was Bartholomew Diaz in 1487, following the ideas of Prince Henry the Navigator who encouraged his subjects to make many voyages of discovery. The reasons for the voyages of the fifteenth century were firstly, to continue the crusade against the Muslims; secondly, to search for gold and ivory on the West African coast; and lastly, to seek an alternative route to the Indian Ocean. This was to enable Portugal to gain control of the spice trade. Throughout the fifteenth century this had been in the hands of the Arabs and the Italian cities of Venice and Genoa.

It was the last reason which provided the main incentive for Diaz's voyage. He erected a pillar to serve as a landmark on the desert coastline, at a place now known as Luderitz in Namibia. On his second visit to the African coast Diaz saw a much more attractive landscape with fertile grassland on which cattle grazed. A second pillar was placed at Algoa Bay, and an excited Diaz turned north, realising that he had rounded the Cape. Only a tired and disgruntled crew prevented him from making further discoveries along the coast. After finding the mouth of the Great Fish River, he turned back and returned home, having prepared the way for Vasco da Gama's historic voyage to India in 1497–9.

Throughout the sixteenth century, the Portuguese developed their empire in the Indian Ocean. The basis for Portuguese power was the control of the seas gained by her merchant shipping fleets. However, Portugal was not strong enough to withstand the challenge of the Dutch and the British who became her great rivals in the seventeenth century.

The establishment of the Dutch presence in South Africa

The Dutch gained their independence in 1572 after being ruled by the Spanish for much of the sixteenth century. The kingdoms of Portugal and Spain were united in 1580 and the Dutch began to attack the supremacy of Spain and Portugal in the Indian and Atlantic Oceans. This was partly to take revenge on the Spanish but chiefly to take over control of the spice trade from the Portuguese.

As well as being the main distributors of spices in Europe, the Dutch wanted to capture the trade from its very source to the point where it reached its final destination. To overcome fierce competition from the English, several Dutch merchants joined together to form the United Dutch East India Company and this organisation proved more powerful than any of its rivals. It is from this period, the middle of the seventeenth century, that the Dutch began to settle at the Cape.

Jan van Riebeeck, under instructions from the directors of the Dutch East India Company, arrived at the Cape with three ships in April, 1652. His

Jan van Riebeeck, leader of the first European settlement at the Cape

instructions were to erect a fort for seventy men, to build a wooden building for sick soldiers and sailors, to establish vegetable gardens for passing ships, and to treat the Khoikhoi with kindness. There was no immediate intention to colonise the Cape but merely to provide a refreshment station for the Company.

Growth of the colony

The number of people living at the Company base varied with the work undertaken by van Riebeeck but by 1662 it had reached 120 persons. The Company was always concerned with the expense of the settlement and in 1671 it was agreed to abandon Company farming on the Liesbeeck River and leave the area to the colonist farmers.

In 1676 Commissioner Verberg agreed that 'a good Dutch colony shall be planted and reared here'. Following this decision, new settlements were established beyond the Cape at Stellenbosch (1680) and de Paarl (1687). By 1685 there were about 150 white families at the settlement, 99 of them being at Stellenbosch and only 30 in Cape Town.

The colony had become self-sufficient by the end of the seventeenth century. Production was going up and as there was only a small group of people to buy goods there was a risk that prices would fall. People were also worried that the Governor, W. A. van der Stel (1699–1707), would try to control trade by hiring agents to control the meat and wine contracts. These **monopolies** were leased to **freemen settlers** to supply the company. The settlers did not allow van der Stel to do this and the company was forced by protests from the settlers to prevent any individual gaining a monopoly within the restricted market. Van der Stel was dismissed for corrupt practices, that is he was dismissed for being a dishonest Governor, who could be bribed by others to do what they wanted.

From the eighteenth century then, the settlers looked on the Company as a rather grand landlord and tax collector, from whom they could expect little in return. Even defence was organised by way of a **burgher militia**. Every freeman between 16 and 60 years had to enlist in the militia and by 1708 it numbered over 500 men.

The poor prospects for the white settlers at the Cape – very few could be described as wealthy – persuaded the Company not to encourage white immigration in the early eighteenth century, but instead to provide land in the interior for expansion. The Company also provided cheap slave labour for these colonists.

Slavery and attitudes to non-whites

Slavery was well established throughout the Dutch Empire and it was introduced at the Cape in 1657 when West Indian, and later West African, slaves were shipped in to take the place of Khoikhoi servants who would not behave as the early settlers wanted. It is in the first hundred years of the Dutch settlement that attitudes of racial superiority were firmly established. The early Boers believed that the black people of Africa were the descendants of Ham, while they were the descendants of Shem. Ham and Shem were both the sons of Noah. In the

A painting of slave traders

book of Genesis, Noah is reported as saying 'Cursed be Canaan (son of Ham), a servant of servants shall he be to his brethren.' From this interpretation of the Old Testament story there developed the idea of non-whites as a servant class. The importance of this attitude in later South African history should not be neglected for it has been used to justify and explain many illogical and extreme white policies towards the non-whites.

Settlers and land ownership

From 1705 the Company also tried to impose an annual rent for land on the colonists. The Company claimed that all land was its legal property, the ownership of which could be taken back at any time. The small return for their efforts brought many settlers almost to ruin and, disenchanted with prospects in the colony, a number left to try their luck on the interior plateaux. They led a semi-nomadic pastoral existence which always provided a reasonable living because of the constant demand

for meat, plough-oxen and other by-products like soap and butter from the Cape settlements.

The pastoral settlers found it necessary to farm extensively over a large area. Farms were often bigger than 2,500 hectares. Licences were renewed annually but the farmers felt secure because the Company seldom refused to renew a licence. The ruling that only the farmstead and not the land could be sold was generally ignored and farms remained in families for generations. The Company was too small to cope with the ever-increasing pastoral settlers and by the end of the eighteenth century many pastoral farmers were occupying large tracts of land without applying for licences or paying any rent.

The movement of settlers away from the Cape

The northward and eastward extension of the colony went on throughout the eighteenth century and by 1780 the Fish River had become the eastern

A view of Cape Town in about 1750. Note the Dutch trading vessels anchored off Cape Town with Table Mountain in the background

boundary. In 1778 the north-eastern boundary was near Colesberg, and at this time the northern borders were decided by the extreme dryness of the Namaqualand beyond the Roggeveld and Nieweveld Mountains.

Company government at the Cape

The Company governed the Cape settlement mainly in the interests of the Company and the main instrument of government was the *Council of Policy*. This Council was composed of Company officials and they were responsible for all people in the Colony, from the lowest of the slaves to the wealthiest settler. They even made the laws for the area. The settlers were not represented on this Council. They did not demand changes in this system but sometimes they protested about unfair official practices as in the case of Governor van der Stel in 1705. The officials employed to run the affairs of the colony were underpaid and as a result corrupt. This often caused discontent among the settlers. The number of officials rose considerably during the Dutch administration. In 1662 there were 120 officials, by 1732 the number had risen to 1,016. There were 1,645 officials by 1769 and 2,093 by 1794.

Company justice

If the administration had its problems, Company justice was not beyond reproach either. The *Council of Justice*, the main court of appeal, sat in Cape Town, and was appointed by the Council of Policy. This meant that in issues affecting the Company directly, Company self-interest would be upheld.

The lack of independence for the judiciary, (the people who are responsible for the carrying out of justice through the courts), was not the only unsatisfactory aspect, for these judges were not qualified people. They were largely untrained in the law and ignorant of legal procedures. The law itself included many statutes which were out of date, but which had not been withdrawn. It was no wonder that the law was not held in any high regard when the judges themselves, let alone the ordinary settlers, were unsure of what laws were being broken.

The Boer Commando–protection for the invading white settler

The defence of the colony showed clearly the contrasting interests of the Company and the settlers. The Company had been concerned about a naval invasion by an unfriendly European power and so had prepared coastal defences. Much more important to the settler was the security of the interior from Africans resisting the white invasion.

This was why the settlers formed the burgher militia. Later, commandos were formed whose function was partly military and partly as a form of public force. In time neighbouring commandos were brought together under a Veldkommandant who co-ordinated the action against the Bantu on the Eastern frontier. In simple terms, the settlers armed themselves against the Africans with whom they were competing for land.

The white community

There were about 15,000 settlers living at the Cape in 1795. The only towns were Cape Town, Stellenbosch, Swellendam and Graaf Reinet. All four looked like pioneer towns. Around Cape Town and in the town itself the settlers lived in comfortable houses. They had made some progress in agriculture. The other settlers were not so well off and were found mainly on isolated farms. They farmed and hunted for a living. There was no system of education, very few roads and because of the numerous restrictions, there was no manufacturing industry.

Cape Town in about 1800. Note the many two-storeyed buildings and the Lutheran Chapel

Swellendam in about 1808. This was a smaller, more rural settlement than the one at Cape Town. Note the Dutch Reformed Church in the background

Dutch Reformed Church

The most important single factor in the cultural life of the settlers was the Dutch Reformed Church. The doctrine of the Church, centred on the teachings of the Old Testament, was well suited to a people who were struggling to steal the birthright of the Africans, whom they regarded as either servants or slaves. The Reformed Church was able to consolidate the position since it was only after 1780 that other Protestants were allowed the freedom of worship. The Dutch Reformed Church was closely associated with the Company. It was the Company which appointed the two church deacons (leaders) and which approved the appointment of the four elders. The ministers (predikants) were accepted into Company service and appointed to specific churches.

The main ceremonies of the church-baptism and confirmation, were held in great respect by the settlers. Even the pastoral Boers travelled a long way to attend communion. In order to be confirmed, that is become a full member of the Church, the Boers needed to be able to read and the

Church provided this educational service for the settlers. Education did not extend much beyond this elementary level of reading, writing and arithmetic.

Afrikaans – a cultural bond

The settlers were concerned with survival and establishing themselves. It is no great surprise that they produced little of importance in the fields of art, music or literature. The isolation of the settlers was a factor in promoting a feeling of belonging to one community. A language based on the Dutch of the original settlers but later including words from Malay, Portuguese and Khoikhoi developed, which provided the Afrikaner people with a common bond, the forerunner of the modern Afrikaans language.

After a couple of generations at the Cape, the white settler was Africa-orientated and had broken most ties with the mother country. At this stage, the settler of Dutch origin thought of himself as an Afrikaner. By the end of the eighteenth century the white community had established itself firmly in South Africa on the condition that it could have as much land as it liked and could deal with all non-white neighbours as it wished.

Revolt at Graaf Reinet and Swellendam 1795

This independent spirit was greatest among the pastoral settlers on the edge of the colony. The settlers recognised their very vulnerable position on the Eastern Frontier and called for greater protection from the Company against the Xhosa. The Company had neither the resources nor the desire to wage an all-out war against the Bantu. It was in South Africa to make money not to defend the settlers. In 1795 the districts of Graaf Reinet and Swellendam demonstrated their impatience with the Company by declaring their own independence as republics. The main grievances which brought about the revolt were a discontent with the official policy regarding Africans, a dissatisfaction with the trading restrictions and the lack of protection to which they thought they were entitled.

This decision to separate themselves from the Company was the first of similar moves that were to take place in the nineteenth century. These attempts to break away were caused by the settlers' dislike of any kind of authority outside their own rather **puritanical** community. They disliked interference in practices such as the keeping of slaves. In fact they disliked any authority that would restrain them from unlimited exploitation of the Africans.

Relations between the Dutch and various African groups

The precarious hunting life of the San made them most vulnerable to competition from rival groups such as the Khoikhoi, the Bantu and the Dutch. As the land became more densely populated, as the

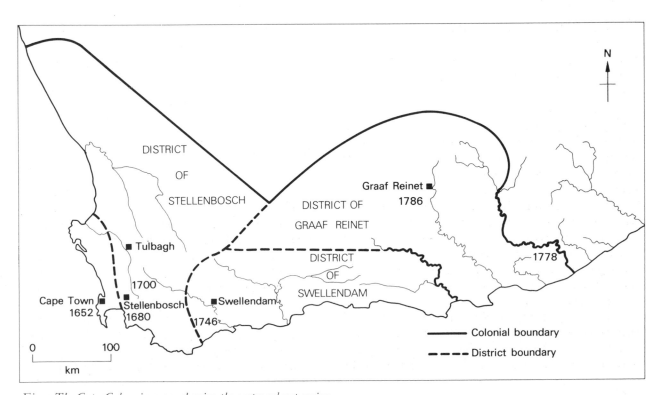

Fig. 7 The Cape Colony in 1795, showing the eastward expansion

Dutch farmers moved further away from the Cape, often driving the Khoikhoi northwards and eastwards, so the San were driven to more isolated and upland areas where they made desperate and heroic attempts at survival. This resistance normally took the form of cattle-raiding when game became scarce. These raids occurred at regular intervals during the first half of the eighteenth century but were always met by ruthless Boer retaliation. The Boers had no respect for the San, treated them as animals and hunted them down as such. San captured by the Boers, usually women and children, entered a life of slavery. Survivors of these manhunts withdrew to the desert margins to the north and the Drakensberg Mountains to the northeast, but even here they were not secure from the indiscriminate shooting of the Trek-Boers. Even as late as 1870 there are reports of San being trapped and shot in their cave homes in the Drakensberg.

The Khoikhoi were affected in a number of ways from contact with the Dutch. Of major importance was the loss of traditional grazing land to Boer settlers. The Khoikhoi were forced into stock-raiding as a means of revenge for the loss of their grazing land, but were compelled to accept the change in land ownership by the strength of Boer arms. Many of the Khoikhoi entered into service on Boer farms or became migrant labourers. Other Khoikhoi near the Cape were tempted to part with their cattle to Dutch traders in exchange for beads, tobacco and alcohol. In time as a result of their poverty they became dependent on the Dutch.

With the loss of land and cattle, the social and political structure of the Khoikhoi was destroyed. The 'horde' broke up into smaller groups and this dispersal marked the end of a separate culture. That the Khoikhoi culture did not survive at the Cape as a separate culture was due partly to the disintegration of the hordes but also because of the ravages of smallpox epidemics. It is estimated that in 1652, the Khoikhoi population at the Cape was about 200,000 but by 1805 after the epidemics of 1713, 1735 and 1767, the population was little over 20,000.

The Khoikhoi who moved away from the Cape before the advancing Boers had adopted many of the characteristics of the Dutch settler – his dress, his religion, his pastoral way of life and often his

The best produce of the Colony being brought to Willem van der Stel in about 1700

language. In time these refugees established important settlements beyond the Cape. These refugees included the Griqua (under Adam Kok), who settled near the Orange River, and the Nama who eventually settled in Namibia.

Conflict was bound to happen as the Trek-Boers moved across the Eastern Cape towards Bantu-held land, and it was the Xhosa near the Great Fish River who bore the brunt of the early clashes with the Boers. Bantu resistance to Boer expansion and land-grabbing was to be one of the central themes of the eighteenth and nineteenth centuries. The Boers found that they were not able to overcome this resistance as easily as they had overcome San and Khoikhoi resistance.

Boer and Bantu relations on the Eastern Frontier 1779–1803

The friction between the Boers and the Bantu resulted partly from their different attitudes to land ownership. The Bantu relied on a subsistence economy. They did not fence land or lay down firm boundaries. Each group claimed a particular area and considered that land to be its own country, but there were no definite boundaries. In most groups there was a feudal system of land tenure by which the chief controlled the use of the land and did not allow private ownership. The Boers on the other hand, were supreme individualists. If they found unoccupied land which looked suitable for grazing they took it over without asking too many questions about who owned it.

Most of the Boer farmers did not live together in small villages but led fairly isolated lives on their farms. Many opportunities existed for the Bantu to go on cattle-raiding expeditions. There has been a tendency to consider cattle-stealing as an end in itself but it needs to be remembered that the differences between the Boers and Bantu were related more to land than to cattle. There is strong evidence to show that it was not a lust for colonial cattle, but a passion to defend their own land which kept up this struggle.

In the south-east the Bantu had absorbed the Koranna, the Khoikhoi and the San by the end of the eighteenth century, the earliest known clash

The exterior of a Boer home

being in 1702. There seems little doubt that before the coming of the Europeans, the Bantu were in control of the Eastern Cape and Natal. In 1816, the LMS (London Missionary Society) missionary, Joseph Williams, lived within 5 kilometres of the Great Fish River, at the 'great place' of the paramount chief, Gaika. As this would have been in the centre of his territory it is easy to imagine how big this must have been.

The First Kaffir War or War of Dispossession as the clashes between Boer and Bantu came to be known, was in 1779. Xhosa chief Rarabe crossed the Fish River and invaded neighbouring Khoikhoi villages in search of Xhosa cattle. Boer cattle were taken in the raid and although the Xhosa defeated the local Boer farmers, the Boer Commando was called out and eventually the Xhosa were driven back across the river, losing 5,000 cattle in the process. The clash was over in 1781 but not before the Xhosa had demonstrated how vulnerable to attack the isolated Boer settlements were.

The Second War of 1789–93 began with an expansion of Xhosa clans across the Fish River to settle the Zuurveld, occupied by the Boers at the time. To begin with the Boers were prevented from evicting the Xhosa by the government official, Maynier. He persuaded the government that it was the Boers' attitude which was the greatest threat and not the fact of Xhosa expansion. A severe drought in 1792–3 brought an end to the peace. Raiding and counter-raiding took place. A Boer Commando invaded Xhosa land and stole cattle. The Xhosa raided Boer land between May and August 1793 and took over 60,000 head of cattle. Maynier was unable to recover the cattle and an uneasy peace was made, more to the advantage of the Xhosa than the Boers. The Boer discontent with the government's attitude to the frontier expressed itself in the Boer revolts at Swellendam and Graaf Reinet in 1795.

The Third War took place in 1799–1803, and it coincided with an uprising against the new British authorities by Boer settlers. The Xhosa took the opportunity of a white versus white struggle to drive out the Boers from the Zuurveld. In early 1803, a great Commando was raised by the Acting British Governor to fight the Xhosa but before it could take its toll a peace was agreed in February 1803. The terms of the peace allowed the Xhosa to stay in the Zuurveld, a decision which might have

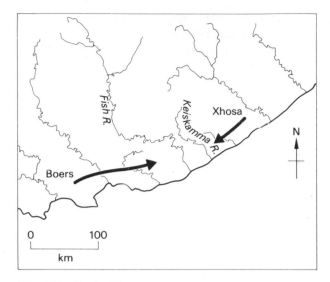

Fig. 8 The Border Wars, 1779–1846

been influenced by the fact that the British were about to hand over the Cape to the Batavian Republic anyway.

The decline of the Dutch East India Company

The fortunes of the Dutch East India Company followed very closely the fortunes of the Dutch Empire. The seventeenth century was the outstanding period for the Company's commercial enterprises, and **dividends** and **share** prices rose appreciably, shares reaching seventeen times their starting level. By the beginning of the eighteenth century, the Company began to decline in importance. The reasons for this decline were firstly, the financial centre of the western world had moved from Amsterdam to London; secondly, the expansion of the English and French East India Companies provided too much competition for the Dutch; and lastly, the main shipping lanes were now dominated by ships of the British Navy.

By 1783 the Company had paid its last dividend. In 1794 it had to announce its bankruptcy, (a position which is reached when individuals or companies cannot pay off all their debts), as it had debts of ten million pounds. The Cape had proved a considerable liability to the Company and had contributed to its eventual downfall. At its height the Company had not allowed the free development of trade and had imposed too many restrictions on the colonists. It paid its officers very low salaries and as a rule corruption was allowed to go on unchecked. Murmurs of discontent against the old order led to the revolts at Swellendam and Graaf Reinet. As the revolt broke out in Swellendam, nine British warships sailed into Table Bay in 1795.

Summary of Chapter 3

Early Dutch settlement
Organised by Dutch East India Company.

1652 Van Riebeeck's refreshment station.

1676 Commissioner Verberg agreed to a Dutch colony – expansion to Stellenbosch (1680) and De Paarl (1687).

Slavery and superior attitudes: slavery introduced 1657 – Dutch justified treatment of non-whites from the Bible – 'hewers of wood and drawers of water'.

Expansion of Colony: settlers moved to interior plateaux to escape Company rules – semi-nomadic pastoralists – large farms – little or no rent – 1780: eastern border at the Fish River.

Company government
Council of Policy: no representation for settlers; corrupt officials and discontented settlers.

Council of Justice: protected Company interests –

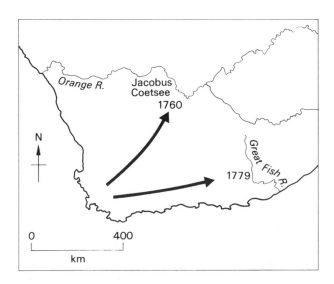

Fig. 9 Boer expansion, 1760–79

untrained lawyers; obsolete laws – no respect from settlers.

Defence: coastal defence by Company; burgher militia by the settlers.

White community
1795 15,000 settlers; comfortable living conditions only in Cape Town; pastoral farming and hunting in the interior; no education; few roads; no industry.

Dutch Reformed Church
Emphasised Old Testament and predestination; justified settler attitudes to Africans; well-established before other churches allowed after 1780; closely associated with Company; provided basic literacy for confirmation.

Afrikaans
Evolved from Dutch and local languages; provided a cultural link between isolated settler farmsteads.

1795 Revolts
Graaf Reinet and Swellendam; discontent over;
1 Company policy to Africans.
2 lack of protection.
3 Company trade restrictions.

Relations between Dutch and Africans
(a) *San:* extermination – withdrawal to deserts and margins.
(b) *Khoikhoi:* loss of land and cattle – migrant labourers – smallpox epidemics – refugee groups.
(c) *Bantu:*
    1779–81 War of Dispossession.
    1789–93 Xhosa occupation of Zuurveld – raiding across the border.
    1799–1803 Xhosa allowed to stay in Zuurveld.

Short questions on Chapter 3

1 Name two Portuguese sailors who explored the route around Southern Africa.
2 Who led the first Dutch settlement at the Cape, and when?
3 What were his four main instructions?
4 Name two settlements, other than Cape

Town, set up by the end of the seventeenth
century.

5 When was slavery introduced at the Cape?
6 On what Bible story did the Boers base their
own racial superiority?
7 How large were the Boer farms?
8 When did the Fish River become the Eastern
Frontier of the colony?
9 What was the Council of Policy?
10 What was the main church at the Cape?
11 What is 'Afrikaans'?
12 What were the three main reasons for the
revolt at Swellendam and Graaf Reinet?
13 When did the British sail into Cape Town?

Longer questions on Chapter 3

1 What were the circumstances which brought
Europe into contact with the Cape?
2 What were the reasons for the settlement of the
Cape by the Dutch East India Company?
3 Why did the settlers want to move away from the
influence of the Company?
4 How did slavery become an accepted feature of
life in the colony?
5 Explain the reasons for the decline of the Dutch
East India Company.
6 Describe the reasons for and the course of the
conflict between Boer and Bantu between 1779
and 1803.

4 Britain's interest in the Cape

Europe at the end of the eighteenth century

The French Revolution of 1789 was one of the most important political revolutions of modern times. The revolution was against bad government, the injustices of the courts, the privileges of the ruling classes and the Church. It was in favour of giving more **liberty** and **equality** to the individual. The great aims of equality, liberty and **fraternity** were not achieved immediately but the seed had been sown. Other European countries supported the French monarchy against the **Revolutionaries**. The wars against France, from 1789 to 1802, were known as the Revolutionary Wars. They were partly responsible for Britain becoming directly involved in the affairs of South Africa.

When the French invaded the Netherlands in 1793, King William V fled to Britain and asked Britain to protect the Dutch colonies. Britain was by this time an important imperial power with possessions in India, Canada, the West Indies and Australia, and was only too pleased to occupy the Cape and safeguard the sea passage to India.

The first British occupation of the Cape in 1795 was only achieved after a combined sea and land attack which was necessary to break the resistance of the Dutch Governor. The British stay at the Cape was short-lived: in 1803, the Cape was restored to the Batavian (Dutch) Republic as part of the 1802 Peace of Amiens. This treaty provided a short breathing space before the next wars with France – now led by Napoleon – and a coalition of European powers. The new series of wars have been called the Napoleonic Wars since it was Napoleon's grand design to extend French control all over Europe.

The Cape under Batavian rule

The new government at the Cape was no longer the Company but was representative of the new republic. In the short space of three years the administration, led by Governor Janssens and the Commissioner General, Jacob de Mist, had an important and lasting effect on the Cape.

They brought with them the new European ideas about liberty and equality of the individual. There was an extension of the freedom of public worship to 'all Religious associations which for the furtherance of virtue and good conduct respect a Supreme Being'[1]. The Roman Catholic Church was quick to accept this new opportunity. Education was of a very elementary kind and in 1805, de Mist produced a comprehensive plan for extending education. Although abandoned because of the

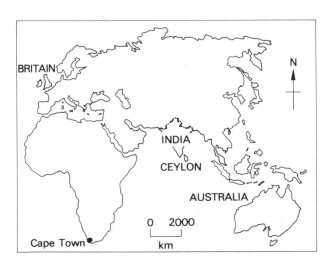

Fig. 10 Importance of the Cape to Britain in 1800. Britain needed to control the only route to India, which was around the Cape. India was a rich part of the British Empire

Jan Janssens, Governor of the Cape between 1804–06

J. A. De Mist, Commissioner General at the Cape between 1803–06

second British occupation, this plan promoted thought and discussion in the colony. By the mid-nineteenth century these ideas had been largely adopted in the Cape by the British. The Cape Church learned about the new religious ideas from Europe and became more liberal itself as a result. The same cannot be said for the churches in the interior who were suspicious of all new ideas. They retained their belief in the Calvinist teachings of the early Dutch Reformed Church.

The greatest single improvement made in the economic field was the introduction of the merino breed of sheep from Spain. The merino has the ability to withstand high temperatures and dry conditions and at the same time develop a rich, thick fleece. Later, the merino was to find its way to Australia from where it has made a world-wide impact. In South Africa in the early nineteenth century the merino made farming in the interior much easier.

The Batavian administration must not, therefore, be regarded as an extension of the old Company rule. It brought with it new ideas of freedom before the law, freedom of worship and an extension of education. These ideas were to concern later British administrations and provide points of conflict between the British and the Boer settlers.

Having said this, it must be borne in mind that these ideas were meant to apply only to white men. All white men regarded the Africans as inferior and none of these new ideas was considered to apply to them.

Second British occupation 1806

The Batavian Republic was an ally of Napoleon and consequently Britain's enemy. When war broke out in Europe between France and her European neighbours it was only a matter of time before the British re-occupied the Cape. In 1805 Britain had won a critical victory at sea at the Battle of Trafalgar, which showed her mastery of the seas. The British took over the Cape in 1806 when a fleet of sixty-one ships was met by only a token resistance from the Governor.

Britain at the beginning of the nineteenth century

To understand Britain's administration at the Cape in the first half of the nineteenth century it is as well to understand the major social and political movements within Britain at the time.

Early nineteenth century government in Britain

Despite being directly involved in the American War of Independence of 1776, Britain avoided similar political revolutions. The government of Britain in the early nineteenth century was controlled by the privileged **upper classes** who, afraid that there might be a British revolution like the French one, followed policies which were conservative, that is allowing for little change at best, and very repressive, that is introducing many laws to keep the poor people in their place, at worst. It was not until 1832 that some parliamentary reform was allowed, and then only for the wealthier **middle class**. In other words, when the British re-occupied the Cape there was no parliamentary democracy operating in Britain, the House of Commons being very unrepresentative of the mass of the people.

Social reform in Britain

If there was little change in political representation in Britain at the end of the eighteenth century, significant changes were taking place in the social and economic life of the country. Britain was the first country to industrialise and with this Industrial Revolution came many social problems: bad housing, child labour, slavery, poor working conditions – all of which could have led to a political revolution. That a revolution did not happen has been partly explained by the religious revival of the eighteenth and nineteenth centuries. It was a movement of **non-conformists**, especially the Methodists, led by the Wesley brothers, and the **evangelical reformers** of the Anglican church. The Methodists worked to help the poorer people, and the social reforms of the nineteenth century were largely the result of the influence of Methodist leaders on the political leaders of the day. The political leadership of the country was controlled by the wealthy **aristocratic** families and the religious non-conformists tried to make them help the poorer people, by introducing such things as a shorter working day.

The history of the Cape Colony in the first half of the nineteenth century was to be somewhat similar. The administration was attempting to sort out problems as it met them. It did not want to introduce changes unless they were absolutely necessary. However the missionary element in the colony was producing evidence of worsening relations between whites and non-whites and persuading the administration that certain actions, such as abolishing slavery, were essential and in line with ideas about freedom as practised in Britain.

The British at the Cape

White settlement at the Cape underwent a fundamental change after 1806. In the first 150 years of white settlement the dominant cultural influences had been Dutch. All the whites shared the same religion, language and law. Any settler who was discontented with the government packed his bags and went to the interior where there was greater independence and fewer restrictions. By the time the British arrived, the Colony included a large proportion of settlers who were opposed to the existing administration. This attitude was reinforced by confrontations with a new administration which was obviously foreign, spoke and imposed a foreign language, and which also did not agree with the main ideas and practices of the law and religion of the settlers. After 1806 the history of South Africa became closely related to the conflict between the cultural values of the British and the Boers.

Making the Cape more British

British policy in the early nineteenth century was aimed at getting control over a colony of widely separated settlements away from Cape Town. The aim was to maintain peace on its frontiers and increase the economic prosperity of the colony. But there was also the desire to turn the colony into a territory which was more British. The different aspects of life which underwent change were: settlement; education; language; the press; the judiciary and the way government was carried out.

Settlement

Britain was becoming more and more urbanised by the nineteenth century and it is no surprise that the early British settlers remained in Cape Town. They established themselves in business and the professions and developed such popular activities as cricket, horse racing and hunting. By 1811 there were forty-two small retail shops in Cape Town. British settlers elsewhere in the colony were not so numerous until the influx of the 1820 settlers doubled the British population. These settlers were better educated than most British people at the time, and so were well aware of their rights and were prepared to appeal to powerful groups in Britain if they found themselves in total opposition to the policies of the government.

Education

An obvious way to anglicise the colony was to introduce English as the language used in education. By the 1812 Proclamation there were incentives for anyone prepared to teach in English in the country districts. Public schools with instruction in English were set up at Graaf Reinet, George, Stellenbosch, Tulbagh and Caledon in 1822. Many of the schools in the rural areas failed because the course of study was considered unsuitable and irrelevant to the needs of the country children. Added to this was the hostility of the Boers to any imposed language.

Language

As well as encouraging the teaching of English in schools, by 1827 the administration had decided that English was to be the only official language. This starting date was postponed for a year to coincide with the Charter of Justice of 1828.

The 1820 British settlers landing at Algoa Bay

Grieg's printing shop. Note the Dutch Reformed Church in the background

Although strictly enforced in the courts, documents, such as acts, proclamations and ordinances or official orders, continued to be printed in Dutch as well as English. By 1853 English was the only language used in the Cape Parliament.

The press

The freeing of the press from censorship (the practice of suppressing what is considered harmful), was a right that the administration were forced to give because of the efforts of two British settlers, Pringle, and Fairbairn. They applied to start a newspaper in 1828. Their application was refused by the Governor, Lord Charles Somerset, who eventually had to admit that newspapers were allowed but not magazines. The *South African Commercial Advertiser* was printed by Greig who refused to submit it for censorship by the Governor. Greig was expelled but he appealed to influential journalists working for the London *Times*, and Somerset's decision was reversed. The agitation for freedom of the press was just one of

the factors that brought about Somerset's recall to London in 1826. Two years later freedom of the press was instituted.

Judiciary

To bring the Cape Colony into line with the rest of the British Empire, the British legal system was adopted. Circuit courts were introduced in 1811, court sessions were made public in 1813, and trial by jury was established through the *Charter of Justice* in 1828. Jury service was obligatory for Boers whether English-speaking or not. Translation in the courts was frequently done by non-whites, and this undermined the Boers' feeling of superiority over them. The Charter of Justice left the Roman-Dutch civil law undisturbed but English criminal law replaced the harsher Roman-Dutch version.

Administration

From 1806 to 1825 the Governor ruled the Colony and his only superior was the Colonial Secretary in

35

London. The Colonial Secretary was responsible to the British Parliament. In 1825 a Council of Advice was set up at the Cape, consisting of the Governor and four officials. It was only a short step towards a more representative form of government. The Governor could still, in emergencies, act independently of the Council. In 1834 a Legislative Council was set up for the Cape. The Council comprised the Governor, plus four senior officials and from five to seven senior citizens appointed by the Governor. It had its limitations, but no order from the Governor could be introduced without its consent. In 1836 an ordinance passed by the Legislative Council allowed for elected **municipal** councils.

While the new British administration was settling in and transforming the Cape into a British colony, there were two problems with which the Governor was constantly pre-occupied: the extension of freedom before the law for non-white people of the Cape, and the problem of the Eastern Frontier.

More freedom for the non-white people of the Cape

At the time of the second British occupation there were coloured slaves who enjoyed no civil rights, that is rights to such things as freedom and equality. There were the Khoikhoi, who although technically not slaves, were not able to refuse demands made on them by their white employers. By the end of the eighteenth century, Britain had become the centre of a more liberal approach to social reform, with people like Granville Sharpe, William Wilberforce and John Wesley paying special attention to living conditions in Britain and the British Empire. Slavery was the great international evil which aroused the conscience of many people in Britain. The power of these social reformers found expression in the Mansfield Judgement of 1772 by which slavery was made illegal in England, and in the Abolition of the Slave Trade Act, in 1807. After the passing of this Act, a movement began which aimed to improve the position of slaves. This led eventually to the abolition of slavery in the British Empire in 1834.

In the Cape Colony attempts to promote more freedom for the slaves and the Khoikhoi met with more resistance than in other parts of the Empire. Arguments pointing out the inefficiency of slave labour which had been accepted by plantation owners in the West Indies had little attraction for the South African farmer. For the Boers, slavery was of a more domestic nature, that is most slaves were servants in Boer households, and therefore the argument that slaves worked less efficiently than free men and therefore produced less was not relevant. Slavery had been part of an established social order for nearly two hundred years and the Boers resisted the change in the official attitude.

Between the Abolition of the Slave Trade Act in 1807 and the Abolition of Slavery Act in 1834 there were a number of measures passed in South Africa aimed at improving the conditions of the slaves. Lord Charles Somerset, the Governor from 1814 to 1826, was sympathetic towards the slaves from the start. In 1816 he arranged for the official registration of slaves and produced a series of regulations by which slave numbers could not be increased except by births. No person could be regarded as a slave unless he or she had been registered. A registry office was opened in each district with a Protector of Slaves as the chief official. In 1817 the Governor established a school for all Government slave children. In 1823 Lord Somerset's Proclamation included limitations on

Lord Charles Somerset, Governor of Cape Colony between 1814–26

working hours. It also allowed Christian slaves to attend church on Sundays and tried to provide protection for slaves from over-brutal treatment by slave-owners.

Despite these good intentions the goodwill necessary for the acceptance of these policies did not extend much beyond the government officials. By 1830 the officials had been persuaded by the farmers to withdraw the need for punishment records to be kept except in the area within thirty-two kilometres of Cape Town. This prevented any real check being made on the degree of brutality imposed on the slaves.

When slavery was abolished in 1834, it was agreed that the freed slaves should remain apprenticed to their masters for periods of up to six years and that compensation at the rate of about one-third of the slave's market value should be paid to the owners. This money was to be collected in London and although this was no great problem for the West Indian plantation owner, for the South African farmer it meant the engagement of an agent who frequently claimed too large a commission. The Boers were unhappy about the compensation. They felt very aggrieved that they should be penalised by a country which only shortly before had accepted slavery.

The position of the Khoikhoi was more open to local interpretation than the slave question had been. The Caledon Proclamation of 1809 tried to limit personal freedom among the Khoikhoi by encouraging them to take employment with white farmers. The Khoikhoi were obliged to carry pass certificates from one district to another when in search of work. Without the correct pass they were liable to heavy punishments. (The pass system has continued as a focal point of African anger at the white domination of the black majority in the country.) In practice the Khoikhoi were forced to live either on white farms or on mission stations. They were given some protection by the clause in the Proclamation which made the master provide board and lodging. They had the right of appeal to a court if wages were withheld.

In a letter written in 1808, Read, a member of the London Missionary Society, complained about the cruelty and injustice which Boers practised towards their servants. Many similar accusations were made until Lord Charles Somerset invited the Circuit Courts in 1812 to make a thorough investigation of all complaints. This was the famous 'Black Circuit'

The Boers executed at Slachter's Nek in 1816 became martyrs for Afrikaner nationalism

which went to the outlying districts of the colony, hearing serious cases and examining complaints made by the missionaries. In most cases the missionaries had the greatest difficulty in proving their claims, but in a few instances there was sufficient evidence to confirm their complaints. The 'Black Circuit' caused great unrest in the Colony. The missionaries were looked upon with hatred and suspicion. The fact that the administration had been prepared to follow up their complaints seemed to indicate that the government sympathised with the missionaries' position. Worst of all, the Boers resented being brought to court to face the Khoikhoi on equal terms.

Three years after the 'Black Circuit' an incident occurred known as 'Slachter's Nek'. In 1815 a police patrol went to arrest Bezuidenhout, a frontier Boer who had ignored repeated court summonses to appear on a charge of cruelty to a coloured servant. He resisted arrest and tried to raise the district to revolt but failed in the attempt. With four other men he was tried and hanged at Slachter's Nek. In the eyes of the Boers these five men became martyrs to British oppression. The

Dr John Philip

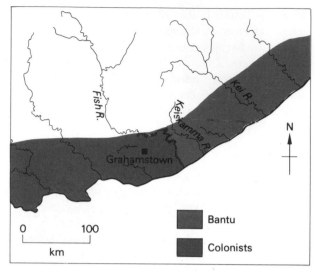

Fig. 11 Eastern Frontier: First solution, 1812–racial separation along the Fish River

incident helped to make the split between the Boers and the British even greater.

The missionaries' campaign, particularly through Dr John Philip, to abolish the pass system in the Cape achieved success when Ordinance 50 was introduced in 1828. This measure continued the process of promoting equality before the law. The farmers deeply resented the abolition of the pass system, the banning of **apprenticeships** contracted without parents' consent, and the introduction of yearly **contracts** between masters and servants. This slow movement towards a society based on equality before the law was opposed by many of the Boers. After the passing of the Abolition of Slavery Act of 1834 many of them saw their own society being gravely undermined within the Colony. They began to prepare for a move away from British control. They wanted to continue their own way of life without interference.

Like the Company before them, the British were faced with the problem of an expanding frontier being met with considerable resistance from the Africans. But the conflict was much greater in the nineteenth century than in the previous century. The first solution tried by the British to guard the frontier, was the setting up of a series of forts centred on Grahamstown. This was attempted in 1812 but only produced greater unrest among the Xhosa people some of whom had had their land

taken away. The frontier commandant had been given a free hand to deal with the unrest. In March 1812 the Ndhlambi (a Xhosa clan) had been driven across the Fish River. This was claimed to be as a punishment for cattle stealing. But the Ndhlambi said in 1811, 'This land is mine. I won it in war and intend to keep it[2].' This suggests that the reason for the attack on Boer farms was more complicated than the desire to increase the size of their cattle herds. We know that the eviction of 20,000 Ndhlambi into an area already settled by Gaika and his people created further pressure on the land to the east of the frontier.

Another cause of friction between Ndhlambi and Gaika was the recognition of the latter as paramount chief of the Xhosa by the British authorities. Gaika was considered too friendly towards the British. This attitude may have contributed to the Makanda Rising of 1819, in which Makanda, a prophet and a soldier, was joined by Ndhlambi in an armed revolt against Gaika. This spark of Xhosa nationalism led to a battle with Gaika on the Amalinde Flats (near the site of King William's Town.) When Gaika asked for government assistance Makanda's attention switched to the government barracks at Fort England. The attack on the barracks failed and Makanda was captured and imprisoned on Robben Island. He drowned while trying to escape from the island.

The Governor, Lord Charles Somerset, tried to

A frontier post on the Great Fish River in about 1822. Note the defensive position behind the stockade.

separate the races along a line. This failed. Then he tried to strengthen the frontier by clearing the land between the Fish and the Keiskamma Rivers of both settlers and Xhosa. This experimental neutral zone was bound to fail as both sides wanted the land separating them. In 1820, after Makanda's attack, 5,000 British settlers arrived to live in the Albany area. They farmed much smaller land units than their Boer neighbours and formed a loyal British community on the difficult Eastern Frontier. Although many of the farms were

abandoned a few years later, the settlers made a valuable contribution to the cultural development of the colony. They emphasised the need for freedom of the press, the extension of educational opportunities and the value of libraries to the community. They also introduced aspects of town life such as the retail trade, the growth of small service industries and the development of a variety of entertainments common to most towns in the British Isles.

To understand what the Governor, Lord Charles

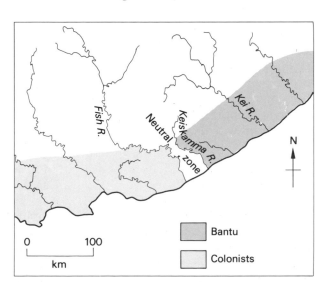

Fig. 12 Eastern Frontier: Second solution, 1819 – neutral zone between the Fish and Keiskamma Rivers

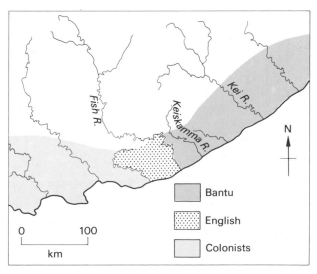

Fig. 13 Eastern Frontier: Third solution, 1820 – British settlement on small farms

39

Somerset called: 'numerous murders and extended robberies of which the Borderers so loudly complain[3],' it is necessary to enquire into the relations between the white settlers and the Bantu on the Eastern Frontier.

The neutral zone between the Fish and Keiskamma had proved unworkable and by the early 1830s Xhosa groups had been allowed to return there. They were warned that further outbreaks of 'cattle raiding' would lead to their expulsion.

Governor D'Urban and the Xhosa raid 1835

Governor D'Urban arrived in 1834 and one of his immediate aims was to set up a better frontier organisation. Dr Philip was sent to the Xhosa chiefs to prepare for the Governor to meet with them. Unfortunately, this meeting was delayed while he dealt with the abolition of slavery in the colony and the Xhosa began to feel that they had been tricked into keeping the peace. Matters were made worse by an extended drought and a small Xhosa raiding party which burst over the boundary and did damage amounting to £300,000 on Boer property.

Sir Benjamin D'Urban, Governor of Cape Colony between 1834–8

D'Urban prepared to bring land between the Kei and Keiskamma Rivers under European control in order to give the farmers compensation for their losses and to expel the Xhosa beyond the frontier. At this point, a report sent by Dr Philip to London influenced the Colonial Secretary, Lord Glenelg, to such an extent that D'Urban's plans were shelved and the land was returned to the Xhosa. It was clear that if the white settlers took the land previously occupied by the Xhosa, then conflict was inevitable. The just claims of the Xhosa had been ignored in the past and, in any event, annexation would prove very expensive. Andries Stockenstrom, Commissioner and Lieutenant General for the Eastern Frontier, 1822–33 and 1836–38, entered into treaties with the Xhosa chiefs, but this did not reduce the raiding.

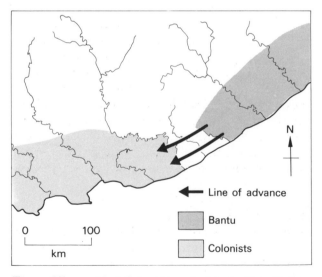

Fig. 14 *Xhosa raid on their old homeland in the Cape Colony, 1834 (adapted from Marquard,* The Story of South Africa, *Faber, 1963)*

British Kaffraria 1848

Eventually annexation took place. In 1848 the land between the Fish and Keiskamma Rivers became Victoria East, and a separate colony was created between the Keiskamma and Kei Rivers called British Kaffraria. This annexation or act of taking possession of a piece of territory, which occurred along the Eastern Frontier, resulted in the reduction of African land. It limited the chiefs' authority. It extended British control through magistrates, traders and missionaries. Before 1847 the favoured policy was to annex territory which could provide land for European settlement. After 1847, annexation involved white administration of African areas. A policy of non-interference in African affairs was followed. This land became known as the Reserves and was the area which today forms the basis of the modern Bantustan, such as the Transkei, which has been set aside by the present South African Government to give expression to the idea of separate development or apartheid (see section on the Transkei pp. 145–9).

African reaction to colonial expansion

Contact between the Xhosa and the white settlers started about 1700. Despite attempts by both the Company and the British administration to limit this interaction it took place on three levels: economic, religious and political.

Economic interaction

Some of the Xhosa traded with the settlers. They provided meat and ivory and in return received metal, beads, blankets, tobacco, guns and horses. By 1831 Grahamstown was exporting from its fair £50,000 of goods, including hides worth £27,000, and ivory worth £3,000. Those Xhosa who wished to enter the colony either to attend the fair at Grahamstown or Fort Wiltshire on the Keiskamma, or to seek employment in the colony were obliged to have written permission – a pass – from the frontier official. It was not unusual for Xhosa women to seek employment in the Eastern Cape and by 1826 refugee Mantatees (an Nguni clan) were employed as servants or herdsmen.

Religious interaction

Missionaries were usually the first white people to settle in African territory and their impact was enormous. An outline of their significance in Southern African history will be given later (see Chapter 11) but at this stage it is worth noting that the missionaries were accepted by the Africans. From contact with the missionaries modern education began. Their society was based on a settled existence, the acceptance of European values of work and a Christian education.

Political interaction

Wars of Dispossession
Trade and mission work brought about important contacts between the settlers and the Xhosa. But there was mainly hostility to the white settlers. It was inevitable that conflict would occur between the two groups of people, each competing for a limited amount of land. From 1779, when the Boers reached the Great Fish River, until midway through the nineteenth century, the Xhosa waged a series of wars known as the Kaffir Wars, or the Wars of Dispossession. There were about nine wars, an indication of the desperate struggle of the Xhosa to defend land which they considered rightfully theirs. The first three wars were in 1779, 1789 and 1803. The fourth, which involved the *Ndhlambi outbreak* was in 1812, the fifth is known as the *Makanda Rising of 1819*, and the sixth was in 1834, led by Macomo and Tyali. The seventh war broke out in 1846. Amongst the reasons for this war were the bad harvests and the plague of locusts which occurred in that year. A British force of 1,500 men tried to defeat the Xhosa chief, Sandile, but before this could be done Colonel Hare, the leader of the British, was ambushed and defeated. Although the victorious Xhosa invaded the colony they were forced back by the Governor, Sir Harry Smith. He proclaimed, after a dramatic meeting with the chiefs, that there were to be no more treaties. This was the beginning of the new British policy of annexation, or in simpler terms, direct colonialism.

Mlanjeni Rising 1850–53
Annexation did not solve all Britain's problems immediately, and the eighth war of 1850–53 was the first Xhosa attempt to rise against the new British rulers. Previously the British had been regarded as invaders. Governor Sir Harry Smith had ordered a meeting of chiefs. Sandile and most of the chiefs

41

refused to come and Sandile was deposed by the Governor as a rebel. The Xhosa were encouraged by a diviner, Mlanjeni, to sacrifice cattle to their ancestors. He claimed that he could give the Xhosa warriors immunity from the white man's bullets by turning them to water.

Having suffered the loss of their land, numerous defeats and the rejection of their religious beliefs by white missionaries, the Xhosa were prepared by this time to put their faith in their old religious traditions once more. Although the prophecy was not fulfilled and the Xhosa were heavily defeated, faith in the traditional beliefs persisted.

Xhosa cattle killings 1856–57

Mhlakaza, adviser to the Xhosa chief, Sarili, had taken on a similar role to Mlanjeni as a respected diviner. In March, 1856, one of his women diviners, Nonquase, said that all the Xhosa cattle and grain should be destroyed so that the Xhosa might purge themselves of witchcraft. She promised that all the past Xhosa heroes would be raised from the dead and that the Europeans would be swept into the sea. Most of the Xhosa believed the prophecy and obeyed Nonquase's commands. When, on the promised day in October, the dead did not rise, action was taken against the un-believers, who were blamed for the failure of the prophecy. By February 1857, the whole area was starving. During the year many Xhosa moved into the colony as labourers, some went to live among their neighbours, and it was estimated by the missionary Brownlee that about 20,000 died. Other incidents, such as the Mlanjeni War and the uprising in Zululand in 1905–6 suggest that there was nothing unique in the background of the Xhosa famine. Whatever else it may have been, it was clearly a resistance movement which hoped to drive the whites into the sea and reclaim the lost Xhosa land.

It is not true that relations between the British and the Xhosa were always hostile and warlike. In between the different frontier wars there were periods of negotiated peace. Outright war was usually a desperate measure to offset some natural calamity such as a drought or to avenge an obvious wrong. In the end the desperate position of the Xhosa can be seen in the reliance on the traditional

A painting of the Eighth Kaffir War of 1850

beliefs and a rejection of Christian values. One of the remarkable aspects of the conflict between the settlers and the Xhosa was the way both sides respected certain unspoken rules of war. Women and children were always unharmed and missionaries were equally secure. An attack was on soldiers and property, and enormous herds of cattle were stolen as well as property destroyed.

Results of military defeat

Unfortunately for the Xhosa, the final results of their courageous struggle against the colonial influence was a loss of land, military defeat, and a decline in their traditional way of life. Eventually it also led to a growing reliance on the white settler for employment in the more menial tasks on the farm, in the home, mine and factory.

The total impact of British colonialism was to destroy the economy of the Xhosa and to reduce these people to a state of poverty. It is this situation that drove the Xhosa to work for low wages and it still drives them to work in the poor conditions that exist in the factories and mines of South Africa.

Representative and responsible government at the Cape

The Legislative Council set up in 1834 during the governorship of Benjamin D'Urban was a marked improvement on the previous administrative machinery but was still not an elected assembly. It would have been surprising had there been a more directly representative body, bearing in mind that Britain itself was far from a parliamentary democracy and also that the Cape was still very dependent on Britain, economically and for security. Added to this was the very unstable situation on the Eastern Frontier.

Municipal Boards (town councils) were elected on a householder qualification (the head of each house was given the vote). There was no legal colour bar involved but only a small amount of representation was ever achieved by the non-white population. The non-whites failed to advance after the emancipation of 1834 since the householder voting qualification guaranteed white control of the town councils and subsequently the Parliament. But it is worth noting that a nominal opportunity

was available for some non-whites in the Cape. Elsewhere in South Africa there was no such opportunity.

Representative government – that is a system where the people elect their representatives but the power to actually pass laws and decrees is outside the control of the elected council – was not introduced until 1853. A House of Assembly and a Legislative Council were to be elected by adult males, irrespective of colour. The vote depended on a property qualification, which meant that men living in houses who were capable of earning £25 rent a year were given the vote. It was also given to people earning more than £50 a year. All the executive power, that is the power to pass laws, remained with the Governor, who had the authority to dissolve Parliament or to overrule decisions made by Parliament.

The demands for responsible government – where the elected representatives are responsible for the law-making in government – were not too insistent while the Governor did not overrule the opinions of the representative Parliament. Things were peaceful during Sir George Grey's term as Governor. But when tensions grew between the Governor and the elected council, the demands and petitions for responsible government increased.

Sir Philip Wodehouse, who followed Sir George Grey as Governor, although a very able administrator, was not always very tactful in his dealings with Parliament. Wodehouse left the Cape in 1870 and by this time the economy was much sounder and security was much greater. It was thought a convenient time for a change to responsible government, and in 1872 John Molteno became the first Prime Minister at the head of a cabinet which was answerable to Parliament. On all internal affairs, the Governor was obliged to accept the rulings of the elected Parliament.

In reviewing all these developments, it is important to explain why Africans did not gain access to the Assemblies and form majorities. The point is that the British, like the Boers, did not want to offer the African a chance. Africans were still regarded as inferior, and the property and income qualifications were used to prevent them from voting and being represented in government. After the destruction of their economies, few Africans could hope to meet such requirements. Colonialism had made the Africans poor, the same process now barred them from exercising their rights as citizens.

Summary of Chapter 4

A *Setting up a British Colony at the Cape*

1 *Settlement*: Britons in business, professions, retail trade; traditional British leisure activities; 1820 settlers.

2 *Education*:
1812 English imposed as the language of instruction.
1828 – only official language.

3 *The Press*: Pringle and Fairbairn;
1828 – freedom of the press.

4 *Law*:
1811 Circuit Courts;
1828 Trial by jury – translation in courts often done by non-whites.

5 *Administration*:
1825 Council of Advice.
1834 Legislative Council.
1836 Elected Municipal Councils.
1853 House of Assembly and Leg. Council – limited franchise.
1872 Responsible Government – Molteno, first P.M.

B *Extension of freedom before the law*

Position of slaves:
1807 Abolition of Slave Trade Act (in British Empire).

at the Cape
1816 Registration of Slaves.
1817 School for government slave children.
1823 Proclamation: limited working hours; allowed church attendance; some protection against brutality.
1834 Abolition of Slavery Act – freed slaves 'apprenticed' for further six years.

Position of Khoikhoi
1809 *Caledon Proclamation*: limited freedom by introducing pass system, master responsible for board and lodging.
1812 *Black Circuit*: investigation of allegations of cruelty.
1828 *Ordinance 50*: abolition of pass system; yearly contracts: no apprenticeships without parents' consent.

Although on the statute book, many of these measures were disregarded and abused by the white population.

C *The Eastern Frontier*

Conflicting attitudes to land ownership:
1 African – held in common.
2 European – a belief in private ownership.

Wars of Dispossession (Kaffir Wars)
1779–81 Xhosa raid across Fish River – eventually pushed back by Boers.
1789–93 Xhosa occupied Zuurveld across Fish River – drought '92–93: raids between Xhosa and Boers – peace agreed with Xhosa still in Zuurveld.
1811–12 British forced Ndhlambi across the Fish River.
1819 Makanda Rising.
1834–5 Xhosa raid between the Kei and Keiskamma Rivers (later Queen Adelaide Province).
1846–7 Xhosa lost the Kei River to Governor Smith.
1850–1 Mlanjeni Rising.
1856–7 Xhosa Cattle Killings (not strictly a war, more a reaction to colonial rule.)

D *African reaction to colonial rule*

Economic: increased trade: meat and ivory for metal, beads, blankets, tobacco, guns and horses – usually balanced in Europeans' favour.

Religion: emergence of literate African peasant society on mission stations; later a rejection of Christianity in favour of the more traditional beliefs.

War: Wars of Dispossession outlined above; results of military defeat: loss of land; decline of traditional life; greater reliance on white-owned farms, homes, mines and factories – general impoverishment.

Short questions on Chapter 4

1 Britain agreed to take over the Cape to protect the .... route to ....

2 When was the Cape returned to the Dutch?

3 Who were the two main officials of the last Dutch Government at the Cape?

4 When did the British take over the Cape for the second time?

5 What prevented a political revolution in Britain during the eighteenth and nineteenth centuries?

6 What elements of government by the British at the Cape underwent change after 1806?

7 Why should the Boers object to changes in education and language?

8 When was slavery abolished in the British Empire?

9 When was Lord Charles Somerset Governor of the Cape?

10 What was the Boer attitude to land ownership?

11 Which areas were included in British Kaffraria?

12 On what three levels did Africans react to the colonists at the Cape?

Longer questions on Chapter 4

1 How did the British try to make the Cape Colony more British after 1806?

2 What attempts were made to improve the position of slaves and Khoikhoi in South Africa, and how did these attempts affect the slave owners and employers of black labour?

3 Write a short paragraph on each of the following:
a) the Black Circuit.
b) Slachter's Nek.
c) Ordinance 50.
d) the Makanda Rising.
e) English settlers at Albany.

4 How did the British try to solve the disputes over land on the Eastern Frontier between the Boers and the Bantu?

5 Describe incidents which show a return to traditional religion by the Xhosa and the desperate steps taken to resist European expansion.

Notes to Chapter 4

1 M. Wilson and L. Thompson, (ed.), *Oxford History of South Africa*, Vol. 1, Oxford University Press, 1969, p. 275.

2 W. M. Macmillan, *Bantu, Boer and Briton*, Oxford University Press, 1946, p. 26.

3 A. K. Millar, *Plantagenet in South Africa*, Oxford University Press, 1964, p. 93.

5 The Afrikaner Exodus

The Great Trek

The expansion of European settlements at the Cape continued during the early part of the nineteenth century. The Boers were as dissatisfied with the British authority as they had been with the Company. They moved as far away as possible from the control of the colonial administration. The Trek Boers were those that had become semi-nomadic pastoralists requiring large areas of land. They often abandoned land when it became too uneconomic to farm. As a group, the Boers were much more puritanical than their fellow settlers at Cape Town. They thought of themselves in South Africa as being the 'chosen people'. They argued that since they were God's Chosen then undoubtedly the non-white population was inferior and suitable only to do the lowest work as servants and labourers for the Boers.

Small groups of Boers had made independent decisions to move but in 1835 there was a mass exodus from the Cape. To understand why so many settlers moved out at much the same time one has to look at the changing conditions in the Cape in the

A painting of a trekking party moving away from the Cape with wagons, animals and servants

nineteenth century. It must be remembered that only about 20 per cent of settlers of Dutch descent left the colony, the other 80 per cent remaining reasonably contented there.

The major British changes which the Boers could not support were the greater equality before the law and the revolution in the practice of land ownership. From 1825 the administration followed a more liberal and humanitarian policy towards the Khoikhoi. This change of policy was brought about as we have seen through the efforts of Dr John Philip. He was convinced of the abilities of the non-white people in the country which were not being given the opportunity to develop. As the liberal influence increased, so the Boers became more dissatisfied with the government. It was weakening their basic belief in the superiority of the European.

Increased freedom before the law

In 1812, through the Circuit Courts, the Khoikhoi were given the chance to bring about complaints and disputes with their employers to court. This put the servant on an equal footing with his master. The incident of 'Slachter's Nek' in 1815 created resentment among the Boers. They could not respect a law which allowed servants to accuse masters of mistreatment.

Reasons for the Great Trek

The *Fiftieth Ordinance of 1828* removed all restrictions on the Khoikhoi and allowed them equality before the law with the white population of the Cape. No longer were they tied to the Boer farm. They were allowed to move about without needing to produce a pass on demand. The Boers accused the British of providing no protection against the newly freed Khoikhoi. Many of the Khoikhoi left the farms and went to the towns, leaving the Boers very short of workers. The abolition of slavery in 1834 by the British Government was also resented by the Boers, who lost their slaves. They were forced to employ agents to collect compensation money in London. A whole way of life was being upset at the Cape by the British who only recently had accepted the same system themselves. Connected with the increased

freedom before the law for the non-whites was the imposition of English as the official language of the courts. Many of the Boers did not know English and were embarrassed to witness non-whites acting as court translators for their benefit. Boers were not used, and did not like, to have to be helped by non-whites in this way.

Control of land ownership

A system of land registration and rent control introduced by the Dutch East Indies Company had not been successful. This was partly because the farmers had refused to co-operate. The British insisted that land should be bought by an annual rent scheme. They said that land should be fenced and that there should be legal documents to prove ownership. Farmers were not supposed to abandon land to move to new land and all selling had to be done by auction.

War on the Eastern Frontier

Further trouble on the Eastern Frontier also contributed to the emigration of Boers from the colony. The Sixth War of Dispossession (1834) in which 1,200 Xhosa raided their old homeland, now part of the new colony, led to Governor D'Urban's decision to clear all Xhosa from the Kei-Keiskamma area and annexe it to the colony as Queen Adelaide Province. This, together with the promise of compensation for loss of property encouraged the Boers. Their optimism was short-lived for the missions opposed the annexation and eventually the Colonial Secretary in London reversed D'Urban's plans and the new province was abandoned. This made the Boers very angry. They had three choices. They could give in and accept British control. They could rebel against the British in the colony. They could leave the colony altogether. Rebellions in 1795 and 1815 had been absolute failures. They thought that another revolt would not change the British. Therefore, in 1835 group after group crossed the Orange River to escape the authority of the British. The aim of the Trek, as outlined by their leader, Piet Retief, was to establish communities organised on traditional Afrikaner lines and free from British interference.

The course of the Great Trek

The Trek began in 1835 but it is not easy to determine when it ended. The organised move from the colony went on steadily for about five years. The Boers settled in the areas of Natal, Transvaal and the Orange Free State. By 1843, when the Natal trekkers gave in to the British Crown, the first trek was over. The second trek began with the withdrawal from Natal to what is now the Orange Free State. There was also a northward movement of the trekkers into Southern Transvaal.

Why is it called 'Great'?

During the first ten years of the exodus, about 14,000 people moved away from the colony. This number on its own does not justify the description 'Great' for the migration. It cannot be said that the trekkers had to face very great danger when one compares the trek with the experiences of the

pioneers in North America. The high plains were largely uninhabited, the Bantu were armed mainly with the short assegai, and the Boers moved slowly. The reason it is called 'Great' is that it was the most important event in the history of European expansion in Southern Africa.

Before 1835 the main problem for the colonial authorities was the large area inhabited by the Boer pastoralists. They had tried to solve the frontier problem by separating the rival groups, at first with a neutral zone and then with the English settlers. All attempts had failed because the Xhosa and the Boers demanded more land. The trek into new territory had provided more land for European settlement. But this increased the administrative difficulties. From 1835 it was no longer possible to deal with the problem of the different races by separating them. By moving into the Bantu areas the Boers had made this kind of solution impossible. Now the problem was trying to govern Bantu, Boer and British together.

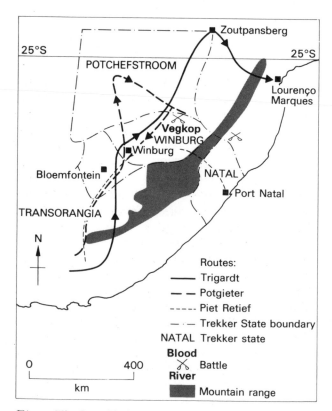

Fig. 15 The Great Trek

Trigardt's Trek

Louis Trigardt, the first of the trekkers, provided a very clear picture of what it was like to embark on such a journey. He wrote a detailed description in his diary. There were many disasters and most of the party died. In the end no settlement was founded. Although the trek was unsuccessful Trigardt's Trek must have strongly resembled other treks which followed. In the early stages of his trek, Trigardt was joined by Van Rensberg's party, which eventually struck out on its own towards the Portuguese territory at Delagoa Bay. Travelling with nine wagons, the group consisted of nineteen men, about the same number of women, nearly sixty children, and a few San servants. Progress was slow. They crossed the Caledon River and then passed over the plains of the eastern Orange Free State towards the Vaal River. They never travelled more than 8 kilometres a day. One of the greatest problems was to try and keep as much as they could of the culture they were leaving behind. Education for the children was limited to a few classes at the beginning and the end of each day. In between, they were expected to look after the cattle. The days were very busy for the men and women. The men

A painting of the Battle of Vegkop of 1836. The Boers defended their 'laager' (protective circle of wagons) against the Ndebele

had no spare time when the wagons were on the move. When they stopped, repairs to the wagons were always necessary. The hunting of wild animals provided food for the party and guns and equipment had to be maintained.

For a year, Trigardt's trekkers settled in the Zoutpansberg of the Transvaal. They built small houses, a small school, and life was altogether as good as it had been in the colony. The advantage was that they were beyond the reach of the administration. They still had 500 head of cattle and the surrounding countryside was very rich in game. As time passed, the isolation of their position began to cause grave problems. The trekkers contracted fever, their domestic animals fell sick, there was a shortage of consumer goods and food. Worst of all, there was a shortage of gunpowder. Trigardt made desperate attempts to contact Lourenço Marques for the supply of provisions. Neither of his messages met with much success, although the Governor at last sent **askaris** to lead him and his party to the coast. It took eight months to reach the coast. Of a party of over 100, only 27 survived to see Lourenço Marques (modern Maputo).

The Battle of Vegkop

The land which the Boers found beyond the colonial boundary was not completely uninhabited. Early bands of trekkers were careful to cross the Vaal far to the east to avoid the Ndebele patrols. Later groups were not so careful, and by the end of 1836 there had been fighting between the Boers and the Ndebele. Mzilikazi had destroyed early trek parties led by Liebenberg and Erasmus. Potgieter, an outstanding trek leader, considered it sensible to bring all the fifty wagons in the locality to a protected camp. This was to be the site of the Battle of Vegkop – 19 October 1836. The wagons were chained together and the gaps filled with thorn bushes. This circle of wagons was called a 'laager'. The Ndebele could not break through the laager as long as the Boers had plenty of gunpowder and there were enough men to defend all parts of the circle of wagons. Although they did not destroy the Boer laager, the Ndebele managed to drive off all the Boer sheep and cattle.

Soon after joining up with one of the early leaders, Maritz's group, it was decided that revenge should be taken on the Ndebele. A commando group led by Potgieter, sprang a surprise attack on the Ndebele kraal. This completely successful expedition captured 7,000 cattle, a number of lost wagons, and three American missionaries. A further defeat for Mzilikazi forced the Ndebele northwards and left the Orange Free State for Boer settlement.

The Battle of Blood River

In April 1837 Piet Retief was invited to become Governor of the United Laagers. These had previously been led by Maritz, the Potgieters and the Uyses. At the age of fifty-seven, Retief had much more experience than his younger colleagues, but he did not have many supporters. In his party there were nearly 2,000 people whose differences were often as many as there were family units. Retief intended to establish some form of political organisation before the trekkers finally settled. He was also enthusiastic about taking the laager to Natal. Before settling there it was thought necessary to come to an agreement with Dingane, the Zulu leader, as Natal was Zulu territory.

Retief returned from a meeting with Dingane, believing that all he had to do to have Natal was to return to Dingane cattle stolen by a neighbouring people. He accomplished this task without much difficulty. When he returned to the royal kraal there were a few days of negotiation and celebration. On 6 February 1838, a final draught of beer was being drunk by the unsuspecting Boers. But at a signal from Dingane, 'Kill the wizards', the waiting Zulu warriors killed the Afrikaners.

The killing of Retief and his party was probably the first stage in Dingane's plan to rid Natal of the growing trekker menace. The second phase of the scheme was not so successful. In mid February, the Zulu destroyed almost all the eastern Boer camps. But they did not follow up this success in the west, where the Boers forced the Zulu to withdraw. The Boers had to wait for revenge until November, when Pretorius was appointed Commandant-General. On 15 December, Pretorius and his commando band camped on the banks of the Blood River. The following day, a Sunday, the Zulu attacked. This time they were armed with a few muskets, but despite their overwhelming numbers the Zulu were defeated by the superior fire-power of the defending commandos. Pretorius moved on to the royal kraal, which he found deserted. After burying the bodies of Retief and his party, Pretorius returned to camp where the Boers rejoiced in the victory after months of uncertainty and terror. To this day, the Boers celebrate this victory annually, arguing that the land they took from the Africans was conquered through the shedding of their own blood. In March 1839 Dingane agreed to return all captured equipment and 19,000 head of cattle, and agreed not to cross the Tugela River without permission. Dingane's rule came to an end when his brother, Mpande, overthrew him. Mpande was supported by the Boers. Dingane managed to escape to Swaziland and Pretorius proclaimed Mpande, King of the Zulu.

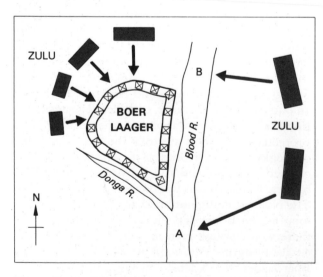

Fig. 16 Battle of Blood River, 1838. Note the good defensive site of the laager between the donga and Blood River (the river was crossable only at two points A and B)

The significance of the Great Trek

It was no longer possible for the British to control or separate Boer from Bantu. The major result of the Trek was that the interior was opened to European settlement. This led to the eventual setting-up of the Boer republics. Further political problems came from the discovery of diamonds

A laager

and gold under the new land. Southern Africa was now divided into a group of politically independent units which were to become more involved with each other towards the end of the nineteenth century. The cultural differences between the Boer and the Bantu were clearly defined as both people held fast to their own traditions. In the Cape, the Fiftieth Ordinance was generally accepted and led to more tolerant and liberal attitudes. In the Boer republics and Natal the difference between the races remained. The relationship between master and servant continued in the tradition laid down by the Afrikaners.

The Great Trek needs to be considered as part of the general expansion which had been going on in the Cape Colony from the earliest days. The major difference was that the trekker Boers were not interested in expanding the colony but rather with leaving it behind. The direction of the Trek was determined by the resistance of the Xhosa in the area of the Keiskamma River. The Boers, did not take the more favourable parts near the coast but moved to the drier areas of the Transvaal and Natal.

Andries Pretorius, leader of the Boers at the Battle of Blood River

British relations with the trekkers

Britain's first reaction to the mass exodus of the Boers was to attempt to maintain control over them without actually stopping them leaving the colony. By the Cape Punishment Act of 1836 it was declared that the trekkers were still under the control of the British Crown as far north as latitude 25°S and that the trekkers were still to be regarded as British subjects. As a result of this policy, Natal was annexed to Cape Colony in 1843.

Between 1845 and 1852, the British, through the efforts of the new Governor, Sir Harry Smith, tried to organise and govern the newly settled areas. He annexed British Kaffraria as well as the land between the Orange and the Vaal Rivers known as the Orange River Sovereignty. He found his forces thinly distributed over the area and was never strong enough to control the outbreaks of war in the new districts. By 1852, the policy of involvement gave way to a policy which hoped to save both men and money by granting some self-government to the Boer settlements. This meant giving up responsibility for the Bantu. Two important conventions (meetings at which agreements are made), took place with the Boers:

(a) *the Sand River Convention of 1852*
It was agreed that the Transvaal Boers should have self-government and a free hand in their dealings with the Bantu north of the Vaal River;

(b) *the Bloemfontein Convention of 1854*
According to the terms of this the British agreed to withdraw from the Orange River Sovereignty. After the signing of the Convention the area was renamed the Orange Free State and thereby became a Boer republic ruled by the Boers themselves.

The Boer republics after the Great Trek

Natal 1839–57

Reasons for British annexation 1843

Only four years after its optimistic beginning as a republic in 1839, Natal was annexed by the British in 1843. The eastern border of the Cape was again upset by warfare because of disorder in Natal. Annexation seemed the best way of dealing with the unrest. A secondary reason was that traders had been calling at Durban (Port Natal), establishing contacts with the Boers. Durban was now threatening to rival Cape Town as a commercial centre. Annexation seemed one way of controlling such a development. The desire to bring the Natal Boers back under British control was not a major factor in the decision to annex the territory.

Weakness of the Natal Republic

(a) *Inexperienced government*
The greatest weakness in the early years of the Republic was the inability of the Boers to establish a secure and stable form of government. They had proved to be accomplished commando fighters, but once settled they divided into a number of destructive groups with divided loyalties. After the death of Piet Retief, there was no obvious leader upon whom they could centre their respect for the Republic. Consequently, there were continuous quarrels between the Commandant-General, Pretorius, and the Volksraad (People's Council). The Volksraad made errors in policy, the greatest of which was the giving away of large units of land. On their arrival in Natal, land had been given to all trekkers over the age of fifteen. Large gifts were made to the widows of Boers killed in fighting with the Bantu. The leading officers of the Republic often had up to ten farms, each of 2,430 hectares. In this way the Republic's main asset lost its value. The amount of money which could be gained from selling or renting land was drastically reduced.

(b) *African re-settlement of Natal*
To begin with the Boers had a severe labour shortage but eventually many thousands of Bantu refugees returned to their homelands in Natal after the period of absorption by Shaka twenty years earlier. On their return they either grazed cattle as before or were forced to work for the Boers. By 1843 there were 50,000 Africans in Natal and the Boers were outnumbered seven to one. From a crisis of labour shortage, the situation had changed to one of insecurity for the Boers. Pretorius decided that the Pondo and Bhaca communities should be driven south of the Mzimvubu, a boundary agreed with Dingane. Governor Napier warned that that

kind of policy would cause racial problems on the Cape's Eastern Frontier. He said the Cape would not tolerate the action which Pretorius was considering.

Annexation by Britain

In May 1842, Captain Smith arrived at Durban with troops sent by Napier. At first he was driven back by Pretorius. Then, with support from Port Elizabeth and Cape Town, Smith forced Pretorius to accept an uneasy truce which lasted for another year. The Colonial Secretary's commissioner, Henry Cloete, began a series of discussions with the Volksraad, trying to persuade them to accept British rule. The divisions among the Boers persisted. Some were prepared to stay in a British colony, others preferred to cross the Drakensberg to the High Veld of the Transvaal. The British

annexed Natal to the Cape Colony in August 1843.

Natal becomes a British colony 1856

In the ten years after annexation, the European economic sector in Natal developed slowly. Its European population in 1856 was no more than 8,000 in a country inhabited by 150,000 Bantu. A little economic headway was made in the growing of cotton, coffee and sugar. Cotton and coffee suffered from pests, and sugar could only be considered promising if adequate labour was available. At first Natal was ruled directly from Cape Town but experience was gained in managing Natal affairs through municipal and county councils until eventually there was a growing demand to be separated from the Cape. Natal became a Crown Colony in 1856 and was administered by four officials and twelve members elected to the Council.

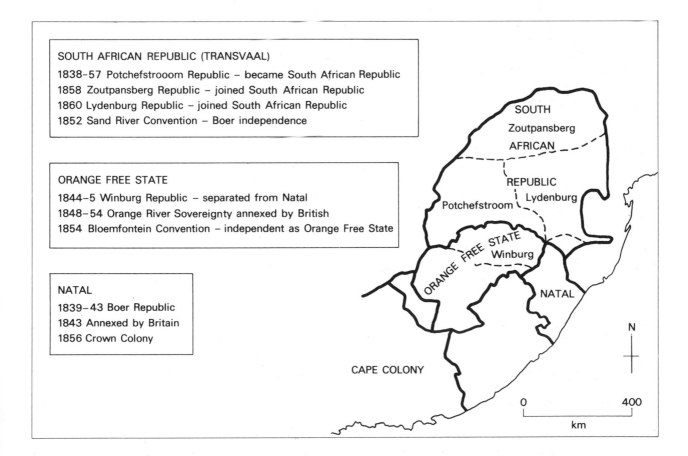

SOUTH AFRICAN REPUBLIC (TRANSVAAL)

1838-57 Potchefstrooom Republic – became South African Republic
1858 Zoutpansberg Republic – joined South African Republic
1860 Lydenburg Republic – joined South African Republic
1852 Sand River Convention – Boer independence

ORANGE FREE STATE

1844-5 Winburg Republic – separated from Natal
1848-54 Orange River Sovereignty annexed by British
1854 Bloemfontein Convention – independent as Orange Free State

NATAL

1839-43 Boer Republic
1843 Annexed by Britain
1856 Crown Colony

Fig. 17 The Boer Republics up to 1854

Orange Free State 1836–54

The movement to Boer freedom 1854

In the first ten years after the start of the Trek, the population beyond the frontier of the colony was very scattered. It followed a broken line from Philippolis round to Durban, skirting the Bantu areas of British Kaffraria and Basutoland. The thinnest part of the line was in the middle of the Orange River Sovereignty, which in 1846 was ruled by the Resident, Major Warden, with the support of a legislative council of officials and burghers. When Sir George Cathcart took over as High Commissioner in 1852, delegates from Bloemfontein demanded constitutional changes aimed at self-government for the Sovereignty.

Cathcart was already a convert to an abandonment policy. He is said to have remarked that the Sovereignty men had better be given their independence and left to it. Sir George Clark was sent out from London as a Special Commissioner to sort out the affairs of the Sovereignty. In February 1854, the Bloemfontein Convention was signed. Josias Hoffman, and a committee of six were now in control of a territory of 12,000 Europeans, isolated from the rest of the world and outnumbered twelve to one by the Basuto. A constitution was set up in which the president was to be elected for five years. Hoffman was elected the first President of the Orange Free State in September 1854.

Transvaal 1836–52

Independence for the die-hard Trekkers, 1852

To the north, the Transvaalers were separated from the Cape, not only by a greater distance than the people of the Sovereignty, but also by basic attitudes. They represented the die-hards who had trekked farthest from the Cape. There were many who had trekked a second time across the Drakensberg from Natal. They considered themselves virtually independent even before 1852. Potgieter became the first Head Commandant of the territory in 1844, but the arrival of the Natal trekkers in 1846 complicated matters. For a number of years there was a struggle for power between Potgieter and Pretorius. By January 1851, it was decided that there should be four Commandants-General, Willem Joubert, Potgieter, Pretorius, and one other to be selected by the inhabitants of Magaliesberg, who eventually chose Pretorius.

In November 1851, two Special Commissioners, Hogge and Owen, arrived to deal with the situation outside the colony. Their main conclusion was that the Transvaal was too far removed from the Cape to be controlled from there. This was accepted by the signing of the Sand River Convention of January 1852.

Economic development up to 1860

The most significant fact of the late eighteenth and nineteenth centuries was the competition for land between the Europeans and Africans. The Boers created large farms of about 2,400 hectares on land claimed by Africans as theirs. This Boer invasion created a land shortage for the African. At the same time as taking over African land, the Boers created a situation in which Africans remained on their land in a number of different ways: as squatters, as migrant farm labourers or, in the case of people who had lost all contact with their traditional way of life, as permanent farm labourers.

In spite of the differences between the British and the Boers, there was basic agreement on a policy which would secure a permanent supply of non-white labour for white farmers.

In the twenty years from 1834, the year of the Great Trek, there was an uneven development in the economies of the various parts of South Africa. There was too much insecurity on the Eastern Frontier of the Cape Colony for any sizeable advance to be made. On the other hand many African communities became relatively prosperous, especially when not under threat from European settlement. External trading in meat, hides, ivory and metals along with a reasonably efficient use of farm land produced viable economies. Most African states were capable of producing a grain surplus in readiness for a bad future harvest, and this continued until European land-grabbing, a rise in population and a 'shrink-

Merino sheep were well-suited to the dry 'veld' and brought wealth to the Cape

ing' land resulted in over-grazing, overcropping and soil erosion by the turn of the present century.

The greatest improvements in the white areas were made in the Cape Colony. Wool production rose from 70,000 kilograms in 1834 to 9 million kilograms in 1845, and by 1862, the Cape was exporting 11 million kilograms of wool a year, over half the total value of exports. Important advances had taken place in arable farming, viticulture (vine growing) and fruit farming as well. There was a large increase in white population at this time. By 1865, there were 180,000 Europeans and 310,000 non-whites at th Cape. The increase in Europeans can be attributed partly to increased immigration. In 1857, 4,000 British soldiers were settled by Sir George Grey in British Kaffraria, and in 1858–9 about 2,000 farmers from northern Germany were also settled in the same area.

The white population outside the Cape was estimated as follows:

Orange Free State	35,000
South African Republic	30,000
Natal	18,000

The Boer communities were nowhere near as prosperous as either the Cape or the African states. The trekkers settled the open veld and practised a pastoral economy which required large tracts of land for each family. They grew cereal crops only for their own consumption, and their methods of land use were both wasteful and inefficient as compared with the African peasant farmer. Natal had the smallest white population at this time. Sugar estates were introduced in the late 1850s to stabilise and encourage further settlement in the colony. Africans could not be persuaded to work on the estates so cheap Indian labour had to be imported. In time the Indian community established itself in the towns and posed a serious threat to European employment, particularly in the Durban area.

Despite the slow development in most of the country, some of the requirements for rapid expansion were evident by the 1860s. Road links with the interior were improving, and the beginnings of a rail network had been started. The first railway in South Africa was the three kilometres stretch between Durban and the Point. Communication through a penny post and telegraphic services had been established.

Summary of Chapter 5

Great Trek 1836
Movement away from British control
Grievances:
1 Land policy
2 Policy towards Africans
3 Border disputes
Purpose:
1 To establish communities beyond British control.
2 To establish communities based on Afrikaner principles.

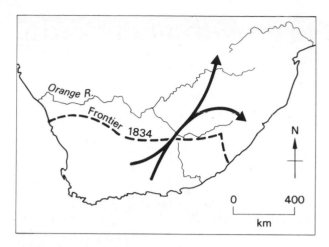

Fig. 18 Direction of the Great Trek

Directions: across the High Veld to Transvaal to Natal.

Results:

1 European settlement inland.
2 End of South African unity.
3 Separation of Boers and Bantu no longer possible.
4 Isolation of the trekkers.

Boer Republics after the Great Trek

Natal: problems of government – Zulu infiltration – potential conflict.

1843 annexed by the British.
1856 Crown Colony.

Orange Free State: Boer population scattered – ruled by Resident Warden – difficult to control. Governor Cathcart prepared to grant independence.

1854 Bloemfontein Convention.

Transvaal: furthest from Cape.

1844 Potgieter was the first leader.
1845 Natal trekkers arrived.
1852 Sand River Convention.

Early economic development

Mainly subsistence farming by both Africans and Europeans outside Cape Town where there were the beginnings of a market economy.

Reduction of African land

European annexation of African land – Africans became squatters, migrant and permanent farm labourers – government policies have always secured a permanent supply of cheap non-white labour.

Mid nineteenth century developments

Slow progress – mostly at the Cape – wool production (over half of country's exports by value).

Cape: arable, pastoral and vines.
Natal: fruit, sugar, tea.
Orange Free State: cereals and sheep.
Transvaal: pastoral.

Improving communications: roads, railways, telegraph posts.

Short questions on Chapter 5

1 When did the Great Trek begin?
2 What proportion of Afrikaners left the Cape on the Great Trek?
3 What two changes made by the British forced the Boers out of the Cape?
4 Which areas were settled by the Boers?
5 What is a 'laager'?
6 Who was Piet Retief and where did he intend to lead the United Laagers?
7 Who was the leader of the Zulu at the time of the Great Trek?
8 Who won the Battle of Blood River?
9 In the Battle of Vegkop the trekkers fought against ....
10 The Transvaal Boers were promised self-government by the .... convention of ....
11 The Orange River Sovereignty gained self-government by the .... of ...., and was then renamed the ....
12 When was Natal annexed by the British?

Longer questions on Chapter 5

1 What were the main reasons for the Great Trek?
2 What were the results of the Trek?
3 Write a short paragraph on each of the following:
   a) Lord Somerset; b) Dr John Philip; c) Piet Retief; d) Louis Trigardt; e) Battle of Vegkop; f) Battle of Blood River.
4 In what ways did the British attitude change towards the trekkers between 1836 and 1854?
5 What were the reasons for the annexation of Natal by Britain in 1843?

6 The Mfecane and the growth of the Zulu nation

Two themes dominated the first half of the nineteenth century. One was the opening up of the interior of South Africa to white settlement which had started in 1700. From 1835 this movement of white settlers into the interior took place on a much bigger scale with the Great Trek. The other major theme was the upheaval among African societies which took place during the first thirty years of the nineteenth century. This upheaval was called the Mfecane by the Nguni speakers and the Difaqane by the Sotho speakers. It led to the creation of strong African states and helped the growth of the Zulu nation in what is now Natal.

At the end of the eighteenth century the Nguni were divided into clans. A clan was a unit consisting of all those persons claiming descent from a common ancestor. There were a number of these lineages (lines of descent), including the chief's central lineage. The Nguni were cattle-keepers, for whom cattle were important for reasons of ceremony and dowry as well as providers of food and clothing. They were also cultivators, who grew millet and maize along with other crops. This mixed economy enabled larger numbers of Nguni to stay together.

The clan areas among the Nguni were usually small. For example, it is likely that there were about two hundred clans in Natal, one of which was the Zulu. We have to understand why these joined together into nations at this time, and why it was that the Zulu clan was central to this development.

Reasons for the growth of large states

Four main reasons have been suggested for the change from small political units into large multi-clan states, such as the Zulu Kingdom. Firstly, it has been suggested that a chance meeting between Dingiswayo, a member of the royal lineage of the Mthethwa clan, and a European military surgeon, gave Dingiswayo the military ideas to establish a new enlarged state. There is no evidence to support this suggestion. It may have been invented by early European historians to claim some of the credit for what happened among the Nguni.

The second possible explanation concerns the expansion of the white settlers eastwards from the Cape and the blocking of the natural line of Nguni advance to the south-west. This may have been one of the reasons. It does not explain why the expansion took place among the Zulu who were several hundred kilometres from the Colony's Eastern Frontier, and not among the Xhosa, who were directly involved in the border fighting. The third reason which has gained great support in recent years is that there was a big increase in population in the Zululand area. Being good farmland, there was greater competition for the land and this encouraged re-grouping and joining together in larger groups. This theory does not explain why the Xhosa, who also suffered from severe land shortage, did not develop in the same way. A fourth theory is that the need to join together came from the desire to control trade through Delagoa Bay. This theory may be true, as might be the population theory or any of the others, but it should be made clear that at present these are only theories.

The best that we can say is that a combination of all these factors occurred in Zululand at this time and this led to the Mfecane. We can be more certain when we deal with the exploits of people like Dingiswayo and Shaka. It is possible to recognise two distinct phases in the building up of larger political units. The first phase was from about 1800 until the death of Dingiswayo in 1817. The second

Shaka, the founder of the Zulu nation

phase involved the rise of the Zulu nation led by Shaka.

Phase one: 1800–17

Before the 1790s warfare between Nguni chiefs was little more serious than cattle-raiding. As conditions changed, warfare could often mean not only the loss of cattle, but also grazing lands and other vital economic resources. With an increased shortage of grazing land, fighting between the clans became more serious. Some of the old traditions had to be changed. Circumcision ceremonies inevitably reduced the number of young men able to fight so such traditions were abandoned. This meant that in times of need regiments could be formed from groups of men of the same age. The formation of such regiments made greater unity among the Nguni possible. During this early phase many of the clans joined together into one of three main groups: the Mthethwa Kingdom of Dingis-

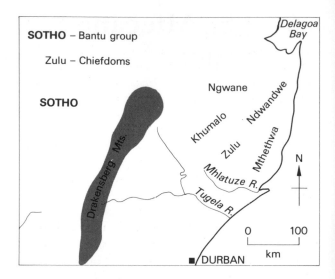

Fig. 19 Chiefdoms among the Northern Nguni

wayo; the Ngwane (later Swazi) Kingdom of Sobhuza and the Ndwandwe Kingdom of Zwide. Conflict was bound to break out between these three groups, all occupying this small part of southeast Africa. The first major struggle was between the Ndwandwe and the Swazi. After being defeated by Zwide, Sobhuza moved north-eastwards towards what is now Swaziland, where he settled and where the Swazi nation was eventually established. The fight for Zululand was then between Dingiswayo and Zwide. In the year 1817–18, Dingiswayo, while watching a battle from a hilltop, was ambushed and killed by Zwide's men. The impact of his death on the Mthethwa was so great that they fled from the Ndwandwe before being attacked.

Phase two: Shaka and the rise of the Zulu nation

His early life

The only fighting force which remained intact as a unit among the Mthethwa was led by Shaka, a young commander of Dingiswayo's. It was the underestimation of the fighting genius of this young man by the Ndwandwe which was to cause Zwide's downfall. This caused a movement of people whose effect was to be felt as far north as the equator.

Shaka's father, Senzangakona, was chief of a

minor clan called the Zulu. While still a boy and before his circumcision, he struck up a friendship with Nandi, a girl from a neighbouring clan. The birth of Shaka to Nandi was not welcomed by the Zulu elders. Although Senzangakona married Nandi, the title of 'unwanted one' remained with Shaka for much of his childhood and early manhood. Shaka was brought up among his mother's people, where he and Nandi were sent by his father after frequent displays of ferocious temper by his mother in the Zulu chief's household. Shaka's early childhood was a determined struggle for recognition despite the constant humiliation which he underwent at the hands of his age-group. In time, through his athletic prowess and great strength of personality, he succeeded in demonstrating his superiority over his fellows.

His military genius

Shaka joined Dingiswayo's regiments and soon established himself as a courageous and natural leader. He strengthened his own regiment, or impi, by introducing new military methods. He was a military genius. The main tactic used by Dingiswayo's army was to advance on the enemy and to hurl spears or assegais which might or might not pierce the enemy's defences. Shaka reasoned that instead of throwing the spear it would be used to better effect at close quarters. The efficiency of the short stabbing assegai was accepted by his own soldiers and demonstrated many times in engagements with the enemy. Tactically, Shaka favoured the pincer movement of the 'horns of the buffalo', in which the two outside edges of his regiments advanced round the flanks of the enemy, thus preventing any organised retreat from a fierce frontal attack. His soldiers fought bare-footed which, in Shaka's opinion, made them more mobile. The other major change made by Shaka (although it may have been introduced by Dingiswayo) was the idea of the standing army. This meant that his regiments stayed in military camps and therefore were always well-trained, well-disciplined and ready for any emergency. This was the most radical change. It altered the traditional customs of his people. A number of the initiation ceremonies, circumcision for example, were abandoned because they did not suit the required pattern. Age-groups were formed into regiments responsible for the protection of the clan. The traditional initiation ceremonies could not be performed without endangering the life of the clan because newly circumcised youths were not in a condition to fight in the event of war.

Zulu warriors, armed with spears

Shaka's military campaigns

Both the well-drilled efficiency of the Zulu troops and the genius of Shaka's leadership were needed to defeat the armies of Zwide. To begin with, Zwide sent a relatively small force to deal with the Shaka menace. This force was not strong enough to stand against the determined Zulu. Zwide then attacked with nearly all his armies and Shaka, not risking a battle, retreated. He destroyed crops as he went until the exhausted and starving Ndwandwe turned near the Tugela River to return to their own land. Zwide's armies were followed by Shaka on their journey northwards, and at a well chosen spot on the banks of the Mhlatuze River, the Zulu regiments attacked their half-starved opponents. The Ndwandwe fled in confusion, leaving Shaka in control of Zululand.

It was eight years before the Ndwandwe felt strong enough to challenge Shaka's power. In 1826 Shaka fought them again and crushed the remaining Ndwandwe resistance. The Zulu gradually extended their empire by a series of annual campaigns which took them far into the Northern Transkei. Shaka was creating a military state. For the conquered, three options lay open. One was to join Shaka. Many did join Shaka's impis, thereby expanding the kingdom. Others could continue with their resistance. Again many did, keeping Shaka busy all his life, especially at the borders. The third alternative was to emigrate, and again many did, spreading the effects of the Mfecane into far-off lands. Shaka has been accused of being tyrannical and destructive. This is not necessarily true. He started great changes which would have been difficult for anyone to control.

Thus began the Mfecane in which defeated clans embarked on journeys which took them to distant parts of Southern, Central and East Africa.

The Mfecane

It is convenient to divide the emigrant clans into three groups:

(a) *Defeated groups who set out on their own careers of conquest*

1 The Qwabe led by Nqeto who established themselves on the edges of Pondoland.

2 The Tlokwa, led by the woman, MaNthatisi, who moved westwards from the veld towards Botswana.

3 The Ngwane, led by Matiwane across the Drakensberg from Natal:

(b) *Refugees who merged into new nations strong enough to stand against the Zulu*

1 Swaziland which was created by the efforts of Sobhuza and Mswati.

2 Lesotho which was created as Basutoland by Moshesh.

(c) *Zulu formations which struck out on their own*

1 Soshangane took the Shangane northwards into Gazaland where they absorbed and conquered the Tonga.

2 Mzilikazi led the Ndebele across the Drakensberg and finally settled in what is now Zimbabwe (Rhodesia).

The results of the Mfecane

(a) *Depopulation*
The most obvious result of the Mfecane was the depopulation of large areas of Southern Africa and the concentration of people in smaller, more easily defended, regions. These were Natal and the areas which were later called the Orange Free State and Transvaal. They had been very under-populated yet they were very fertile. But the open grasslands of the veld did not provide adequate security from the persistent attacks which people began to expect.

(b) *Empire-building*
Groups of people who fled from Shaka tended to do one of two things. They set out to build their own empires. This took many to the far north of the region. These groups included the Shangane and Ndebele. Others preferred to remain near to their local area, setting up their own kingdoms.

(c) *Defensive kingdoms*
The Basuto, the Swazi and the Bapedi were the most successful in achieving this kind of security. They carefully chose mountainous areas which were not as open to attack as the veld. The Bapedi established themselves in the Zoutpansberg of Eastern Transvaal. They became so strong by the

This hilltop stronghold in Basutoland was an effective defence during the Mfecane

1870s that they caused the annexation of the Transvaal by Britain.

The nation building in the first half of the century shows that it is possible to unite many different groups into one unit. This can be achieved in a relatively short time. One would expect the best examples of this process to be found among the Swazi and the Basuto. Even among the aggressive empire-builders, such as the Ndebele, their wars of conquest were accompanied by successful policies of integrating conquered and conquerors.

The influence of the Mfecane was extended northwards by military groups who did not intend empire building. They did absorb conquered people as they moved on. Examples of such people were Zwangendaba, who reached Zambia in 1835 and Nxaba, who followed much the same route, settling eventually in the Lake Malawi region. Their importance was that they destroyed the surviving Shona Kingdom of Monomotapa and severely weakened other Shona chieftaincies. These were unable to resist later invasions by the

Ndebele and eventually by white empire builders in the late nineteenth century.

(d) *Impact on the Xhosa*

The area of Southern Africa which suffered the most was that of the Southern Nguni – the Xhosa people. They were in the unenviable position of being caught between two powerful groups. To the west was the Cape Colony. By the 1830s there was a great desire to extend its Eastern Frontier at the expense of the Xhosa and for the benefit of white settlement. To the east the pressure was from the Zulu regiments. Refugees were constantly moving westwards away from the advancing Zulu impis. These circumstances, one would have thought, would have led to joint action and alliances between the different Xhosa clans and the central Nguni groups such as the Thembu. No such alliances were made.

(e) *Trekkers settle in empty land*

If conditions had been peaceful in South-East Africa things might have returned to the way they were before the Mfecane. This return did not take place because of conditions in the Cape Colony. Here, increased population and greater pressure on land were persuading settlers of the need to extend the area of white settlement. This movement into the largely uninhabited areas of Natal and the veld coincided with the Mfecane. The Boer settlers were able to take over land left unoccupied as a result of the Mfecane. So the Mfecane takes on a greater significance when it is related to the development which is known as the Great Trek.

The political organisation of the Zulu nation

Hundreds of chiefdoms in Zululand were united by their king. Each chiefdom occupied and defended a certain territory. Apart from their common language, the Zulu were united by their military background as warriors. The king enforced the law and administered the Zulu lands. He was expected to fulfil these duties with generosity and justice. His major responsibilities were the care of his regiments and of his people in times of crisis. He took part in religious ceremonies and performed ritual acts for

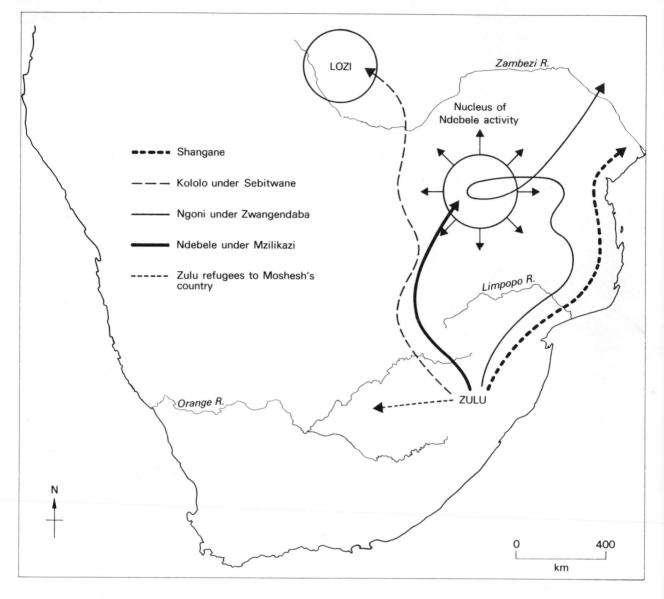

Fig. 20 *The movement of Bantu groups, 1820–40 (adapted from Fage,* An Atlas of African History, *Edward Arnold, 1958)*

the benefit of his people. The people believed that these increased his abilities as a military leader.

The advisory council of the Zulu had the power to speak before the king on matters of national importance. It was valuable to have councillors who were strong enough to be critical of ideas introduced by the king. During Shaka's reign the role of the council was largely redundant as the Zulu entered a brief but exciting period of military conquest.

Normally, kings ruled with the support of brothers and uncles. This prevented the king becoming too powerful. Shaka was assassinated,

Dingane was deposed and later murdered, but princes and chiefs usually plotted against each other rather than against the king. Cetshwayo succeeded Mpande only after defeating his brother Mbulazi who had been favoured by Mpande.

Integration of defeated groups into the Zulu nation

The Zulu nation included many groups. They ranged in size from a few hundred to several thousands. If the chief of the clan was defeated in battle he became a vassal of the king. This meant that from then on his authority was subject to the will of the king and he had to provide military support whenever the king needed it. The king sometimes recognised the existing chief, as in the case of Mzilikazi, or else imposed a member of the royal family on the clan. The kings would normally consider it worthwhile to follow the custom by which the son inherited his father's position, except when the heir was obviously incompetent. They were reluctant to interfere in the succession problems of the larger clans as this could create dangerous opposition to their rule.

The clans who made up the Zulu nation maintained their individual identity and carefully guarded their own traditions and customs. Shaka, particularly, practised a system of 'divide and rule', that is he made the most of these separate loyalties. He eventually moulded the different clans into a nation based on their allegiance to the king.

The death of Shaka and the Zulu nation

In organising his kingdom on such efficient military lines, Shaka had taken all the political power into his own hands. He paid occasional attention to his military indunas and ignored the traditional chiefs. These were reduced to the position of administrators of purely local affairs. This was resented by some, particularly, by his brothers Dingane and Mhlangana. They plotted to murder Shaka in 1828. There had been at least one other attempt on his life in 1824, but in 1828 the assassination was arranged by close members of his family. Mkabayi, a full sister of Shaka's father was the chief plotter. She suspected that Shaka had killed his mother, Nandi, and was looking for a way to avenge her death. She was able to gain the support of Shaka's half-brothers. A suitable time for the attempt on Shaka's life came when a Zulu army was sent out to defeat the Soshangane. Dingane and Mhlangana returned to the royal kraal on 24 December. They killed Shaka in broad daylight. A potential rival who had been favoured by the dead chief was also murdered by the brothers. Dingane then had Mhlangana killed. By the time the army arrived at the kraal Dingane was in complete control. The army did

not attempt to overthrow Dingane on their return, as they were exhausted after their defeat by the Soshangane. Dingane also promised them a period of rest after the many wars they had fought and the impis accepted the new state of affairs.

Results of Shaka's rule

One of the most important results of the life of Shaka was that he united the Zulu nation, which was to remain independent and intact until 1887, when it was brought under colonial rule. Shaka built on the work of Dingiswayo, who had united hundreds of clans in a common allegiance to himself. Shaka, by organising age-groups into regiments and stationing them in the royal household, inspired a loyalty firstly to himself, secondly to the regiment and thirdly to the nation. Its military spirit and common language and culture helped to unite the Zulu nation. Despite the defeat of the Zulu army in the late nineteenth century, the unity of the people remains.

Dingane's reign 1828–40

Dingane ruled Zululand from 1828 until 1840. During his reign the white settlers became more interested in Natal and Zululand. Shaka had had contact with traders from Port Natal (later Durban). The settlers assisted Shaka in his decisive battle against the Ndwandwe in 1828 but it was not until after his death that they took a greater interest in Natal.

Natal – a threat to Zulu independence

Dingane became more concerned with Natal because of the increase in white settlers. Also African refugees from Zululand used to go there. By 1835 there were 30 whites and 2,500 Africans in Port Natal. Dingane attempted to deal with this double threat by making an agreement with Captain Allen Gardiner, a British naval officer turned missionary. Gardiner agreed to return Zulu refugees to Dingane, who in exchange undertook to respect the position of the white settlement in Natal. In this way Dingane would have ensured that Natal would not help to harm Zulu independence. Unfortunately, Gardiner was unable to keep his side of the agreement. The Natal whites would not have anything to do with it. By this time the Boer trekkers were moving into Natal. One of the Trek leaders, Piet Retief, reached Port Natal in October 1837.

Threat of Boer trekkers

Dingane was now faced with a very different problem. Retief was demanding Natal for white settlement. Dingane, like Shaka, had avoided conflict with the whites until this point. Now he had to deal with an opponent who had just defeated the formidable Ndebele led by Mzilikazi and was making threats and demands. Dingane had no-one who could give worthwhile advice and help. He eventually decided that the threat must be met by force, although he signed away Natal to the Boers on 4 February 1838. Two days later, Piet Retief and his party were murdered. It is likely that Dingane intended this action to be followed by an attack on the white settlers in Natal, driving them out of the country. The Zulu, despite a number of isolated successes against Boer settlements, were unable to expel the Boers by September. The arrival of Andries Pretorius spoilt Dingane's plans. Pretorius organised a commando of some 500 men and they formed their wagons into a laager, or protective circle on the banks of the Ncome River. The Zulu attacked ferociously but were unable to overcome the firepower of the Boers who fought from a good defensive position. On 16 December the Zulu were defeated at Blood River as it was later named.

This marked the end of Zulu resistance to the Boers. It forced the Zulu to surrender control of areas south of the Tugela River and threatened to destroy the Zulu nation. The Zulu were divided between Dingane and his brother Mpande. Mpande allied himself with the Boers. In February Dingane was killed by a band of Swazi as he fled northwards. Mpande was proclaimed King of the Zulu by Andries Pretorius. He was now a vassal of the Natal Republic. Mpande's reign was one of the longest in Zulu history and lasted for thirty-two years until 1872.

Mpande's reign 1840–72

Mpande's long reign was an uneventful period of relative peace and prosperity for the Zulu people. Mpande was not interested in expanding Zulu influence. He was well aware of the superior weapons of the Europeans. He avoided any open conflict and even allowed some white settlement in his territory. Even though his vassalage with Natal ended in 1843 he maintained this policy of avoiding conflict throughout his reign. This may have been what the Zulu needed to recover from the upheavals of the previous generation. But this point was not always appreciated by the younger Zulu.

The Zulu nation had been founded on military success. For many of the Zulu Mpande's reign had been a humiliating experience. Long before the end of his reign a succession struggle began between Mpande's eldest sons, Cetshwayo and Mbulazi.

Cetshwayo's reign 1872–84

Succession dispute decided 1856

The succession dispute to Mpande's throne was settled in 1856 when the two factions led by Cetshwayo and Mbulazi fought each other in a tremendous battle near the mouth of the Tugela River. Cetshwayo was the winner and he was assured of the eventual leadership of the Zulu nation. Cetshwayo had taken on the responsibilities of kingship long before his father's death in 1872. The Zulu people, once again, had a leader who was prepared to rebuild the military strength on which their nation had been established. By 1873, the Zulu had recovered their prosperity and their self-confidence. Cetshwayo was crowned in 1873 by Sir Theophilus Shepstone, Natal's Secretary for Native Affairs. In the first years of his reign he concentrated on reforming the age-regiments and rebuilding the feeling of Zulu nationalism.

The British at this time were intent on bringing the two British colonies and the two Boer republics into some form of political union or federation. Before this could be achieved, the South African

Republic (Transvaal) had to be persuaded that federation was worthwhile. An extension of Transvaal territory near the Blood River together with a reduction of Zulu power was made in order to demonstrate British goodwill to the Boers. It was decided to give the Transvaalers a section of land near Blood River which had always been claimed by the Boers. But the judicial commission, when it reported, awarded Cetshwayo more land than he had demanded, and found that the Transvaalers' claim was completely unjustified. The High Commissioner was convinced, however, that if the award was not made to the Boers then they would lose the chance of a peaceful federation, which is when a number of previously independent areas unite for reasons of security but remain independent in local affairs. The British High Commissioner, Sir Bartle Frere, used a raid by some of Cetshwayo's warriors into Natal territory as an excuse to insist on the disbanding of the age-group regiments and the breaking up of the Zulu political organisation.

Anglo-Zulu War 1879

Not unnaturally, Cetshwayo refused to agree to these demands and in January 1879 Zululand was invaded by 13,000 British troops, commanded by Lord Chelmsford. Almost immediately, the British suffered an embarrassing defeat at the Battle of Isandhlwana, in which a whole British regiment was destroyed.

Battle of Isandhlwana

Eighteen hundred soldiers, part of Chelmsford's central column, had been stationed at the Isandhlwana Camp, about eleven kilometres to the east of Rorke's Drift on Natal's border. There were 950 British soldiers and 850 of the Natal Native Contingent under British officers. The British were quite unaware of the great Zulu 'impi' which was

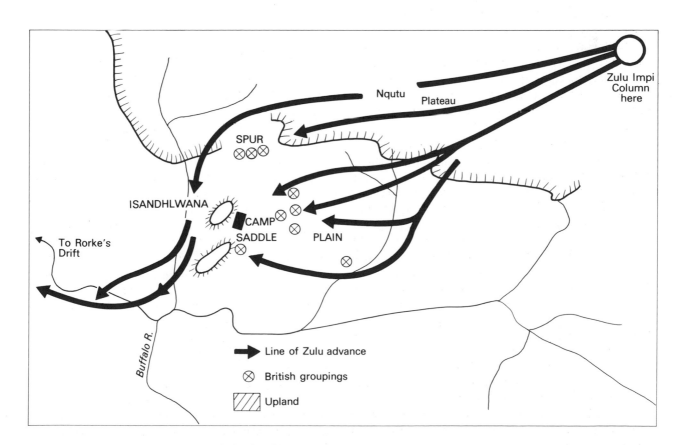

Fig. 21 Isandhlwana campaign, 22 January 1879

concealed on the nearby plateau and was about to pour down on the camp. They made no preparations to withstand a surprise attack and in fact spread their forces thinly, to the north of the camp, on the plain to the east and in the pass to the south. Even ammunition supplies were left stored away for the forthcoming campaign.

When the twelve Zulu regiments emerged from the ravine on the Nqutu Plateau, they were able to advance on the camp systematically destroying the inadequate outposts on the plain and on the hill. The ruthless, tactical efficiency of the Zulu was never more vividly illustrated. The tactical formations and the courageous discipline of Shaka's day had not been forgotten, and at the end of the battle very few of the British forces survived, in all only 55 British and 300 Natal Native troops. Chelmsford had left 2,000 oxen at the camp for future transport but these were slaughtered by the Zulu. The Zulu themselves had suffered terrible losses in the battle, perhaps as many as 2,000, but they had shown tremendous courage and great tactical skill against the ill-prepared British troops.

Isandhlwana was followed by the attack, on *Rorke's Drift* by over 4,000 Zulu led by Dabulamanzi, Cetshwayo's half brother, in command of the Undi Corps. This section of the Zulu impi had formed the right 'horn' of the Zulu advance on Isandhlwana. Against Cetshwayo's instructions they had advanced into Natal at Rorke's Drift and were eventually driven off by a small British force of 150 men. The attack lasted about ten hours and the dreadful hand to hand struggle ended with the withdrawal of the Zulu. The impi had been on the move for six days, had not eaten for four days, and had fought two exhausting battles within twenty-four hours. Dabulamanzi recognised that his men were incapable of further action. The defence of Rorke's Drift had only been possible because of the superior British weapons and the concentration of their soldiers within the small area of the hospital.

Battle of Ulundi

The battle of Ulundi on 4 July allowed Chelmsford to regain a little of his reputation and dignity which had been lost at Isandhlwana. The Zulu were forced to defend their chief's camp in unfavourable circumstances. The Zulu were unable to penetrate

Cetshwayo, who revitalised the Zulu nation before he was defeated at the Battle of Ulundi in 1879

the large British square because of the powerful Gatling guns. These prevented the Zulu from approaching any nearer than thirty yards. When the Zulu retreated with terrible losses the mounted British lancers attacked and the defeat of the Zulu was complete. In the wall of stone archway marking the site of the British square there is a tablet inscribed:

IN MEMORY OF THE BRAVE WARRIORS
WHO FELL HERE IN 1879 IN DEFENCE OF
THE OLD ZULU ORDER.

Cetshwayo was brought to London in 1882 and, although reinstated as chief a year later, he was unable to regain the loyalty and support of his people. He was forced to seek refuge in a Reserve and died at Eshowe in 1884. In the civil war which occurred after his death, one of the rebel leaders, Dinizulu, asked for Boer support to gain the Zulu throne. This assistance was gladly given and Dinizulu was made chief. In return, the Boers proclaimed a new Republic over north-western Zululand and claimed that they were the protectors of the Zulu.

The Zulu political system had been drastically altered on two occasions in the nineteenth century. Firstly, because of the wars of conquest in the 1820s, Shaka had had to adapt the traditional methods of government in order to control the many defeated nations included in the new Zulu nation. The second radical change came after the defeat of Cetshwayo. The military power of the Zulu nation was broken and with it went one of the major unifying factors of the nation. The development of agriculture and, in particular, the introduction of the plough threw more responsibilities for the farms onto the men's shoulders. Zululand was divided into thirteen magisterial districts with the chiefs required to assist the government in administrative matters. The chief official was the magistrate, a European, who had overall responsibility for the district.

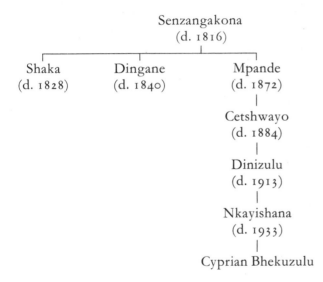

Zulu Paramount Chiefs

Summary of Chapter 6

The Mfecane
Causes of the Mfecane:
  1 Growth of population in South-East Africa.
  2 Scarcity of grazing land.
  3 Career of Shaka.
Shaka's military tactics:
  1 stabbing assegai
  2 'horns of the cow'
  3 bare-footed soldiers
  4 a standing army.

After defeat of Zwide annual campaigns led to:
  1 Depopulation of Zululand and Natal.
  2 Movement of people away from the wrath of Shaka.

Different groups of the Mfecane:
a) *empire builders:*
  1 Shaka and the Zulu.
  2 Mzilikazi and the Ndebele.
  3 Shangane and the Soshangane.
b) *defensive nation-builders:*
  1 Moshesh and Basutoland.
  2 Sobhuza and Swaziland.

Rise and fall of the Zulu nation
Shaka 1818–28
  Growth of Zulu nation based on:
  1 Hundreds of clans united in allegiance to the King.
  2 Age-group regiments which inspired a three-fold loyalty: to the King, the regiment, the nation.
  3 Military strength.
  4 Common language.
Dingane 1828–40: White settlers in Natal a greater threat than previously – unable to defeat the Boer trekkers completely; after the death of Retief, 1838 defeat at Blood River; Boers assisted by his brother Mpande.
Mpande 1840–72: A quiet period of Zulu history, although peaceful and prosperous, discontent among young Zulu warriors;
  1856 succession dispute won by Cetshwayo.
Cetshwayo 1872–84: Rebuilding of Zulu military strength. 1879 Zulu drawn into a war with the British – Isandhlwana – Rorke's Drift – Ulundi. Zulu military power destroyed. Cetshwayo succeeded by Dinizulu, a tool in the hands of the Transvaalers.

Short questions on Chapter 6

  1 What were the three main groups which developed among the Nguni at the beginning of the nineteenth century?
  2 Who were their respective leaders?
  3 What changes did Shaka make to the usual methods of waging war?
  4 At what battle did Shaka defeat Zwide?
  5 What was the most obvious result of the Mfecane?

6   Name three groups who established successful defensive kingdoms.
7   What were the main functions of the King or Paramount Chief of the Zulus?
8   How long did Dingane rule?
9   What event marked the end of Zulu resistance to the Boers?
10 How was the succession to Mpande's throne decided?
11 When was Cetshwayo crowned?
12 What happened at Isandhlwana?
13 On what condition did Dinizulu gain the Zulu throne?

Longer questions on Chapter 6

1   What four suggestions have been made for the grouping together of clans among the northern Nguni?
2   Describe the rise to prominence of Shaka.
3   Describe the effect of the Mfecane on the history of South Africa.
4   Describe the rise and fall of the Zulu empire during the nineteenth century.

7   Nation building during the Mfecane

Other clans saw the need for strong kingdoms as a defence against the Zulu, and later the Boers. The Basuto of Moshesh and the Swazi of Mswati are examples of united peoples who maintained their separate identity and achieved political independence in recent times. The activities of Shaka and his regiments resulted in the depopulation of Natal and of vast areas of the interior plateaux. Fleeing Zulu formations separated from Shaka and carried Zulu ideas and methods far into the interior. Mzilikazi and his Ndebele are the best example of such a migration.

Mzilikazi and the Ndebele

In 1818, the year that Dingiswayo died, Mzilikazi became the leader of the Khumalo. After being allied with Zwide he switched his people's allegiance to Shaka. He and his regiments filled a unique position in Shaka's army. They were a lineage regiment led by its own chief. Perhaps it was a small enough unit not to form a threat to Shaka's rule. But the loyalty of the regiment must have been centred on Mzilikazi rather than Shaka. Shaka did not like indunas who did not deliver all the spoils of battle to the royal kraal. Mzilikazi did not risk Shaka's anger when, after a campaign in northern Zululand in 1821, he did not return all the captured cattle. First of all, he insulted the royal messengers, and then escaped across the escarpment into the interior.

On his flight he smashed all opposition and in 1824 he reached the Olifant River. He settled at Eku Pumelani. Here he rested for a time, reinforcing his ranks with captured women and children and sending out his warriors to crush his enemies and capture more cattle. However, Eku Pumelani was too close to Shaka, and Mzilikazi began to move towards central Transvaal. This was devastated and depopulated by the Ndebele between 1825 and 1828. Constantly searching for security, Mzilikazi was still threatened by the Zulu and by bands of Koranna and Griqua. Dingane sent an army against him but the battle was indecisive. Mzilikazi stifled the threat of half-caste groups by an attack on the Taung led by Moletsane, after which the Ndebele moved westwards to Mosega.

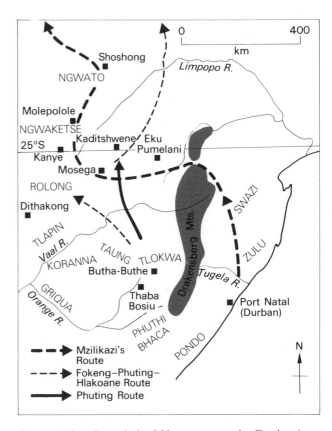

Fig. 22 The effect of the Mfecane across the Drakensberg Mountains

They systematically destroyed Tswana opposition on the way.

Having escaped from the Zulu, Mzilikazi was faced by a more dangerous enemy. In 1836 Boer trek parties entered his territory unannounced. He mistook the Erasmus and Liebenberg trek parties for raiding expeditions and destroyed them. A further attack on Potgieter's party is remembered as the Battle of Vegkop (see p. 49). In an attack on Mosega on 2 January 1837, the Boers defeated the Ndebele. In October Potgieter defeated Mzilikazi again and forced the Ndebele into Shona territory (modern Zimbabwe).

Mzilikazi has been accused of being a tough leader in the same mould as Shaka, but during his lifetime the security of his people was all important. He was completely uncompromising in his dealings with other groups to achieve it. It must be said in his favour that because of his great personal authority his land and his people were governed with law and order.

Moshesh and the Basuto nation

Mention has been made of one reaction to the Mfecane, that of groups setting out on aggressive wars of conquest for new homes far to the north of Zululand. These people – Mzilikazi, Sebetwane, Soshangane – as well as the Zulu themselves, were a great threat to groups living as neighbours of the Nguni. These groups reacted in a very different way. They tried to build up nations from different elements who wished to survive. The best examples of defensive nation building are Moshesh's Basuto nation and the Swazi nation of Sobhuza and Mswati.

From 1820 onwards traditional leaders had to face great pressures. These added pressures required a more radical policy than many leaders were prepared to introduce. For much of the nineteenth century insecurity was accepted as normal. The clans faced the danger of fierce attacks by other Africans. Later there was the added problem of the Boers moving into the interior. The uniting of clans, the adoption of new military methods, the use of diplomatic strategies when military conflict was avoidable – these were some of the radical changes which the more conservative

leaders found hard to make. One man who emerged as a leader with the necessary foresight was Moshesh. This remarkable chief became the central figure around whom the history of the interior plateau revolved in the nineteenth century.

Early leadership

Moshesh was born among the Makoteli, a small ethnic unit. Like many other groups this had separated from its parent tribe, the Kwena, over land succession disputes and land rights. As a young man, Moshesh showed qualities of considerable intelligence and personality which singled him out as being exceptional among his own folk. Moshesh was one of the first to recognise the defensive possibilities of the many flat-topped hills in Basutoland. He gathered together men of his own age-group and established a well-protected fortress on the mountain Butha Buthe. In 1821, the Hlubi crossed into Basutoland, attacking and defeating the powerful Tlokwa led by the

Moshesh, an outstanding leader of the Basuto

Sekonyela, leader of the Tlokwa

MaNthatisi. The Hlubi were the first of the ethnic groups to sweep northwards from Zululand; the impact of the Hlubi gives some idea of the upheaval caused by such movements. The Tlokwa were forced into a period of wandering which brought them into contact with Moshesh and his warriors on Butha Buthe.

Attacked by the Tlokwa

The fortress justified Moshesh's faith in it. The camp remained intact even though most of Moshesh's cattle were captured by the Tlokwa. The Hlubi and the Tlokwa extended their activities into the area which is now the Orange Free State. But Moshesh was never sure how long this peace would last. In 1824 the Tlokwa, this time led by Sekonyela, turned back on Moshesh. Only an alliance with another tribe saved Moshesh and his

people from starvation after a long siege. After the near disaster of the Tlokwa attack Moshesh realised that he needed to find somewhere more easily defended. Somewhere that would also provide adequate food supplies should there be another siege. After a hard journey across Basutoland he found a new fortress, Thaba Bosiu. He had to have peace in the neighbourhood. This meant gaining the support of the Phuthi, the first Bantu to live in Basutoland. After a short fight Moshesh treated Moroosi, the Phuthi chief, with such generosity that he got his support.

Political organisation

Other groups were attracted by the security of Basutoland. Moshesh had to organise all these different groups. He placed small ethnic units under the control of his own family. He allowed larger groups to keep their own leaders provided they were loyal to him. He wanted to encourage a growth of nationalism among all these different peoples. He brought them together at councils and public assemblies at which important matters could be discussed. This was the traditional Sotho pattern of organisation. The growth of the Basuto nation under Moshesh was different to the development of the Zulu nation under Shaka. Shaka built up a military organisation in which many of the traditional practices were broken. Moshesh followed a system which saw the value of peaceful agreements. He recognised the need for military solutions on occasions but always tried to provide justice as fairly as possible.

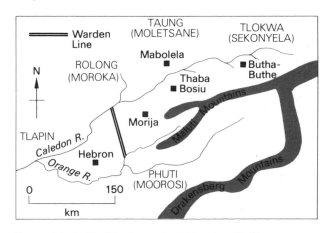

Fig. 23 Moshesh's Kingdom and neighbouring chiefdoms

Defeat of the Ngwane

Moshesh was attacked by Matiwane, chief of the Ngwane, before he had strengthened his position on Thaba Bosiu. Matiwane had defeated the Hlubi. He had made himself the most powerful leader on the inland plateau. He forced Moshesh to pay very heavy tribute. To escape this crushing tax, Moshesh played Shaka off against Matiwane. Matiwane was attacked by a small Zulu group. The struggle was not decisive but Matiwane was forced to search for new lands after a struggle with the Ndebele. Moshesh was blamed for much of the Ngwane trouble and a weakened Matiwane was urged to launch a last assault on Thaba Bosiu. The Ngwane were driven back by the Basuto. Matiwane had to withdraw to the eastern border of the Cape Colony. There was a further fight with the Ndebele. Moshesh escaped with great diplomatic skill. This helped to weld the different groups together in loyalty to their chief. The Griquas and the Koronnas were attracted from the Orange Free State by the riches of a stable populated Basutoland. Moshesh defeated them with mounted soldiers. This adaptation later resulted in greater mobility in the Basuto regiments.

Moshesh and the French missions

In 1832, Moshesh heard about the work of the white missionaries. He realised that with the growing number of white farmers in Basutoland, he would require experienced advisors. He asked for missionaries to be sent to him. Originally he requested help from the Church Missionary Society, but it was three French missionaries who came from the Paris Evangelical Society – Arbousset, Casalis and Gosselin. It was made very clear that these men, who were given many privileges, remained Moshesh's men. They were always responsible to him and were expected to advise him in his dealings with other Europeans.

By 1840, Moshesh had created the beginnings of a nation out of the various refugee groups, but the rest of his reign was complicated by a much more difficult problem – the question of the immigrant farmers. They had moved into Basutoland after 1835. These people were not willing to be part of the Basuto nation. They were not satisfied with a small portion of Basuto land. The British authori-

ties of the Cape kept changing their minds about these immigrant farmers. This made Moshesh's position much more difficult.

Relations with the British and Boers

From the time of the Great Trek his problems were twofold. He had to unite the different groups in Basutoland into one nation while keeping the loyalty of each individual group. The coming of the white farmers was the second problem. Until his death in 1870, Moshesh was concerned with protecting his land and promoting unity among his people. For most of this period he tried to gain the protection of the British Crown without giving up too much of his own authority. Moshesh made his first application for British recognition in 1842. He hoped that this would prevent more of the Boers coming into Basuto territory. The Napier Treaty of 1843 warned the Boers not to extend their own lands at the expense of the Basuto. But there was little force to support the Governor's policy, which had hardly any effect on the farmers. In 1845 Moshesh was prepared to set aside a small part of his country for white settlement. But he wanted the land to remain Basuto land. The Boer farmers who lived outside this selected area did not want to move. The British Resident was unable to force them to move.

In 1848 the new Governor, Sir Harry Smith, decided that the only way to prevent a serious outbreak of war between the Boers and Basuto was to bring the whole area between the Orange and the Vaal Rivers under British control. This extension of British power could have been possible if the British Government had provided enough money and men to exert an influence over the Boers. Such assistance was not available to the Governor. He and his Resident in the Orange River Sovereignty, Major Warden, found that the area could be governed only with the support of the Boers. This did not calm the Basuto fears and suspicions. The Warden Line of 1849 was a new boundary which took a triangle of land 32 kilometres long, between the Orange and lower Caledon Rivers away from Moshesh. The Resident intended to establish white settlers in a much larger area than that agreed in 1845. This would have undermined Moshesh's authority by giving more power to lesser chiefs, such as Sekonyela and Moroka. Moshesh saw that this plan not only meant the loss of a great deal of land, but also threatened to wipe out the achievements of twenty years of nation-building.

A diplomatic victory over Cathcart

Warden went on trying to break Moshesh's power, but completely underestimated the power of the Basuto. The Basuto defeated his combined force of British and Rolong troops. They retreated to Bloemfontein. A further humiliation was suffered by Governor George Cathcart when he insisted on Moshesh paying a fine of 10,000 cattle for Warden's defeat. Moshesh supplied 3,500 cattle on the appointed day. Cathcart was not satisfied and marched against him. The Basuto attacked unexpectedly when the British were capturing 4,000 more cattle. A semi-victory for Moshesh was turned into a triumph when he sent a message to Cathcart asking him not to punish the Basuto further and hoping that the captured cattle would be sufficient compensation. Cathcart accepted this tactful offer of peace and marched back to the Cape. It was a quarrel between the Orange Free State and Moshesh which forced Basutoland to seek British protection.

Under threat from the Boers

In 1854, the Bloemfontein Convention was signed, giving the Orange River Sovereignty its independence as the Orange Free State. The Boers were promised non-intervention by Britain and they were also promised supplies of gunpowder. This was denied to Moshesh and the other African leaders. To begin with, relations between the Basuto leader and the first President of the new republic, Josias Hoffman, were good. But Hoffman was replaced by Boshof because he was considered to be too friendly with Moshesh. Because of the advantages given to them the Boers became much stronger militarily and tried to force Moshesh to accept the Warden line. One attack was driven back by Moshesh. He was prepared to accept terms suggested by Governor Sir George Grey which gave him a little more land than the Warden Line had. This was only a temporary halt to the fighting, which began once again in 1865. The Treaty of Thaba Bosiu left Moshesh with only a very small

Moshesh's stronghold of Thaba Bosiu, which was attacked by the British in 1865

area of land. Although he signed the peace treaty, Moshesh would not accept the terms in practice and war broke out in 1867.

Move towards British protection

The Basuto were in a desperate state. They faced both defeat and starvation when Sir Philip Wodehouse announced a protectorate over Basutoland on 18 March 1868. When Wodehouse arrived as Governor in 1861 he had received two requests from Moshesh that his land and people should be taken into British protection. Wodehouse had not been able to make such an agreement without the support of the British Government. At the end of 1867, the British Government agreed that the protection should be given to Moshesh, providing that Basutoland was annexed to Natal, with the consent of the Orange Free State.

Wodehouse decided to interpret this decision very liberally and annexed Basutoland as a Crown Colony. Firstly he cut off ammunition supplies to the Orange Free State. A new boundary was agreed between Wodehouse and President Brand. This improved the settlement of Thaba Bosiu for the Basuto, but they still lost land north of the Caledon River and land between the Caledon and Orange Rivers.

Moshesh died in 1870, but not before the survival of Basutoland was assured. For more than forty years he had collected together many different peoples, who eventually acknowledged him as their rightful leader. Having built up this nation, he was successful in defending it. His greatest quality was probably his diplomacy. This had turned Cathcart away when he was setting off on a campaign to punish the Basuto. He played off one power against another, as in his struggle with Matiwane. He was determined to fight to the last, as he showed in the war against the Orange Free State.

Growth of the Swazi nation

The leading people in Swaziland from the sixteenth century had been the Nkosi-Dlamini clan of the Nguni. They had gained control over the neighbouring Ngoni and Sotho people. This control lasted for over three hundred years. At the beginning of the nineteenth century, the Ngwane, led by Sobhuza, were defeated by Zwide's Ndwande. The Ngwane retreated to Swaziland and began to conquer and absorb the clans that lived there.

Sobhuza I 1814–40

Sobhuza I, who reigned from 1814 to 1840, led this growing community. During his reign, eight more clans joined the group, accepting the overall control of the Dlamini. Refugee groups fleeing from Zulu regiments to the south-east found security among the mountains and caves of Swaziland. They were only too pleased to promise loyalty to Sobhuza in exchange for their safety.

Sobhuza allowed a fairly loose political control. Separate groups were allowed to keep their own chiefs. Unlike Shaka and Mzilikazi, Sobhuza did not try to impose the way of life of his group on the others. He was not strong enough to challenge the

military power of the Zulu, so he tried to live in peace with his more powerful neighbours. He married one of Zwide's daughters and gave young princesses as gifts to Shaka. Even when these princesses were murdered for becoming pregnant and thus providing problems of succession, Sobhuza did not try to avenge their deaths.

By keeping the peace with his aggressive neighbours, Sobhuza provided a period of peace and increased prosperity. But Sobhuza's position was more secure in Shaka's time than in Dingane's. Dingane needed new grazing grounds for his raiding parties and Sobhuza had large herds. Sobhuza kept away from major fighting until 1839 when the Boer attacks at and after Blood River, forced the Zulu to withdraw from Swaziland. Dingane was killed by the Ngwane and a year later Sobhuza himself died.

Mswati 1840–68

Mswati succeeded his father in 1840. His long reign lasted until 1868. During this period the Swazi saw a development in their political and administrative organisation. Mswati had a much more aggressive foreign policy. He succeeded in making the Swazi one of the more powerful Bantu peoples. The Zulu leader at the time, Mpande, was a rather passive ruler. Mswati gained control over his neighbouring people. As late as 1860 he was trying to extend his influence over the Shangane Kingdom of Mozambique. He was not successful and by 1862 the Limpopo was accepted as the boundary between the two states.

Gradually, during the 1840s and 1850s the different clans in Swaziland developed into a kingdom with clear national elements. Nation-building in Swaziland was not based on military power and authoritarian rule as it was in Zululand. But the Swazi did borrow ideas of organisation from both the Zulu and Sotho structures of government.

Swazi government and military organisation

The kingdom was divided naturally into a number of chieftainships. Some had been established before the Ngwane invasion. Some were directly related to the Ngwane. Although the king had households in different parts of the country, the local chiefs had considerable local power. They also formed part of a council which discussed national affairs. As well as this council there was a meeting of adult men who met occasionally to discuss and even criticise the king. This assembly resembled the pitsos of the Sotho people.

The Swazi had age-regiments but they were not organised as a standing army. This was quite adequate to control neighbouring Sotho peoples but not enough to face the Zulu with any confidence. The nearest to a standing army was the recruitment of young men to serve in regiments at the royal homesteads. In peaceful times the age regiments were always available to local chiefs. This provided a balance to the king's power without being dangerous to the system.

One other major difference between the Swazi and the Zulu was the position of the Swazi queen mother. If the king was the centre of government, the queen mother was almost an unofficial head of state. She had no real political power but was expected to have a stable influence on the king and act if necessary as regent. This is the title given to the person who is appointed to rule when the real king is too young or for some reason unable to rule.

Swaziland and the Europeans

As early as 1845 Mswati had given land occupied by the Sotho people to the Transvaal Boers. Later in 1864 the Swazi helped the Boers to defeat the Poko clan. Without being too suspicious Mswati allowed Boers to move into Swazi territory. The advantage of Swaziland to the Transvaalers was that it provided a reasonable route to Kosi Bay, giving the Transvaal an outlet to the sea. Relations between Transvaal and Swaziland remained cordial until the death of Mswati in 1868 after which the Boers took a more direct interest in Swazi affairs. A succession dispute followed Mswati's death and the Transvaalers supported the claims of Mbandzeni for the paramount chieftaincy.

There is some evidence of an agreement which would have given the Transvaal a substantial control over Swazi affairs. Even though this agreement was never confirmed by the Volksraad (Transvaal Assembly), the evidence was strong enough for Natal to insist that the independence of

Swaziland was guaranteed by the Convention of Pretoria at the close of the first Anglo-Boer war in 1881.

In spite of being unable to carry out their political ambitions in the country, the Transvaal Boers had been able to gain considerable land concessions from Mswati and Mbandzeni. As well as land concessions, extensive mining and trading rights were granted to the Boers. But the Swazi did not consider that the concessions had affected their own right to use the land.

There was an attempt by the Boer residents in 1893 to have the area administered by the Transvaal without being part of it. Mbandzeni died in 1889, and the Queen Regent sent a deputation to London asking for protection. At this time Britain was opposed to the German-Transvaal railway to the coast, but she did not want to take on any more responsibilities. As a compromise Britain agreed at a convention in December 1894, that the Transvaal should have 'all rights of protection, legislation, jurisdiction and administration over Swaziland' with the provision that Swaziland would not become part of the Transvaal.

At the end of the Anglo-Boer war of 1899–1902 the Transvaal was made a colony. The Queen Regent of Swaziland asked for her country to be joined to the new colony but the British Government decided to treat Swaziland separately. Britain took responsibility for legislation and jurisdiction without annexing Swaziland as British territory.

Moshesh was considered the most important man in South African politics by many European politicians in the middle of the nineteenth century. He deserves his leading place among all African leaders since he was able to build a nation, withstand pressure from outside, prevent annexation by the Boers, and leave Basutoland as a British possession. The Swazi followed much the same path but gave up much of their land to the European settlers during the reign of Mswati and Mbandzeni.

Faku and the Pondo

One African leader who played an important part in the events of the Mfecane was Faku. He was the leader of the Pondo. The Pondo position to the south of Port Natal (Durban) always made them vulnerable to attack from Zulu raiding parties. There was also pressure from the refugees escaping from Zululand. Throughout the period of the Mfecane, Faku was able to hold his people together by his strict rule. In many ways he was a forgiving man. He rarely had to use the death penalty except in cases of witchcraft. He always kept the loyalty of his people who in 1800 numbered some 80,000. Like Moshesh, he favoured diplomacy more than warfare. He faced his greatest problems after the death of Shaka, when he was threatened by the Qwabe led by Nqeto. Nqeto fled from Dingane in fear of his life and established his people on the edges of Pondoland. Tension built up between the two groups and eventually Faku was able to select the place for the important battle. He did not allow the Qwabe to form ranks and use their superior fighting methods. Instead the battle took place among thorn trees by a river. In the hand to hand fighting here, the Pondo, because of their greater numbers were able to defeat the Qwabe. Faku did not take cattle which by right belonged to Dingane. Dingane was therefore pleased that Faku had defeated Nqetho.

Faku, like many other African leaders, was threatened by Boers planning to seize land between the Mzimkulu and Mzimvubu Rivers. He requested help from the British who sent a small force to protect him. After the defeat of the Qwabe, the only important powers in Pondoland were Faku and Ncaphayi, the leader of the Bhaca. War between the two was inevitable, despite attempts to form an alliance through marriages. Land was in short supply and the two groups were very different culturally. Faku finally defeated Ncaphayi, had him killed, and ended his last threat.

Faku had secured the position of the Pondo despite attacks from the Zulu, the Qwabe, the Bhaca and the Boers. Although the authority for the clan passed to the white colonial government, Faku deserves recognition as a great African leader. He did his best to help his people survive in very difficult times.

The Fingo – a refugee band

The depopulation of Natal resulted in large groups of people wandering beyond the borders of Zululand. The devastation and poverty often destroyed clans. Sometimes, groups of refugees would band together to form one people. Such a people were the Fingo (meaning 'beggars') who settled among the Xhosa. They were formed from remnants of Matiwane's combined Ngwane and Hlubi army and from the Mdingi and Bhele, after their defeat by the Bhaca led by Ncaphayi.

There were between 5,000 and 6,000 Fingo near Butterworth on the coast. To begin with they were unpaid herdsmen for the Xhosa. This led to a great deal of resentment among the Fingo and in the 1834 Kaffir War they saw their chance. They were promised land under British protection and although annexation did not actually take place, they were settled on lands for which the Xhosa had fought for so long. This resulted in great hostility between the two peoples. Perhaps to protect themselves the Fingo adapted themselves to European ways rather better than the Xhosa. They took full advantage of educational opportunity. One of their educational successes has been the eminent Jabavu family.

The Tswana, the Mfecane and Chief Khama III

There are many things we do not know about the early history of the Tswana people. Legend suggests that Kwena, Ngwato and Ngwaketse, the three sons of Masilo, a great Sotho chief of the mid-seventeenth century, gave their names to the three main tribes of modern Botswana. The Bangwaketse finally settled in the area of Kanye, the Bamangwato around Shoshong and the Bakwena in the neighbourhood of Molepolole.

If there is uncertainty about the early history of the Tswana there is no doubt that the Botswana region suffered the shattering experience of invasion from a whole series of refugee groups escaping from the anger of Shaka at the beginning of the nineteenth century. The followers of MaNthatisi, led by her son Sekonyela, left a path of destruction as they marched to the north-west of the country. Marauding groups created chaos as they were pushed westwards across the Vaal River by the Hlubi, the Ngwane and Tlokwa. The Phuting, after crossing the Vaal, moved north and destroyed the Hurutshe capital, Kaditshwene. The Fokeng joined forces with another group under the leadership of Sebitwane and moved away westwards in search of new land. The Fokeng were later called the Kololo.

Dithakong, the capital of the Tlapin, with its rich herds of cattle was an obvious target for these wandering bands. The Fokeng, Phuting and the Hlakoane all became involved in skirmishes over cattle, but news of the advancing Tlokwa (under Sekonyela) and increasing starvation drove many people down into Dithakong. The Tlapin were unable to protect themselves and enlisted the help of the missionary, Moffat. Moffatt, father-in-law of David Livingstone, persuaded the Griquas to join forces and fight the coming invasion. On 26 June 1823 the half-starving invaders were defeated by the more mobile Griquas mounted on horseback.

Mzilikazi and the Ndebele proved more formidable opponents than the Tlokwa. The Ndebele were under pressure continually from raiding Zulu regiments. They were always in search of a more secure place to settle. The effect of their movement through Tswana country was general devastation. Large areas were depopulated, towns were set on fire and in particular the Bakwena were almost exterminated, never to regain their early prominence. Eventually, the Ndebele decided to move towards what is now Zimbabwe, taking the northerly route through Ngwato territory along the edge of the Kalahari Desert before moving northwards.

Chief Khama and the Protectorate

During the second half of the nineteenth century what is now Botswana was dominated by Chief Khama of the Bamangwato. It was Chief Khama III who was clever enough to recognise the growing white interest in the area. His contribution to the history of the period makes him one of the outstanding African leaders of his day, comparable with the great Moshesh.

As a child he grew up in a normal African environment but his attendance at a Lutheran mission school provided an insight into another culture and another religion. He was baptised into the Christian faith in his early twenties. His conversion made a deep and lasting impression on him and all people who met him. Conversion was often confused by both missionaries and the new converts with the assumption of a western way of living, and Khama provoked great family conflict over his acceptance of western dress, culture and religion. He disobeyed his father's command to take a second wife, and would never accept alcoholic drinks. Despite a number of attempts on his life by his father and brothers, Khama reacted with charity and never lost his respect for his father. That this respect was returned by his father, even if unwillingly, can be understood from one of his father's reported sayings: 'We think like that', he once said, as he drew a circle in the sand, 'but Khama thinks like that,' and he drew a straight line[1].

Khama became chief in 1875 and immediately set about changing the whole pattern of his people's life. All alcoholic drinks were banned, bride-price was forbidden, the killing of one of twin children was stopped and witchcraft was abolished. Khama also invited the London Missionary Society to establish a school at the royal kraal. Khama was far-sighted enough to see the benefits of western

From left to right: Chiefs Sebele, Bathoen and Khama III of Bechuanaland. Chief Khama III saved the country from the Boers

culture and tried to incorporate them into his own society. He was no less clever in recognising the threat of Boer greed for Tswana land. His first appeal to the British Government for protection failed in 1876. Ten years later his persistence led to the setting up of the requested protectorate. It must be recognised that German presence in South-West Africa was a more powerful reason for British involvement in Botswana than the persuasive qualities of the chief.

Khama still needed to be very alert when the possibility of a Rhodes take-over of Bechuanaland was proposed. He, and chiefs Bathoen of the Bangwaketse and Sebele I of the Bakwena, were quick to see the danger. After successfully lobbying the British Parliament and Queen Victoria it was agreed that Rhodes should be allowed a strip of land to build a railway northward. The Tswana would remain under British rule with the promise that the chiefs would continue to rule their own people much as at present. Thus Khama, like Moshesh, was successful in preventing his country coming under the influence of either the Boers or the colonialist Rhodes. By doing so he helped create the opportunity for political independence in the twentieth century.

Summary of Chapter 7

Mzilikazi and the Ndebele
Leader of the Khumalo – became allied to Shaka – retained leadership of his own regiments.
1821 Broke with Shaka and fled from Natal.
1825–28 Devastated central Transvaal.
1836 Battle of Vegkop.
1837 Defeated by Potgieter at Mosega – forced into Shona land.
1868 Death of Mzilikazi.

Moshesh
Makoteli clan – obvious powers of leadership – stronghold on Butha-Buthe.
1824 Attacked by Tlokwa (Sekonyela) – new fortress at Thaba Bosiu – gained support of Phuti (Moorosi). Suffered attacks from Ngwane, Ndebele, Griqua and Koranna.
1832 Missionaries: Casalis, Arbousset, Gosselin.
1843 Napier Treaty: hollow British protection against Boers.
1849 Warden Line: limiting Moshesh's land –

diplomatic victory over Cathcart.
1854 Bloemfontein Convention: gave Boers independence and a freer hand in dealing with Moshesh – led to increased conflict.
1865–7 War with Orange Free State Boers – Moshesh near breaking point – drought and famine.
1868 British protection promised by Governor Wodehouse.
1870 Death of Moshesh.

Swazi nation
Sobhuza I
1814–40 Ngwane joined by 8 refugee groups; safety of hills and caves; policy of conciliation; peace and prosperity; no open conflict with Zulu.

Mswati
1840–68 More aggressive than Sobhuza (Mpande, King of the Zulu). Council of adult men – age regiments but no standing army – unique position of the queen mother.

Swaziland and the Boers
It could give access to Kosi Bay for Transvaalers; Boer interest increased after Mswasi's death in 1868.
1868 Land concessions for Transvaalers in Swaziland.
1889 Death of Mbandzeni; queen mother sent deputation to Britain asking for British protection.
1894 Britain agreed to give Transvaal control of Swaziland without any annexation.
1902 British responsible for Swaziland but not as a colony.

Faku and the Pondo
Preferred diplomacy rather than warfare – secured the position of the Pondo despite attacks from the Zulu, the Qwabe, the Bhoca and Boers.

The Fingo – a refugee band
They were settled on lands for which the Xhosa had fought – adapted to European ways better than Xhosa.

Chief Khama and the Tswana
Area experienced attacks from the Tlokwa, Phuting and Ndebele in the first half of the nineteenth century.

Chief Khama III
Attended mission school – accepted western culture and Christianity.

1875 Became chief of his people; recognised the Boer threat.

1886 Eventually gained a protectorate under British control – saved the country being overrun by Boers and concession hunters.

Short questions on Chapter 7

1 Name two groups who were successful in forming empires after the Mfecane.
2 Which Boer leader defeated Mzilikazi at the Battle of Vegkop?
3 Where did the Ndebele settle eventually?
4 Where did Moshesh settle his age-group in 1821?
5 Which wandering groups did Moshesh have to resist?
6 Which missionaries joined Moshesh in Basutoland?
7 Why did Moshesh ask for British protection in the 1860s?
8 When did Sobhuza rule the Ngwane?
9 What kind of policy did Sobhuza follow towards the Zulu and the Ndebele?
10 What was the advantage of Swaziland to the Transvaalers?
11 When did Britain decide to take over responsibility for Swaziland?
12 Who was Faku and what were his particular problems?
13 Who are the Fingo?
14 Which are the three main ethnic groups in Botswana?
15 When was Botswana's position as a British protectorate assured finally?

Longer questions on Chapter 7

1 Describe the wanderings of Mzilikazi and his eventual settlement in Zimbabwe.
2 What were the qualities which made Moshesh an outstanding leader of the Basuto people?
3 Why and how did Basutoland and Swaziland become Britain's responsibility by the end of the nineteenth century?
4 Describe the circumstances by which Botswana became a British protectorate. (You will need to consult the details on 'the Scramble' in Chapter 8).
5 In what ways can Chief Khama III be considered an outstanding African leader of the nineteenth century?

Notes to Chapter 7

1 N. E. Davis, *Africa in the Modern World*, Oxford University Press, 1973, p. 38.

8   Federation, annexation and the 'Scramble for Africa'

The balance of power before 1867

Were the African states before the 1880s always much weaker, militarily and economically, than the growing Boer republics? Was eventual domination by the Boers inevitable from the time they migrated into the South African interior? The answer may be that a balance of power between the African states and the Boer republics was fairly well established until the discovery of diamonds. It might be that but for the discovery of precious minerals and the great numbers of Europeans who came into the area afterwards, the influence of the Boers might have in time been much reduced.

British power

The only major power in South Africa in the middle of the nineteenth century was the British authority at the Cape and Natal. Its main interests at that time were naval and commercial. As the great conventions of 1852 and 1854 suggest, it had no real designs on controlling the interior. Even so, a population of 250,000 Europeans in the Cape Colony had produced a prosperous economy and an element of self-government. Also, relations with British Kaffraria did not present any great military problems.

Boer weakness

The Boer republics at this time did not present the same picture of prosperity. They were generally able to defend their own territory against attack. They were not too successful in uniting the different Boer groups into a strong centralised government. At moments of critical danger co-operation between the laagers did occur, but it only existed for the period of the emergency. Economically, the Boers were pastoralist farmers. They produced little for export, and what little there was did not sell for a very high price at the Cape. Much of their land use was wasteful. No great progress was made because little emphasis was placed on education and training of any sort. The Boers lacked capital for development. Their prospects were not considered to be very good. When the Orange Free State tried to raise a loan with Cape banking houses it was refused. Neither was the Transvaal successful in getting investment in railway construction from Europe. Therefore, life in the Boer republics could not compare with that of the Cape, but was that of a simple pastoral economy, which was capable of self-defence. Occasionally, when a joint effort was made, the Republics were capable of defeating their African neighbours.

Attempts at federation

In 1837 there had only been one white colonial government in South Africa. By 1860, there were three colonial administrations: the Cape, British Kaffraria and Natal and two republican governments: the Orange Free State and the South African Republic (composed of Transvaal and the smaller ex-republics of Lydenberg, Utrecht and the Zoutpansberg).

The insecurity of the interior, for both African states and Boer republics as well as Natal, began to worry certain British administrators. They felt that Britain ought to have greater influence inland. The way that white settlement was spread out was the major reason for suggesting a federation of all the different regions.

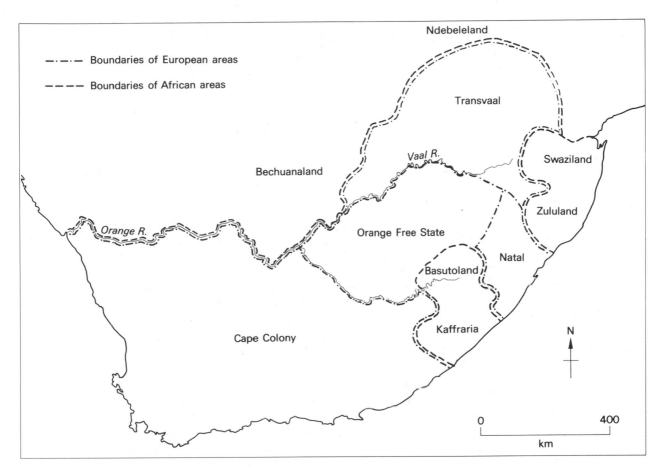

Fig. 24 South Africa in 1870

Sir George Grey and federation

Sir George Grey succeeded the soldier, Sir Harry Smith in 1854 as Governor at the Cape but unlike Smith he sought more peaceful solutions to South Africa's problems. He had time to reflect on the need for the federation of the separate areas. He was convinced that the racial question was the central problem in South Africa. In his statement of the case, he recognised that with separation as it existed, war was almost inevitable somewhere in the country. He said, 'for if a state is successful in a war it is waging, a native race will be broken up, and none can tell what territories its dispersed hordes may fall upon . . . Again, such petty states must be constant foci of intrigue and internal commotion.'[1] He considered the internal affairs of such states to be so small that they would produce no statesmen, provide little educational opportunity, and any money coming from a likely stagnant economy would not be enough for their

Sir George Grey

own protection. This defenceless position would in turn invite attack from neighbouring African groups.

In this message Sir George pointed out the disadvantages of separation. During his five years in South Africa he tried his hardest to federate the British colonies and the Orange Free State as the link between the Cape and Natal. He hoped that the Transvaal would see the need for federation also. His failure was due chiefly to the different racial policies practised in the various areas.

Different racial policies

In the Cape there was supposed to be political and civil equality between the white, coloured and black people. This was based on a voting system which, although common to all residents, provided greater proportional representation for the Europeans than for the non-Europeans. In Natal, the practice was quite different in a situation in which 100,000 Bantu lived in the same territory as about 7,000 whites. To accommodate the growing numbers of Bantu, Theophilus Shepstone, the Natal Agent, set aside eight reserves which together formed an area of just over 404,690 hectares. It had been intended to develop each reserve with training schools, schemes for agricultural training, and a local police force supervised by European officers. Lack of finance severely restricted these ambitious plans. Within the Reserves the Bantu were subject to African law which was administered by local chiefs, supported by European 'Native' Magistrates. Shepstone combined judicial and executive functions in the reserves. It is a tribute to his administrative skill and his great personal influence that Natal enjoyed a relatively peaceful period for nearly thirty years.

The policy of the Transvaal bore no resemblance at all to that of the earliest colony. The frontier followed a policy which was based on the belief that the Africans were 'Divinely appointed hewers of wood and drawers of water'. The main outline of the policy was that local affairs were in the hands of the chiefs. Dependent groups were given land which was only held on the basis of good behaviour. They were not allowed guns, wagons or horses, and were not allowed to make alliances with neighbouring groups. They were also required to pay a labour tax. They had to work when called upon.

Sir George Grey's first aim was to find a definite policy for British Kaffraria. The plan was not to be one of complete segregation. The population, both white and black, were to consider themselves 'inhabitants of one country'. It was intended that the territory should be more self-sufficient economically. In order to achieve this, the British provided a lump sum, an imperial grant and to this was added money from hut tax and court fines. Grey personally concerned himself with the establishment of training schools and the Grey Hospital at King William's Town. This policy was introduced at a time when relations between Moshesh and the Orange Free State were gradually worsening. Grey realised that Moshesh stood very clearly at the centre of South African affairs at this time.

Halfway through the nineteenth century, Moshesh was at the height of his powers. He had to be considered on equal terms by his European contemporaries. Boundary problems arose in the Orange Free State between the burghers and Moshesh after the withdrawal of British authority in 1854. Claims and counter-claims were made by and against the Basuto, and Grey was forced to persuade the two parties to accept the Smithfield Treaty of 1855. Fresh trouble broke out in 1857 when President Boshof tried to play a lesser chief off against Moshesh, Moshesh carried out legitimate reprisal raids on the border, and war began between the Basuto and the Orange Free State. For a time there was talk of a union between the Transvaal and the Free State. Grey maintained that such a union would involve a change in the Conventions by which the republics had gained their independence.

Failure of Grey's federation plan

He raised the question of federation in the Cape Parliament but had to give up his plans when he was told that Britain was not prepared to resume authority for either of the republics. He was recalled to Britain and only allowed to return to South Africa on the understanding that he did not raise the question of federation again.

By blocking the federation scheme, Britain and South Africa lost the best opportunity to correct some of the mistakes and injustices brought about by the division of the country. If the Great Trek divided the country, the discovery of precious minerals in the second half of the century demonstrated the wisdom of Grey's general strategy. The minerals provided an attractive economic incentive to bring about the union of the four areas.

Ownership of the diamond fields

The discovery of diamonds and gold provided a much greater reason for the extension of British influence northwards. After the discovery of diamonds in 1867, there were four years of

Waterboer, Chief of the Griqua, who was awarded the diamond fields by the Keate Award of 1871

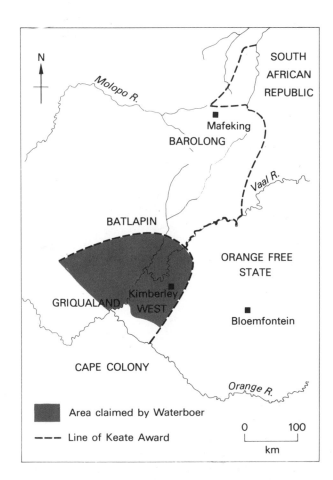

Fig. 25 Griqualand West and the Keate Award, 1871 (adapted from Walker, A History of Southern Africa, *Longmans, 1965)*

uncertainty. Numerous claims were made for the possession of the diamond fields. Even the diggers themselves established a free republic at Klipdrift under the presidency of Stafford Parker, a former able seaman in the British Navy. The five main claimants were the republics of the Orange Free State and the Transvaal, the Griqua chief, Waterboer, and the chiefs of the Batlapin and the Barolong. In retrospect, it would seem that the Orange Free State had the most genuine claim, but at the Keate Arbitration Award of 1871, the Lieutenant-Governor of Natal pronounced in favour of Waterboer. Waterboer immediately put his territory under British protection. The Orange Free State had based its claim on the fact that before 1854 her territory had extended as far as Kimberley. The Orange Free State was compensated for her loss with a sum of £90,000 provided by Britain. In the short term it was probably prudent of Keate to award the area to the Griqua. It was obvious that the Cape would be responsible for organising the diamond fields since there was no one else strong enough, either economically or politically, to accept such a responsibility.

83

Results of the diamond discoveries 1871–4

a) Relations between the Cape and the Afrikaner (Boer) Republics became much worse, the Boers being convinced of their rightful claim to the fields. Only the warnings of the cautious Brand (President of the Orange Free State) prevented the state from embarking on a distinctly hostile policy.

b) Pretorus was replaced as President of the Transvaal by the Rev Thomas Burgers. It was thought that he would be a much more accomplished diplomatist and not as likely to be outmanoeuvered by the imperial statesmen.

c) There were more Europeans in and around Kimberley than had gone on the Great Trek and Kimberley had become the second largest settlement in South Africa.

d) The white population in the country shared in the prosperity. The diamond fields provided a very attractive market for food products, and consumer goods were brought in from hundreds of kilometres away.

e) Because of the international attraction of the diamonds, money was more easily available for railway construction than ever before.

f) Many thousands of Africans came to work in the mining area from all parts of the country. This was the beginning of the modern migrant worker system. Many left Natal, causing a shortage of labour and an increased demand for Indian labour for the sugar and tea plantations.

g) The Transvaal benefited least from the development of the diamond fields, but President Burgers created a feeling of great optimism in the Transvaalers for a future South African federal republic with the Transvaal taking the leading role. The discovery of the goldfields at Lydenburg at this time created a great deal of confidence.

h) Land values in the diamond areas became very high and farms were sold for huge prices.

i) Griqualand West, annexed in 1871, became a

Diamond diggings in the 1870s. Note the division of labour

Crown Colony in 1873, but by 1880 it was under the control of the Cape.

The most important result of the discovery of diamonds and gold on the Witwatersrand was the greater European interest in the interior. This interest was inevitably political and economic. Increased white population in the diamond fields, and later the goldfields, strengthened the white position in the interior. This position had barely been maintained by the Boer republics. As a result of the economic importance of the fields and the wealth which resulted from them it was necessary to establish effective control over the important areas. The main question was: effective control by whom? The eventual result was a growth in the influence of the Cape and a reduced imperial influence. It was the Cape which gained most from the discovery and it was the Cape which was the least prepared to co-operate in any federation plan.

In these respects the mineral discoveries marked a turning point in the history of Southern Africa. The interior became so important to the colonialists of South Africa that the balance of power was tipped firmly in favour of the whites. The African states were eclipsed. Also, any ideas of federation introduced by the imperial government in Britain were likely to fail. This was only partly because of the independent spirit of the Transvaal, but more because of the growing wealth and economic independence of the Cape. Federation schemes were to be attempted but were started in the more vulnerable areas of Transvaal and Natal, not in the Cape.

Further attempts at federation

When the British Prime Minister, Disraeli, took office in January 1874 he promised a progressive colonial policy. Lord Caernarvon was made Colonial Secretary. He had had experience of a federation scheme; therefore he embarked immediately on a course aimed at federation. Conditions at this time were quite encouraging for federating the four European settled areas. The Cape was prosperous and well populated, while the two Boer republics were poverty-stricken. They might have been willing to give up some of their

Lord Caernarvon, British Colonial Secretary in 1874

independence in exchange for a share in the economic prosperity of the Cape. There were, however, a number of reasons why the federation plan failed.

Failure of Caernarvon's federation plan

The Cape was not prepared to accept interference from Britain so soon after gaining self-government. It was not prepared to share its resources with other states. The growing prosperity of the Cape was to be the great obstacle to Caervarvon's plans, because Prime Minister Molteno was not prepared to support an extension of Imperial influence. He was only prepared to consider a federation scheme if it was started by the Cape Colonial government. The Orange Free State was very suspicious of any British initiative, especially after the British annexation of Griqualand West. The Boers of the Transvaal were opposed to giving up any of their newly won freedom. They realised that federation with the Cape would mean the acceptance of the more liberal racial policies of the Cape. Consequently, when Caernarvon called a conference in London, only a delegation from Natal arrived. Caernarvon did not abandon his policy of federation but waited for circumstances to change so that the scheme could be reintroduced.

Annexation of the Transvaal 1877

War broke out between the Transvaal and the Bapedi in 1876 over a piece of land claimed by the Boers but controlled by the Bapedi (for an account of the war between the Bapedi and the Transvaal see page 109). The Boers exhausted themselves and their resources and the republic was left in a state of bankruptcy. The farmers refused to pay their taxes and the Cape banks would not lend any more money. It was at this stage in April 1877, that the British Government annexed the Transvaal. Although the Transvaalers did not agree with this there was little outspoken opposition at first. However, soon afterwards the Boers' nationalist pride made them very angry about the annexation. They looked to their leader, Paul Kruger, to do something about it.

Paul Kruger 1825–1904

Kruger was born in the Cape Colony in 1825. He left the Colony at the time of the Great Trek and was old enough to remember the sorrow of Piet Retief's death. He was proud of the Voortrekkers' triumph over Mzilikazi at the Battle of Vegkop. His early life was full of hunting and fighting. In the first years of the South African Republic (Transvaal), he gained the affection and honour of his fellow Boers through his connection with the early history of the trekkers. He seemed to them to be a typical Boer and a part of the open veld life that they loved.

After the Battle of Majuba Hill in the First Anglo-Boer War, Kruger was the automatic choice for the Transvaal burghers. He was elected as President four times; 1883, 1888, 1893 and 1898. He only came close to defeat in 1893 (before the Jameson Raid). He had a very forceful personality. He was a very persuasive speech-maker. His main asset was that he understood that his people wanted a strong and independent Republic, controlled by Afrikaners. To the people of the Transvaal, Kruger

Paul Kruger

represented all that was best in the independent spirit of the Afrikaner nationalist. He had played an active part as a commando leader in battles against African groups during the early years of the Boer Republics. He had led the resistance movements during the British annexation of the Transvaal.

Caernarvon resigned as Colonial Secretary in 1878 but the new Governor of the Cape, Sir Bartle Frere, was just as keen to implement Caernarvon's schemes. His term of office began badly when he dismissed John Molteno as Prime Minister of the Cape. An attempt to appease the Transvaalers after annexation and persuade them that federation was in their best interests also failed. He wanted to show the Boers how strong the British were but the disastrous British defeat at Isandhlwana did the opposite. It improved the morale of the Trans-vaalers.

First Anglo-Boer War, 1880

The annexation of the Transvaal was authorised by Disraeli's government. The new British Prime

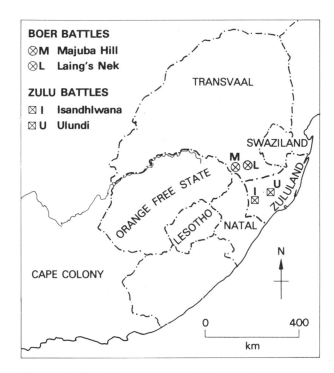

Fig. 26 Anglo-Zulu War 1879, Anglo-Boer War 1880–81

which was well-defended by 2,000 Boers. The British over-estimated the efficiency of their soldiers and underrated the Boers. The results were worse at Majuba Hill, when 500 British soldiers could not defend their position against a Boer attack on the hill. The Boers were allowed to advance up the hill until it was too late. Ninety-two British soldiers died, while the Boers only suffered slight casualties.

The Pretoria Convention 1881

Gladstone had not been happy about the Transvaal situation. He was very pleased to end the war soon after Majuba Hill and to grant internal independence to the Transvaal. It was also agreed in the Pretoria Convention of 1881 that the foreign policy of the Transvaal should be in British hands. Britain was to have limited responsibility for native affairs through a Resident in Pretoria. There was to be no discrimination against British goods by the Republic and the civil rights of the uitlanders were to be protected. The 'uitlanders' were the people

Minister, Gladstone, did not change this. The Boers had hoped that Gladstone would end the annexation. They were disappointed and they rebelled. The incident which started the war concerned a small farmer who was sued for the non-payment of tax. His property was compulsorily sold by the British administration in the Transvaal. A band of 300 Boers took back the property for the farmer. This attack on British authority convinced the rest of the Transvaal that they could take more positive action. The republic was re-established on 8 December 1880, with Paul Kruger as Volksraad President and Joubert as Commander-in-Chief.

Laing's Nek and Majuba Hill

With only 3,500 British troops in South Africa at this time, the initial advantage lay with the Boers. This advantage was maintained throughout the short war. The first engagement on 20 December involved a small British column of 264 men. The relief force was slaughtered by deadly Boer fire and half the British were killed or wounded. General Colley rushed from Natal with reinforcements and immediately began a foolish attack on Laing's Nek

The British defeat at Majuba Hill in 1881

who had entered the Transvaal to exploit the mineral wealth of the country. They had not been allowed to take out citizenship. The number of uitlanders was not very great in 1880, but the discovery of gold in 1885 brought a massive influx of European immigrants. The position of the uitlander was to be much more important by the end of the century.

The discovery of gold 1885

Gold was discovered in 1885 on the Witwatersrand. This time there was no disputing the ownership of the goldfields as they were definitely in Transvaal territory. From being a poverty-stricken state on the verge of bankruptcy the Transvaal was transformed. It became a wealthy, prosperous state with a growing white population and an expanding industrial economy based on the gold and coal fields.

Now the rest of South Africa saw the value and necessity of federation as soon as possible. But with their new-found prosperity the Transvaalers were even less interested in any links with British South Africa. Railways were constructed from Natal and Cape Town to the Transvaal border to provide a link with the coast for the Rand. But President Kruger allowed the Rand to use what was then Lourenço Marques and is now Maputo in Mozambique, as its port, by granting a railways contract to the Netherlands Company. As well as following an isolationist policy, that is, a policy of non-involvement with other countries, Kruger also continued to deny the uitlanders equal civil rights.

Uitlanders in Transvaal

Three years after the discovery of gold, the uitlanders had purchased nearly a third of the Transvaal, and by 1892 more than half the population was composed of uitlanders. The Boers

Goldmining brought wealth and prosperity to the Transvaal

recognised them as a distinct threat to their way of life, and insisted that they live in the country for ten years before they could take out citizenship. In the meantime, the Boers refused them all civil rights. They were not allowed trial by jury and were prevented from speaking English on public occasions. A typical reply of Kruger's to an appeal for equality was, 'Go back and tell your people that I shall never give them anything. I shall never change my policy. Now let the dam burst.'

Colonialism and imperialism

By 1886 the Cape Colonists and the republican Boers were prepared to stand alone and did not feel the need for imperial protection. The Cape had a long history of European settlement. A long period of economic growth had made it virtually self-supporting. The Transvaal, although it had been annexed by Britain was developing rapidly thanks to the goldfields. It was intent on maintaining its independent status. The Cape did not demand full independence but was not very enthusiastic about any plan to federate the different white areas in South Africa. The Cape had people who wanted to extend the white South African influence, but did not want the imperial government involved. Cecil Rhodes was one of these very strong colonialists.

Cecil Rhodes

Rhodes was born in England. He was expected to follow his father into the Church but his health was considered too fragile. He joined his brother on a farm in South Africa. In his early years in South Africa his health recovered. He achieved fabulous success in the Kimberley diamond fields.

Between 1876 and 1881, Rhodes concentrated on consolidating the Kimberley and De Beers Companies. The thousands of individual claims were gradually reduced to one huge operation, the De Beers Consolidated Mines Ltd, controlled by Rhodes. De Beers was to form the basis for Rhodes's political dreams and ambitions. He was convinced of the need for the Cape to dominate the

Cecil Rhodes

government of a united South Africa. To further these aims he tried to increase the Cape's power at the expense of imperial control. He later clashed with Kruger in deciding which brand of colonialism, British or Afrikaner, was going to control a united South Africa. In his extraordinary first will, he bequeathed his fortune (not yet made) to the purpose of extending British rule throughout the world. His views were made less extreme by the ideas of the Afrikaner Cape politician, Jan Hofmeyr, who believed in the need for colonial home rule rather than imperial rule.

Hofmeyr and Rhodes and colonial rule

Hofmeyr had been successful in reducing tensions between Afrikaners and British colonists at the Cape. The development of Afrikaans as a written as well as a spoken language gave the Afrikaners a greater degree of self-respect. Hofmeyr did not resent being part of a British colony, but did not realise until the late 1880s that the interests of the Cape were in some respects hindered by the interests and policies of the Boer republics. Taxes imposed on Cape produce entering the Transvaal affected Cape prosperity. Instead of appointing well-qualified South Africans (Afrikaner Cape Colonists) to important administrative posts, the Transvaal was bringing men in from the Netherlands. Lastly, the Transvaal was trying to develop a working relationship with Germany, an arrangement which, if allowed to happen, would have been to the disadvantage of the Cape.

Rhodes and Hofmeyr had much in common. Neither wanted British interference in South African affairs. They agreed that the future of South Africa depended on the breakdown of hostility and suspicion between Boer and Briton. They wanted South African Union, and also an imperial connection for trade and defence. It was this last that the republican Boers suspected. The alliance between Rhodes and Hofmeyr was intended to encourage the interests of the Afrikaners within the Cape and promote plans for expansion northwards. This policy became known as 'colonialism' (not to be confused with the meaning of the word in the twentieth century).

Rhodes entered the Cape assembly in 1881. Nine years later, with the support of Hofmeyr, he became Prime Minister of the Cape Colony. During his period of office, he followed a policy aimed at 'a government of South Africa by the people of South Africa with the Imperial tie for defence'. He realised that to achieve this there would need to be greater co-operation between the Afrikaners and the British. In trying to further this ideal, he set out on a course which was to prove disastrous for Rhodes personally, and for relations between the Afrikaners and the British.

Rhodes: mining concessions in Rhodesia

In order to extend British interests northwards Rhodes needed to control Bechuanaland, since the chance of a federation with the Boer republics was remote. Bechuanaland was declared a British Protectorate in 1886. The road northwards was now open to Rhodes. He sent agents to Lobengula requesting the right to mine for gold in Mashonaland (modern Zimbabwe). Later he was granted a Royal Charter for his South Africa Company, and in 1890 he established a Company station at Harare (later Salisbury) with Dr Jameson in charge.

Jan H. Hofmeyr, leader of the Afrikaner Bond and an ally of Rhodes's at the Cape

Jameson, who had given up a profitable medical practice in Kimberley to help Rhodes, played a very important part in the negotiations with Lobengula, partly through his medical ability in curing an attack of gout suffered by the chief, and partly through his personal charm. He was later to play a prominent role in the ill-fated Jameson Raid (see p. 99), when Rhodes tried to force the issue of federation with the Transvaal.

Rhodes at the Cape

Rhodes became Prime Minister of the Cape in July 1890, and was then the most powerful personality in South Africa. For as controller of the De Beers diamond empire at Kimberley and of the Goldfields Company on the Rand, and leader of the Royal British South African Company, he had a great influence on South African affairs.

His main contributions to the Cape while he was Prime Minister were dealing with problems of voting and land ownership in African reserves and the annexation of East and West Pondoland. His greatest disappointment was his inability to bring about economic federation with the Transvaal.

Failure of economic union with the Transvaal

As far as economic integration with the Transvaal was concerned Rhodes realised that he did not have enough time. His health had become worse after a fall from a horse in 1891 and this may have persuaded him to try to achieve by force what he had failed to achieve by persuasion and negotiation. (see p.99).

Both Kruger and Rhodes played a part in the Jameson Raid. Kruger made a great error of judgement in his dealings with the uitlanders, but Rhodes can be accused of an unnecessary crime. It is very likely that Kruger, who was gradually losing support among his own people over his uitlander policy, would have been ousted at the next presidential election. The raid only served to revive his declining support and return him once again as president with the same inflexible policy. Rhodes's greatest fault was that he failed to understand the situation. After the miserable failure of the Raid, and after his commitment to it had appeared obvious, he resigned from the Cape premiership in January 1896 and concerned himself for the rest of his career with the development of his financial empire in Rhodesia, until his death in 1902.

The growth of Afrikaner nationalism

When the Afrikaners left the Cape Colony on the Great Trek they were rejecting the authority of the British administration. It had threatened their traditional way of life. But before the discovery of diamonds and the economic revival that this brought, it is difficult to recognise a clear feeling of nationalism in the Boer way of life. The Boers tended to live in isolated farmsteads and did not come together very often except in times of emergency. In normal times, family interests often clashed and differences between groups were

common. Only months after the discovery of gold in 1885, the Transvaal was a sound economic unit and the Transvaalers were beginning to enjoy a standard of living far better than anything they had previously experienced.

Mineral wealth and Boer nationalism

The numbers of uitlanders increased with the mineral wealth of the Transvaal. Many envious eyes were cast on the new-found prosperity of the country, particularly from the south. The Cape built railways close to the Transvaal border in order to exploit the commercial advantage of her position near the sea. The Transvaal had no intention of allowing a growth of British influence in the Transvaal. It pursued a deliberate policy of favouring the Portuguese to the east and the Germans to the west. The Transvaal, instead of being a poor, insignificant country in the 'Scramble for Africa', developed a growing sense of nationalism based on the wealth of the Witwatersrand and a stronger government. This found expression in attempts to move into Botswana and Swaziland. The symbol of this nationalism was the figure of the Transvaal President, Paul Kruger.

Southern Africa and the 'Scramble for Africa'

Ideas about federation and the growth of 'colonialism' at the Cape were blocked by the 'nationalism' in the Boer republics. At the same time international pressures began to build up over tropical Africa. The effects of these pressures were felt in Southern Africa. For most of the nineteenth century Britain had been able to deal with South African problems without fear of interference from any other European country. This all changed in the last thirty years of the century. Rivalry between European countries expressed itself in competition for the control of African territory, and in South Africa it was Germany who intervened in South African affairs. The main reasons why there was this 'Scramble for Africa' were the possible economic advantages of the territory and the desire of each country to increase it's own importance.

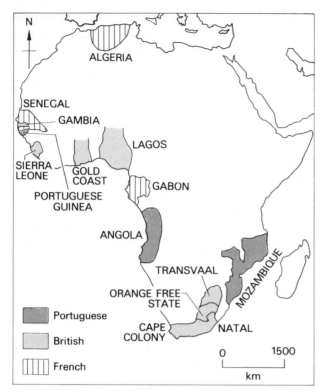

Fig. 27 European colonies 1879

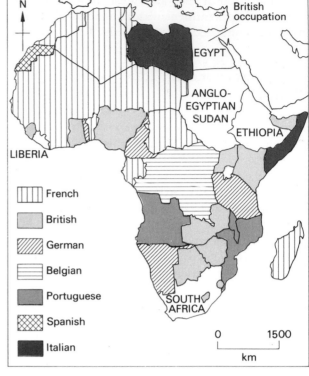

Fig. 28 European 'Scramble for Africa' by 1914

Britain had had little competition from other European countries before the 'Scramble' period. She had expanded her trading interests without much expense to the British Government. With increased European rivalry, effective political control of Africa became necessary and Britain was late to realise this.

German annexation of South-West Africa

The German Rhenish Missionary Society was established in South-West Africa by 1868. The missionaries requested protection from the King of Prussia (later Germany) and sent complaints to the Cape government. A visit by Special Commissioner Palgrave in 1876 almost resulted in the territory placing itself under Cape protection, but the Cape Parliament was not prepared to take on the extra expense which this would have involved. In 1880 war broke out again between the Herero and the Khoikhoi. The German Chancellor Bismarck

asked whether Britain was going to provide protection for the German missionaries. Britain was not prepared to take any action. A German trader, Luderitz, built a trading post at Angra Pequena Bay in 1883 and in 1884 South-West Africa was annexed by Germany after discussions between the Governments of Germany, Great Britain and the Cape Colony.

Botswana

The British annexed Botswana (formerly Bechuanaland) the land of the Tswana, because they needed the route inland between the Transvaal and the Kalahari. They did not want the Transvaal controlling this route. They did not like the idea of further German expansion from South-West Africa. In 1885 the area to the south of the Molopo became the Crown Colony of British Bechuana-land. In 1895 it was included in the Cape Colony. The protectorate was extended northwards to latitude 22°S in the 1890s to include the rest of modern Botswana. There was an attempt to transfer the territory to Rhodes's British South Africa Company, but the transfer was opposed by the chiefs of the Bakwena, Bangwaketse and Bamangwato clans. Bechuanaland remained under the control of the British High Commissioner.

Lesotho and Swaziland

Both countries eventually became protectorates administered by the British High Commissioner. Both areas seemed likely to fall under the influence of the Boer republics. In the case of Swaziland it was not until after the Anglo-Boer War 1899–1902 that Britain took responsibility for the area. As late as 1893–4 in negotiations between the British and Transvaal it was agreed that Swaziland should be a Boer dependency. Despite a Swazi protest delegation to London, the Afrikaners assumed a control which was not transferred to the British until 1902. Lesotho, formerly Basutoland, came under British control at a much earlier date. Moshesh's kingdom was annexed by the British in 1868. Control was given to the Cape Colony. The Colony mismanaged Basuto affairs so badly that it asked the British Government to take over responsibility for Lesotho. This was done in 1884. (For an account of the 'War of the Guns', see p. 108).

In these three separate ways the Tswana, Swazi and Basuto gained for themselves freedom from the 'colonials' and 'republicans' in South Africa. They were never included in the Union of South Africa and were able to take advantage of the decolonisation process after the Second World War.

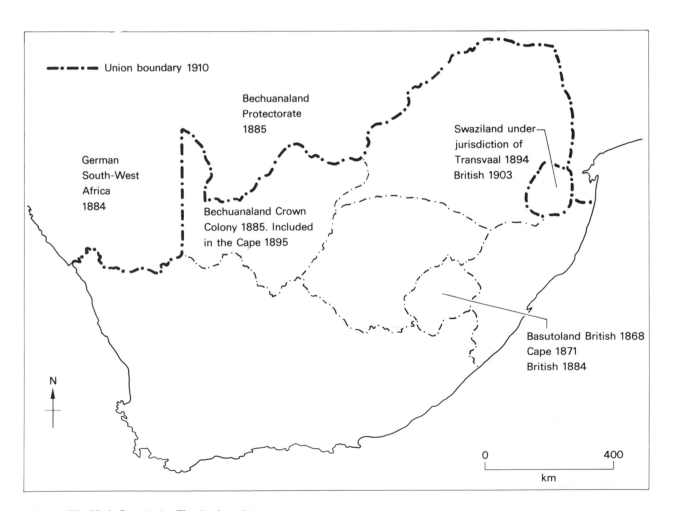

Fig. 29 The High Commission Territories, 1860–1910

Economic changes after the mineral discoveries 1870–1904

The discovery and exploitation of minerals, particularly diamonds and gold, in the second half of the nineteenth century was the greatest single factor in the economic development of the country.

The impact of the diamond fields

Situated in the drier western part of the country, Kimberley suffered, as have many other pioneering mining settlements, from a great shortage in the bare essentials of life. With a growing population moving into the area, Kimberley, the centre of the diamond mining suffered from a lack of communication with the coast. The nearest railway was at Wellington, at the end of the line from Cape Town, some 1,000 kilometres from Kimberley.

Since the expense of constructing railways of this size was beyond the financial capacities of most private companies, the Cape government decided to buy up all existing railways and began a programme of railway extension from the three main ports of Cape Town, Port Elizabeth and East London. Eventually, Kimberley was reached in 1885. At this time no railways had been constructed in the Orange Free State or the South African Republic (Transvaal).

The results of the discovery of diamonds and the building of the railways were:

(a) *A new source of great wealth*
The discovery completely altered the whole economy of the region. Employment, both skilled and unskilled, was available for thousands. South Africa had found an alternative to farming as a major source of income. After the discovery of diamonds, and more especially gold, there was little chance that the Europeans would evacuate the area in the foreseeable future. The minerals increased the interest in the area of the Imperial Powers. Previously Britain had been prepared to withdraw from responsibility for the area.

(b) *A great increase in the demand for farming produce caused by:*
1 The rapid growth of population resulting from immigration. By 1871 Kimberley had a population of 50,000, second only in size to Cape Town.
2 Increase of wealth and purchasing power.
3 Enlarging of local markets by improved transport facilities.

More land was brought under cultivation. With a wealthier farming community, more money was invested in machinery and fertiliser. This resulted in more efficient farming.

(c) *The expansion of transportation and communication*
As well as improvements in the railways, much progress was made with roads, bridges, telephones, telegraphs and ocean communications. The Union and Castle steamship companies provided a regular link between South Africa and England. Kimberley was in contact with Cape Town by telegraph in 1876, and in 1882 the telephone was introduced into South Africa.

(d) *Improved banking facilities*
It was very necessary that with the increase in trade there should be an accompanying expansion of banking facilities. The major banks which established themselves at this time were the Standard Bank, the Oriental Banking Corporation and the National Bank of the Orange Free State. All three absorbed local banks and opened new branches all over the country.

The Cape Colony gained the greatest benefit from the opening-up of the diamond fields, but both Natal and the Orange Free State later made progress. The Transvaal being further inland and far removed from the diamonds, was hardly affected by the boom and made very little progress during the period.

The gold era 1886–1910

Before 1886, the Transvaal had had little more than a poor pastoralised economy. It was this poverty which had persuaded Sir Theophilus Shepstone of the need to annex the Transvaal in 1877. Even after the end of the First Anglo-Boer War in 1881, economic conditions did not show much improvement.

From 1886, Transvaal began to make spectacular progress. An idea of the improvement can be

Railway in the Transvaal. Note the covered wagons and the division of labour

gauged from the change in the value of gold production from 1890–8.

1890	£1,869,000
1894	£7,600,000
1898	£16,000,000

When gold was discovered, there were no railways in the Transvaal, but ten years later the Rand was in contact by rail with the Cape, Delagoa Bay and Durban. It had become the focal point of the economic life of South Africa. The actions of imperial and colonial statesmen in expanding British influence in Bechuanaland, Natal, Basutoland, Zululand and Pondoland forced the Transvaal to search for an outlet to the sea which was free of British control and influence. It was thought that economic pressures would persuade the Transvaalers of the need for a customs union which would form the basis for a later political union of the four regions.

But the Transvaal turned its attention to Delagoa Bay and with the help of the Netherlands Company, the railway link to Portuguese East Africa was completed in 1895. After the opening of the railway, the economic warfare between the Transvaal and the Cape intensified. Other factors such as freight rates, the closure of the 'drifts' and the status of the uitlanders combined to complicate matters, leading eventually, since the struggle could not be resolved at a political level, to the Anglo-Boer War of 1899–1902.

Conditions during and after the war

Reconstruction

The disruption of agricultural and industrial activity, particularly in the Transvaal, was only temporary. Although the value of gold production fell to just over £1 million in 1901 the post-war years saw a greater development than the years before the war. Cape Colony and Natal were able to benefit from the large amounts of money which were spent by the British Government in fighting the war. The war cost Britain about £250 million and a large proportion of this money was spent on supplies provided by the local farmers and traders.

Repatriation and reorganisation was effected smoothly and rapidly under the leadership of Lord Milner, who had been appointed Governor of the Transvaal and the Orange Free State. By 1905, the farming industry was back to normal and developing rapidly. The mining industry was re-established. Railways were extended and improved, and the finances of the two colonies were stabilised.

Confidence in the commercial potential of South Africa grew with the rapid reconstruction of the country. This confidence was translated into an increase in overseas investment, and in the number of immigrants. The European population rose from 630,000 in 1891 to 1,117,000 in 1904, figures which suggest that immigration must have been on a considerable scale during these years. During the same period the non-European population increased from about 2,800,000 to just over 4,000,000.

Summary of Chapter 8

Mid nineteenth century

British Colonies: Cape and Natal – relatively prosperous with no great racial problems.

Boer Republics: Orange Free State, South African Republic – simple pastoral economy – poor prospects – no strong government – little education.

Federation attempts

1 *1857 Sir George Grey:* failed – Britain not prepared to accept responsibility for Boer Republics so soon.

2 *1874 Lord Caernarvon:* failed – Cape not prepared to share prosperity; Transvaal and Orange Free State jealous of own freedom.

Attempts to control Transvaal

1 *1877 Annexation of Transvaal:* in state of bankruptcy after war with Bapedi in 1876.

1879 Anglo-Zulu War: British attempt to appease Transvaal. Defeat at Isandhlwana only encouraged later Transvaal revolt.

2 *1880–1 Anglo-Boer War:* Boers rebelled against British control – Laing's Nek and Majuba Hill. Pretoria Conference: gave internal self-government to Transvaal.

Mineral discoveries

1867 Diamond Fields: under the control of the Cape; discontent among the Boers in the Orange Free State.

1885 Gold: rapid economic growth in the Transvaal; encouraged Boer nationalism.

'Colonialism'

Extension of Cape influence to the north. Rhodes and Hofmeyr – powerful leaders. Imperial control (British Empire) only to be used as a guarantee against foreign interference. Rhodes and Hofmeyr wanted a South African Union.

Boer nationalism

Transvaal suspicious of British involvement in any Union – keen to maintain a strong independence made possible by gold discovery.

Imperialism

'Scramble for Africa' (European rivalry)

1884 German South West Africa.

1885–95 Botswana – to prevent further German expansion and control route north.

1903 Swaziland. 1884 Lesotho – British protection from Boer expansion threats.

Cecil Rhodes 1853–1902

Born in England – went to South Africa for health reasons – gained control of diamond fields through De Beers.

1881 member of the Cape Assembly.

1890 Prime Minister of the Cape, established Company station at Harare (later Salisbury).

1895 Jameson raid: an attempt to overthrow the Transvaal Government and integrate it with the Cape. (See Chapter 9.)

1896 resigned as Prime Minister; continued with Rhodesian interests.

1902 died at the relatively early age of 49.

Paul Kruger 1825–1904

Born in N.E. Cape – took part in Great Trek in Potgieter's party – fearless commando leader in the Transvaal – symbol of conservatism and Boer independence – elected President of the Transvaal four successive times from 1883 until 1898. Forceful character – passionate speaker. He had clear-cut ideas and objectives understandable to the Boers – a strong, independent Transvaal.

Diamonds and gold
1 Source of great wealth.
2 Increased population – increased demand for farm produce.
3 Rapid expansion of transport.
4 Massive influx of Africans to work the fields.
5 Provided money for developing all aspects of the country's economy.

Short questions on Chapter 8

1 Which was the only major power in South Africa in 1850?
2 Name the three colonial administrations in South Africa in 1860.
3 When did Sir George Grey become Governor of the Cape Colony?
4 When were diamonds discovered?
5 The Keate Award of 1871 was in favour of
....
6 Who was the Prime Minister at the Cape in 1874?
7 When was the South African Republic (Transvaal) annexed by Britain?
8 Who was the Transvaal President in 1880?
9 When was gold discovered in the Rand?
10 How did Rhodes amass his great wealth?
11 When was South-West Africa annexed by Germany?
12 When was Basutoland annexed by the British?

Longer questions on Chapter 8

1 What reasons did Sir George Grey give for federating the four areas?
2 How did native policies vary between the British areas and the Boer republics?
3 How was the dispute over the diamond fields settled, and what effect did the discovery of diamonds have on the subsequent history of South Africa?
4 Describe the circumstances which led to the outbreak of the First Anglo-Boer War of 1880.

5 Give the terms of the Pretoria Conference of 1881.
6 Describe the career of Cecil Rhodes, emphasising the acquisition of great wealth and his political ambitions for South Africa.
7 In what way did the discovery of gold contribute to the growth in Afrikaner nationalism?
8 Explain the importance of the gold and diamond discoveries to the subsequent wealth of South Africa.

Notes to Chapter 8

1 E. A. Walker, *A History of Southern Africa*, Longmans, 1965.

9　The Second Anglo-Boer War; conciliation and union

There were two main reasons for the outbreak of war between Britain and the Boer republics in 1899. Firstly, there was a greater British effort to federate the South African areas under the British Crown. Secondly there was the equally determined Transvaal attempt to maintain their independence. Throughout the 1890s one incident after another increased the differences between the British and the Boers until by 1899 war was almost unavoidable.

Railway tariff dispute

The Colonial Secretary in 1895 was Joseph Chamberlain. He was quick to intervene in the customs and **tariff** war which was developing between the Cape and the Transvaal. The Netherlands Railway Company controlled the Transvaal sections of the railway to Durban and the Cape as well as the entire line to Delagoa Bay. The Cape had built up a valuable market in the Transvaal for her own produce. By imposing different tariffs on different sections the Company was able to control the flow of traffic into the Transvaal. The Cape government tried to get round this by sending ox waggons with supplies by road into the Rand. Kruger answered this by closing the Vaal drifts (river fording places) to ox waggons. Chamberlain protested to Kruger, first of all preparing the ground for a military expedition, and in October 1895 Kruger re-opened the drifts.

Surrounding of the Transvaal

In the same year Bechuanaland Crown Colony became part of the Cape Colony. In the east Kosi Bay and Tongaland were annexed by the British. Kruger was offered Kosi Bay as a coastal port for the Transvaal if in return he would enter into a customs union with the Cape. This he refused to do. By missing this opportunity of gaining a sea port, the Transvaalers were hemmed in on all sides, for by then Rhodes had extended the influence of the British South Africa Company into what is now Zimbabwe, to the north of the Transvaal.

1895 was a very critical year for British-Boer relations. It was in 1895 that Rhodes attempted to force events in the interests of the Cape and the

Joseph Chamberlain, British Colonial Secretary during the Anglo-Boer War of 1899–1902

British. His offer of a customs union with the Transvaal had been refused because of the Transvaal's growing economic strength. So he tried to overthrow the Boer Government by an invasion of Boer territory to support a civil uprising by the uitlanders.

The Jameson Raid 1895

The uitlanders appealed to Rhodes and Jameson for help in their struggle for political and civil rights in the Transvaal, and a plan was thought up to overthrow the Transvaal Government. Cecil Rhodes had intended that the raid should support a revolt by the uitlanders on the Rand. As the time for the raid grew closer it became clear that the mining people of the Rand were not very enthusiastic about the plan. Colonel Frank Rhodes, Rhodes's elder brother, who was in charge of the conspiracy in Johannesburg was not the type of person to inspire a rebellion. He might have been more valuable as commander of the raiders instead of Jameson, who had the glamour and dashing personality necessary for the leadership of the revolt in the Transvaal.

Failure of the Raid

There were differences between the uitlanders and Cecil Rhodes. The uitlanders wanted self-government for the Transvaal, Rhodes wanted an association with the rest of South Africa. Rhodes had second thoughts about the possible success of his plan. Jameson was to set out on 28 December, but on 20 December Rhodes cancelled this order. The impulsive Jameson chose to disregard the second order and the raid began with 385 mounted soldiers leaving Botswana for the Transvaal. The Boers knew about his invasion by the morning of the first day. Jameson found that his small band was no match for the Transvaalers, who surrounded the raiders at Doornkop near Krugersdorp and forced Jameson to surrender unconditionally.

The raid caused great excitement in Britain. Jameson was pictured as a hero riding to save the uitlanders from continued Boer oppression, but the British Government did not know what to do about the situation.

Dr L. S. Jameson, leader of the Jameson Raid of 1896

Results of the Jameson Raid

The major result of the unsuccessful raid was that a peaceful solution to the differences between the Transvaal and Britain became almost impossible. In the Transvaal, suspicion of the British was increased while groups in Britain, embarrassed by the failure of the raid, wanted the British Government to intervene in the Transvaal. Paul Kruger was re-elected as President of the Transvaal. Had the raid not happened, the Transvaal might have chosen a more liberal leader. The raid also created a closer understanding between the two Afrikaner republics. The Orange Free State realised that the British designs on the Transvaal could also extend to her. In the Cape, Rhodes was forced to resign as Prime Minister and concentrate his attention on the future of Rhodesia. The alliance between Rhodes and Hofmeyr was destroyed. The white electorate in the Cape was divided. The 1898 election resulted in a narrow victory for the Afrikaner Bond, the major political party at the Cape. Hofmeyr, leader of the Bond, had supported Rhodes in his search for a united South Africa, but the raid destroyed this alliance, and W. P. Schreiner formed a government whose aim was to limit Rhodes's influence and prevent British interference in internal South African affairs. Jameson had a long period outside politics but he returned to lead a pro-British government in the Cape before the Act of Union.

After the raid it was the British Government rather than the 'colonialist' politicians at the Cape, who called for British intervention in the Transvaal. The British representative was High Commissioner in South Africa. Chamberlain realised that if the Transvaal was to become part of British South Africa it would be through the direct efforts of the British Government. He misunderstood the situation in South Africa very badly in three ways. He may not have thought that war was the only way to bring Transvaal into the British sphere of influence but these three errors made war inevitable.

Chamberlain's errors of judgement

Firstly, he exaggerated the Transvaal's threat to British interests in South Africa. At that time there was no united effort among Afrikaners to control the whole area. Had the Transvaal been given time there was every chance that the problems of the uitlanders' civil and political rights might have been solved. Secondly, the Boers could not be easily persuaded to give up their independence to a people that they had defeated at Majuba Hill. The Transvaal quite naturally expected help from the Orange Free State and were given reason to hope that Germany would provide assistance if needed. Thirdly, Sir Alfred Milner was the High Commissioner. He was an arch-imperialist, who ignored the fact that people in South Africa were opposed to war. He exaggerated his feelings against the Transvaal in his reports to Chamberlain. Chamberlain and Milner led Britain into war with the Afrikaner republics. The excuse used to justify British policy was the protection of the uitlanders. The real reason was Britain's determination to bring all South Africa under her control. She would not allow an unimportant Afrikaner republic to threaten her status as a world and imperial power.

Chamberlain prepared for war but before reinforcements could be sent out to South Africa, Kruger demanded the withdrawal of British troops from the Transvaal border. The deadline expired on 11 October 1899, and war was declared on Britain by the Afrikaner republics (Transvaal and Orange Free State).

The war 1899–1902

The war was a test for the Boers as to whether they would be able to retain not only their own culture, but their freedom, their language, their possessions, their racial supremacy, their very existence as an independent people. The British were at first defeated, but the Boers did not follow up their early success effectively. About 80,000 men fought for the two republics and from first to last about 500,000 fought on the British side. It was not a short war as most people had anticipated. During the three years of war there was much cruelty on both sides. This did not help future relations between the two groups.

General Roberts entered Bloemfontein in March 1900. By June he was in the Transvaal capital of Pretoria. The British, although in control of the two republics, still had the problem of defeating the commando bands led by Generals de Wet, Smuts, Botha and Hertzog, who carried on the struggle for a further eighteen months in the Cape and Natal. The Boers were not helped by a European power,

Boer Commandos were fine horsemen and crack shots in the Anglo-Boer Wars

Boer prisoners in a concentration camp. These camps were set up by the British between 1899–1902

as they had hoped. They were further disappointed when their commando raids into British areas did not lead to a general uprising. One of the most famous commando leaders was General Christian de Wet, who time after time attacked and escaped before the British forces had a chance to counter attack.

Modern methods of warfare – scorched earth policies and concentration camps – were used by the British in order to weaken the Boers' fighting spirit. Farms were burnt or blown up, crops and livestock destroyed and women and children made homeless by the British so that the Boers' resolve to carry on the war would be broken. The women and children were herded into tented camps which were overcrowded, disease-ridden and lacking basic supplies of food and clothing. At the end of the war, the camps held 120,000 Boers and 100,000 Africans. It is estimated that about 26,000 Boer women and children died in the camps.

The war continued to go badly for the Boers, but their leaders were not prepared to give up their independence. At a meeting between Lord Kitchener (representing the British) and Boer representatives, it was agreed that the Boer commandos should be given the opportunity to sound out the opinion of their people on acceptable peace terms. Majority opinion was in favour of retaining independence and the five generals, Smuts, Botha, Hertzog, de Wet and de la Rey, were given the task of protecting the independence of the republics at the conference table. When it was clear that this was totally unacceptable to the British they were obliged to return to their people with the British terms. At a meeting of the Boers' delegates at Vereeniging the terms were agreed by a large majority. The generals returned to Pretoria where the Peace Treaty was signed.

At the end of the war, about 6,000 Boers and 22,000 Britons had been killed and a further 30,000 Boer soldiers had been imprisoned in prisoner-of-war camps in and outside South Africa.

A white man's war

One aspect of the war which needs to be emphasised was that it was only carried on between the two white armies. The Africans did not fight. They were bearers or transport drivers. This is not to suggest that Africans did not wish to take a more active part, but the British and Boers considered the war an all-white affair. There was an unwritten agreement not to accept African allies on either side. One obvious reason for this agreement was that neither side was prepared to arm African troops, who could quite easily use their arms in their own interests against either of the white authorities. African armed resistance against colonial rule was still a normal pattern of South

African life at the end of the century. There was the Ndebele and Shona revolt of 1896–7; the Herero continued their fight for independence against the Germans in South-West Africa; and in 1906 there was the Bambata Rising in Natal.

This practice of not arming Africans even in the South African armed forces has continued right up to the present day. When General Smuts led a South African division against the Germans in Tanganyika, he did not conceal his contempt for the fighting potential of Von Lettow's band of African askari. Before the campaign was over, however, Smuts revised his opinion to the point of open admiration for their courage and discipline. Throughout the present century the South African Government has never felt confident enough of its own security to risk such an experiment. They feel that they can count on the undivided loyalty of the armed forces if they are all white.

Peace of Vereeniging 31 May 1902

Smuts and Botha had been keen to sign the peace treaty but General Hertzog had been very reluctant. This was a sign of his nationalism which was to show itself politically soon after the Act of Union was passed in 1910. The peace was a generous conclusion to a disastrous war. The terms of the peace were:

a) The Transvaal and the Orange Free State became British colonies.
b) Responsible government was promised to both colonies in the near future.
c) Vast sums of money and assistance were given to restore the broken countries.
d) The Dutch and English languages were to have equal status.

Afrikaner opinion on the peace was divided between that of Smuts and Botha who were 'preparing to sacrifice much for South Africa', and Hertzog, who said that he was 'aware that a great nation could co-operate with a smaller one without any sense of danger, but that the smaller one could only preserve itself by vigilance, care and, if necessary, by isolation'. That Botha and Smuts adopted an attitude of 'South Africanism' was no small contribution towards the Act of Union in 1910.

Economic steps towards union

Despite the decline in economic activity between 1904 and 1907, important steps were taken towards a union of the four regions. Although attempted previously this had always failed usually because of the special position of the Transvaal. This fourth attempt to unite the country probably succeeded for the following reasons:

a) All four regions were British colonies and were organised in similar ways. This was an improvement on the previous occasions when a large obstacle had always been the different political systems in the Transvaal and the Orange Free State.
b) The formation of the Customs Union of 1903 completed the movement of gradual commercial federation, which provided a common tariff wall against the outside world.
c) During his term as Governor of the two new colonies and High Commissioner, Lord Milner was successful in reducing rivalry between the different railway systems. The railways of the Transvaal and the Orange River Colony were brought under one authority and an agreement was signed between the Cape and Natal railway authorities in 1905. This closer co-ordination of the railways was no small contribution to the later achievements of political union.
d) Political union was also influenced by the need to lower administrative costs: in place of four wholly separate administrations, one common administration had a lot to recommend it. If the idea had been sound in Sir George Grey's term of office, it was even more advisable in a modern South Africa, which in economic terms was expanding very rapidly.

South African Act of Union

There were two main reasons why the Act of Union followed so quickly after the Peace of Vereeniging. The introduction of a customs union developed economic co-operation among the four colonies, and the granting of responsible government to the Transvaal and the Orange Free State in 1907 placed the two former Boer republics on the same political level as the Cape and Natal. In the Transvaal, Botha and Smuts won the election; Fischer and Hertzog won the election in the Orange Free State, and the new government in the Cape depended on the support of Afrikaners. The opportunity was therefore available for a union movement on conditions laid down by the Afrikaner leaders instead of by English-speaking politicians as had been expected.

In 1908 the National Convention met to decide on an acceptable formula for a union constitution. Delegates came from each of the four colonies and observers from Rhodesia also. The nature of the franchise (right of voting at public elections) and the question of racial politics were to be considered by the convention but it was agreed to leave aside the question of African affairs until after union was achieved. This was a victory for the separatist Afrikaners. They would not have changed their firmly held opinions to satisfy the more liberal views of the Cape.

The Cape delegation was the only one which represented both European and non-white voters, and there was a genuine attempt to extend this 'Civilisation Franchise' to the other three colonies. This would have meant that some of the non-whites would have been able to vote and a number of the poor whites would have lost the vote. This was completely unacceptable to the Transvaal, the Orange Free State and Natal. The deadlock was only broken when the three delegations agreed that the Cape franchise for the non-European should remain and that the non-Europeans should be eligible for the Cape and Natal Provincial Councils. But they denied the right of non-Europeans to sit in the Union Parliament. Despite protests against the franchise arrangements, the British Government ratified the proposed constitution in the *Union of South Africa Act* which was effective from May 1910. The main provisions of the new constitution were:

a) The Union Parliament was given supreme authority over the four colonies which in future were to be called 'provinces'.
b) The leading executive officer was to be the Governor-General assisted by an Executive Council of Ministers.
c) The Union Parliament was to consist of a House of Assembly and an Upper Chamber, the Senate.
d) The capital was divided into three with the Parliament at Cape Town, the Executive at Pretoria and the Judiciary at Bloemfontein.
e) The official languages were to be English and Dutch. (There are differences between the Dutch and Afrikaans languages).
f) Recognition was made of the non-white voters

Pretoria in about 1910. This was the capital of the Transvaal and later the executive capital of a united South Africa

in the Cape Province, but Parliamentary membership from the Cape was limited to Europeans. Clauses e) and f) could only be changed by a two-thirds majority decision of the Senate and the House of Assembly sitting together.

One small provision of the Union Constitution ensured that the Afrikaners would always have an advantage over non-Afrikaners. It was decided that in rural voting areas, the number on the electoral roll need only have 85 per cent of the average number of electors; whereas the urban voting areas might have as many as 115 per cent of the average number. Since the rural areas were overwhelmingly Afrikaner, the effect of this provision was to give the Afrikaners more voting areas than their numbers alone would justify.

Only eight years after the bitter struggle of the Anglo-Boer War, the Act of Union was passed. This was a remarkable achievement. That the optimism of the Act was not justified by events after the union can only be explained by the fact that the politicians tended to ignore the emotional content in politics. They overlooked the fact that the differences between the Afrikaners and the English-speaking South Africans would not be forgotten for long. The British Government, by accepting the franchise arrangements in the constitution, gave up its last chance to influence the future of the South African community. The Act of Union was basically an act of conciliation between the two European groups and ignored the needs and demands of the non-white population of the country.

Although they were defeated in the war, the Afrikaner delegates to the conferences did not give up their nationalist attitudes. The war may have weakened them economically, but it reinforced all their feelings about Afrikaner independence. They still believed in the superiority of the Afrikaner over the non-white in South Africa and the need to protect and support the symbol of their national identity, the Afrikaans language. In retrospect it is not so surprising that the Union of South Africa came about on conditions laid down by the Afrikaner politicians. Chamberlain and Milner's ideas of establishing a state committed to British interests could not compete with the Afrikaners' belief that they should be free of all foreign influences.

Summary of Chapter 9

Anglo-Boer War
Incidents leading to war:
1 Tariff Dispute – on railway between Cape and Transvaal; closing of the drifts by Kruger.
2 Isolation of Transvaal.
3 1895 Jameson Raid.
4 Intervention of British Government (Chamberlain). Chamberlain made three mistakes:
   a) Exaggerated Transvaal's threat to British interests.
   b) Transvaal would not give up independence without war.
   c) Ignored existing South African attitudes which were opposed to war.

The war 1899–1902
A white man's war: involved 80,000 Boers 500,000 Britons. Early Boer successes. British gradually gained upper hand. Boers continued with guerilla warfare in the Cape and Natal – Generals de Wet, Botha, Smuts, Hertzog.
Casualties: 6,000 Boers, 22,000 Britons.
Scorched earth policy and concentration camps.

1902 Peace of Vereeniging
1 Transvaal and Orange Free State – British colonies with a promise of early responsible government.
2 Massive restoration funds.
3 Dutch and English languages – equal status.

1910 Act of Union
1 Union Parliament: House of Assembly and Senate.
2 Governor-General.
3 Capital: Parliament – Cape Town; Executive – Pretoria; Justice – Bloemfontein.
4 Two official languages – Dutch and English.
5 Status of non-white voters at Cape to be changed only by two-thirds majority of Senate and House of Assembly combined.

Short questions on Chapter 9

1 Who were the 'uitlanders'?
2 When was the Jameson Raid?
3 How many men fought on the Boer side during the Second Anglo-Boer War?
4 How many men fought for the British?

5 Who were the main Boer leaders?
6 What are the scorched-earth and concentration camp policies?
7 When was the Act of Union?

Longer questions on Chapter 9

1 What were the causes of the Second Anglo-Boer War?
2 How did the Boers continue the war after the capture of their main settlements?
3 Why was there not a much more positive contribution made to the war by Africans?
4 What were the terms of the Peace of Vereeniging?
5 What were the critical issues at stake at the National Convention and how were they treated?
6 Write brief notes on: a) concentration camps; b) responsible government for the Transvaal and the Orange Free State; c) the franchise in the Cape Colony.
7 What were the main provisions of the Act of Union?

African reaction to European control

After the development of the mining industries in South Africa and the decisive intervention of European countries in Southern Africa, political independence and freedom were removed from the African states and their leaders. They tried to react to these threats to their independence and their traditional way of life. But it was difficult for them to know how to deal with these new developments. They needed new tactics in order to survive.

Lack of co-operation between African groups

The African groups saw the problems brought by the extension of European control. They usually tried to resist further expansion. But the chiefs and people did not often unite against the common enemy for a number of reasons. First of all, Africans did not identify with each other on racial grounds. Political associations were based on a similar language, kinship links and cultural similarities. The idea of being African as opposed to European was not an important part of their political organisation. Secondly, there were great cultural differences between the Nguni and the Sotho and these differences led to political rivalry. The Mfecane had thrown people against each other and built up resentment and suspicion of one clan for another. This hostility was too recent to be ignored, even at a time of increased pressure from Europeans. Furthermore the clan was often divided between the people who had been converted to Christianity and those who had not. The

The Maxim gun was a multi-barrelled machine gun which fired 600 shots per minute

Isandhlwana and the remains of the British force after the devastating Zulu attack in 1879

'converts' subsequently rejected some of the traditional beliefs of the clan, while the rest remained faithful to the old ways. Also, because the Europeans spread out in small groups, Africans found themselves separated from each other by a European settlement. In this way the Zulu were isolated from the Southern Nguni by the Natal settlement. Co-operation between the Bapedi, Venda and Tswana was made difficult by the Afrikaner republic settlements. Divisions on religious lines were not the only differences found within the clans. Succession disputes were common and chiefs frequently asked the Europeans to help them keep their positions. There was always a price to pay for this help and many Africans failed to see the significance of the European advance until it was too late. Opposed to this divided reaction to the Europeans, was the single-minded determination of the whites to extend European culture and domination as far as possible, even at the expense of traditional African ways of life. The Europeans also had the added confidence of knowing that militarily they were far superior to any African army. This confidence is summed up in the following phrase:

'Whatever happens we have got the Maxim gun and they have not'.[1]

There was no single African reaction to European control because the Europeans were different and this resulted in different African responses. The difference was between republican, colonialist and British control. Generally a link with the imperial power, Britain, was considered preferable to annexation by the colonial government at the Cape or the Afrikaner republics. Control by the Boers was resented most of all by the Africans.

Protection rather than annexation

A number of chiefs realised that, being under threat from the Boers, they would perhaps have a better chance of survival if they were under the control or protection of the British Crown. They made every attempt to achieve protectorate status for their areas. Chief Khama of the small Bamangwato clan was particularly successful in this strategy. He gained a protectorate for his people. When it appeared that Rhodes's British South Africa Company might take over from the imperial authority, he travelled to Britain with two other chiefs to protest to the Colonial Secretary Chamberlain about the proposed transfer of power. In the event the company did not press for power in what is now Botswana after the disaster of the Jameson Raid (see pp. 99–100). Moshesh, after a lifetime's struggle to establish the Lesotho nation, was able to request protection from the British Crown. This came eventually despite an unhappy interlude when the Basuto were governed by the Cape administration.

Armed resistance had been seen to be on the whole unsuccessful. The occasional victory (as in the case of the Zulu victory at Isandhlwana) was achieved, but it usually led to a far stronger European attack which crushed any further African resistance. The Anglo-Zulu War of 1879 illustrates this. In January 1879, Lord Chelmsford invaded Zululand with about 15,000 men including 7,000 British regular soldiers. He advanced in three lines towards Ulundi, the Zulu capital. He completely underestimated Zulu strength, failed to send out scouting parties in advance of the main armies, and paid the penalty when the Zulu attacked the central party. On 22 January the Zulu killed 1,600 of the British forces. This was the greatest single defeat for the British since the Crimean War in the 1850s. Despite this, the Zulu were unable to take advantage of their position, and better armed reinforcements soon won the war for Britain.

The efforts of the Zulu at resisting foreign domination were not always of a military nature. Mpande, who succeeded Dingane, managed to maintain Zululand and its traditions with the minimum of interference from outside, but this was before the 'Scramble' era. When his son, Cetshwayo, tried the same policy of peaceful co-existence he found that conditions had changed and that peace proved as great a failure.

War of the Guns

The only armed African resistance which changed European rule was the war between the Basuto and the Cape in 1880. This was called the 'War of the Guns'. The Cape had been responsible for ruling Lesotho from 1871 and had aroused much resentment there. In 1878, the colonising government passed the Peace Preservation Act which required all Africans to hand in their firearms. Moorosi, leader of the Phuthi people in Lesotho refused to follow the instruction. After a campaign lasting six months his resistance was overcome and Moorosi himself was killed. Afterwards the Basuto were told that they were to be disarmed, there was to be an increase in Hut Tax, and part of Moorosi's land was to be opened to white settlement. These measures were both badly timed and not very well thought out; they united the southern Sotho chiefs as nothing else could have done.

The Disarmament Proclamation was issued on 21 May 1880. Formal protests were made about it by the Paramount Chief Letsie but these had no effect on the Cape government. Fighting broke out in September but not before Lerothodi, Letsie's son, had improved the defences on Masite, a flat-topped mountain overlooking Letsie's village near Morija. Lerothodi's uncle, Masupha improved the fortifications on Thaba Bosiu also. Fighting in Lesotho occurred mainly in three areas: near Morija and Mafeteng; Leribe; and Maseru. Lerothodi frustrated attempts by Cape forces to reach and capture Morija. He can be considered second only to Moshesh himself in ability and popularity. He

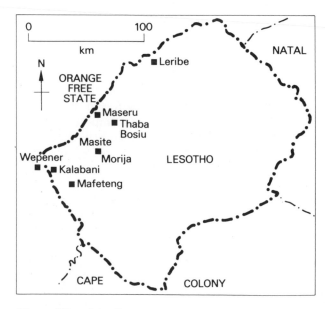

Fig. 30 War of the Guns, 1880

was courageous, an excellent horseman, and an inspiring leader in battle with a fine tactical sense. As a politician he was unyielding, reliable and a good judge of a situation. In all he had about 23,000 armed men willing to fight for him, many of them mounted.

The war lasted seven months and was one of the greatest defences of African interests in nineteenth century South African history. Lerothodi made sure that the enemy's movements were always relayed to him, and he was always able to prepare his plans in the face of the painfully slow progress of the Colony's troops. He avoided where possible the open battle situation favoured by the Zulu. He preferred to harass the invaders by long range rifle fire, and to force them to build secure 'laagers' at each camping place. When the 'square' of Colonial troops advanced beyond the camp they were attacked by mounted Basuto firing at will and choosing their place for the engagement. In this way Lerothodi tried to retain the initiative without sacrificing too many of his men. After most engagements, the Basuto had a greater sense of victory than the Cape forces who were frequently frustrated by an enemy who could escape so cunningly. Two examples from the war will illustrate Lerothodi's tactics.

The aim of the Cape troops was to move along the roads from Wepener in the Orange Free State to Mafeteng and eventually to Morija, but their progress was always slow. In October, Lerothodi positioned 3,000 troops on the small hill behind Kalabani. From this secure position they were able to fire on the advancing columns. A company of Colonials were ordered to dislodge him from his position but it was caught completely by surprise by Lerothodi who counter-attacked down the hill. The ferocity of his attack resulted in the death of thirty-nine Cape troops. The Colonials tried in January to find another way through to Morija by way of Thaba Tsueu. Lerothodi defended nearby Sepechele and at the end of five hours fighting four hundred Burghers had been put out of action by the Basuto and a Cape Yeomanry charge had been driven off. Whereas Lerothodi could gain satisfaction from the action, the Cape could only claim a very 'hollow' victory.

The Basuto always had more men than the Cape since the colony had to be completely self-reliant in the war. Only three British officers were seconded to their army. The Cape officers had great problems in mounting offensives because of the appalling weather conditions, and the fact that they were obliged to defend the various white settlements in the country. It was estimated in April 1881 that a further 10,000 troops would be required to fight the Basuto. The thought of extra troops, money and supplies persuaded most Cape politicians that the war was best ended. The terms of the April peace amounted to a victory for the Basuto. Although the Basuto were asked to register and license their guns, this was a condition that the Cape was never able to enforce. The Cape government requested that the British take over direct responsibility for the Basuto, and in fact offered to hand over the Transkei as well. The British would only accept direct control of the Basuto. The protectorate was restored in 1884.

Sekukuni and Bapedi resistance

Sekukuni claimed the chieftainship of the Bapedi in 1861 after the death of his father, Sekwati. His strongest rival was Mampuru who took refuge with the Swazi after the power struggle with Sekukuni. During the first few years of his reign, Sekukuni and the Bapedi became a focus for African refugee groups escaping from Boer invasion. His policy was to set these groups up on the margins of his territory, knowing that they would resist further attempts to dislodge them. One such group of Swazi led by Umsutu had settled on the top of the Lulu Range by about 1874.

Sekukuni had never accepted domination by the Transvaal, and unlike his father, he considered that Christian missions were a threat to the traditional customs of his people. Therefore in 1864, the missionary Merensky was with no warning dispossessed of his mission at Maandagshoek.

Sekukuni felt reasonably secure by 1875. His capital was protected by the Swazi group on the Lulu Range; the Mosego Hills provided a natural defence for it and even if the stronghold was taken, there was always the cave-ridden hill of Dsjate for his final stronghold. This independence was supported by his half-brother, Johannes Dinkoanyane, who was established in the Spekboom Hills, north of Lydenburg.

Growing hostility and rivalry developed into

open warfare when a false report that the Bapedi had burnt a German mission persuaded Burgers, the Transvaal President to call up his commandos. On 14 July 1876, Johannes's stronghold was attacked by about 2,500 Swazi and 200 burghers. The Swazi were partly successful in their attack. They had to withstand penetrating gunfire from the Bapedi, but were given little or no support by the Boers who were intimidated by the staunch defence of the Bapedi. Many of the Swazi were killed and the rest returned home complaining they had been let down by the burghers.

The Transvaal forces, now 2,000 burghers strong, advanced on Sekukuni's stronghold. Sekukuni concentrated all his forces in the Mosego area and when the Boer assault began on 1 August, the Bapedi defence was more than equal to its task. They were not dislodged from their positions and a counter-attack mounted by Sekukuni on the demoralised burghers resulted in a full scale retreat by the Transvaalers. After this defeat, the Bapedi were harassed rather than attacked by the commandos and were prevented from sowing or harvesting their crops. The fear of famine persuaded Sekukuni finally to ask for peace. Peace was proclaimed along the border by February 1877, but Sekukuni always claimed that he did not sign the peace, stating that he would always remain independent as his father had been.

The British annexed the Transvaal in April 1877, and Sekukuni was allowed to ignore the terms of the peace and retain his independent position. After the defeat of the Zulu, the British under Sir Garnet Wolseley decided to overthrow Sekukuni. In November 1879 a combined force of British troops, Transvaal Artillery, 8,000 Swazi and Boer Volunteers advanced on the Bapedi citadel. The Bapedi, unable to withstand such a force, suffered heavy casualties, and were defeated after a courageous last stand. Sekukuni's son, Moroamotshe, defiant to the end, was killed fighting bravely with his back to a large rock. Umsutu was killed in another part of the battle. Sekukuni was forced to surrender to Major Clarke high up in a cave in the Lulu Range. He was released later in 1881 after the First Anglo-Boer War, but in August 1882 his camp was surrounded by Mampuru and his followers and he was assassinated as he slept. His struggle against white occupation was courageous, resourceful and energetic, but when the British concentrated their forces against him, resistance proved hopeless.

Another African leader who tried to resist European rule was Samuel Maherero, the Herero leader in Namibia (South-West Africa). Because of white settlement in Namibia, the Herero lost much of their land. Many of the Herero's cattle died from disease, and their chiefs lost a great deal of their independence. In a letter to the Nama leader, Hendrik Witbooi, Samuel Maherero wrote, 'Let us rather die together than die through maltreatment, prison or in any other way.'[2] In 1904 the Germans were forced to use 15,000 white troops to overthrow the Herero. At the end of the war about three-quarters of the Herero people had died, most of them in the desert.

Collaboration

Another reaction which must not be overlooked is that of collaboration with the colonial and imperial forces. We should not judge the actions of African leaders by modern standards. Some African leaders were not completely aware of what colonial rule and the loss of political control meant. Neither were they able to forget traditional rivalries and hostilities, despite the more dangerous European threat. Khama helped the British South Africa Company against his traditional enemies, the Ndebele. The Swazi supported the Transvaal against the Bapedi. At this stage the African leaders rarely thought of themselves as Africans. This idea of nationalism had to wait until the smaller communities had been subjected to white domination. Even today there are divisions in the African nationalist movement which threaten it once again.

Reaction and resistance to the arrival of white rule was varied. The lack of successful resistance helps us to understand the collaboration which occurred between African leaders and the European colonial authority. One of the immediate results of the establishment of European rule was either the decline of traditional leadership, or the complete substitution of traditional chiefs by the colonial authority. Lobengula did not have a successor to the Ndebele throne, and Cetshwayo was never able to re-establish himself as the leader of Zululand. His successor, Dinizulu, was little more than a king in name, the colonial government was the real ruler.

African reaction after the establishment of European rule

Independency Movements

As a result of this decline in traditional leadership, resistance came from different levels within the various African societies. Religious leaders took on a greater significance in the resistance movement. There was a reaction against Christianity for a number of reasons. Africans felt that Christian missionaries were too often the messengers of colonial forces. For this reason there was a collapse of confidence between the white missionaries and their African converts. This led to the formation of independent African Churches which had considerable influence on the political development of areas in which they were found. Certainly in Central Africa, and to some extent in East Africa, these independency movements were directly influenced by African experience in South Africa.

A branch of the African Methodist Episcopal Church was formed in 1906 by the Sotho preacher, Zachariah Magatho. His rejection of a white man's concept of Christianity encouraged the idea of self-improvement which he passed on through his schools to the Ndebele chiefs and their sons. The influence of South African black missionaries spread throughout Central and East Africa. As late as 1953 Archbishop Alexander of the African Orthodox Church in South Africa spent eighteen months in Kikuyu, Kenya, working with the leaders of the Kikuyu Independent Schools Association. The visit made a great impression on the Kikuyu leaders who recognised the value of an association which was organised by Africans and had the interests of Africans at heart. The importance of the independency movements should not be exaggerated but certainly, in parts, they did constitute elements of a later nationalism. As we shall see later, they played a significant part in the Bambata Rising in Natal in 1906.

The educated elite

Mention has been made of African resistance and rejection of white rule. A minority had benefited from European influence and had gained a small amount of education which justified them having the title of 'educated elite' – the privileged few. In the last sixty years of the nineteenth century, 3,500 students passed through Lovedale (a London Missionary Society institution). Of these, 700 were in professional jobs – mostly schoolteachers, 100 were clerks, 170 were artisans (craftsmen) and 600 were labourers and farmers. Bearing in mind that there were other important colleges for African students, the number who must have assimilated European ideas and practices was significant. They tended to feel that it was possible for Africans to progress within the colonial system. They did not understand the fact that in countries with a white minority settler population, the likelihood of progress for the masses was remote. The white minorities could not afford direct competition in employment which would have resulted from such progress. Measures concerned with land ownership and job allocation were dealt with by the Union Parliament and it believed in the idea of white supremacy. At the end of the nineteenth century, after the various disturbances described in the earlier chapters, most African people were poor and uneducated. They had little hope of progress beyond the level of unskilled labour in a white controlled economy. It was no wonder that a gap developed between the educated elite and the mass of the people. This gap remained until there was a change in African reactions to white rule in the twentieth century.

The Bambata Rebellion

Changing patterns of African life

The development of the white economy in South Africa was based on the extraction of valuable minerals. This caused the growth of large urban areas and had a profound effect on the African people. A pattern of African life emerged which is still followed today by most of South Africa's non-white population. The Reserves became the areas where the women, children and old people lived while the young men took up temporary residence in the white urban areas where they worked in unskilled jobs.

Lack of land, poverty, disease and taxation drove

Bambata, the leader of the Zulu Rising in Natal in 1906 against colonial forces

In 1906 a resistance message became widespread in Natal:

> 'All pigs must be destroyed, as also all white fowls. Every European utensil hitherto used for holding food or eating out of must be discarded and thrown away. Anyone failing to comply will have his kraal struck by a thunderbolt, when, at the same date in the future HE sends a storm more terrible than the last, which was brought on by the Basuto king in his wrath against the white race for having a railway to the immediate vicinity of his ancestral stronghold.'[3]

The interpretation of the order was clear enough. The white man was to be swept into the sea. The Zulu in Natal followed the instructions with regard to the slaughter of pigs and fowl, against the wishes of Dinizulu, Cetshwayo's successor, who did not identify himself with the resistance movement. The imposition of a poll tax of £1 per head – European, African, Asian or Coloured – resulted in outbursts all over Natal. The tax, involving the payment of the same amount of money by everyone, was resented by Africans when Europeans were earning at least twenty times as much money as they were. The government panicked and enforced extreme measures as punishment. Public executions occurred and fourteen Africans died. A more serious incident took place about 26 kilometres beyond Greytown in another part of Natal. It involved Bambata, the leader of the Zondi people and a chief who had always caused difficulties for the administration. He was ordered to appear personally at Greytown to pay his poll tax together with all the taxable members of his group. Some of his men had not brought their tax money so Bambata failed to comply with the magistrate's order. But he stayed with his men trying to persuade them to comply with the new regulations.

Bambata was ordered to appear before the court a second time but his headman, Nhlonhlo, refused to allow him to go: 'I prefer he should die in our own hands rather than be shot by Europeans out of our sight.'[4] Bambata became a hunted man. He reached Usutu, the place of Dinizulu, and it was here that he gained a .303 rifle, a double-barrelled breech loader and a carbine. After leaving Usutu he made for Mpanza where he ambushed an advance

thousands of Africans into the towns. The basic fact to grasp is that life in these towns meant poverty, insecurity and fear for the Africans while in contrast many of the whites have been able to enjoy lives of wealth and privilege: A resentment, a hatred and a defiance of their white employers, and administrators, grew up in place of the traditional life. Ethiopianism, a separatist religious movement, which used the slogan 'Africa for the African' gained a considerable following among Zulu in the cities. It preached rebellion and the message found its way back to Natal and Zululand.

guard of twenty-six men sent to bring him in. Four of the police died, four were wounded and fifteen horses were killed. None of Bambata's band were killed. This meant that Bambata was able to enrol more men because the engagement had fulfilled the prophecy that they would not be hurt by the white man's bullets.

Bambata moved into Zululand but was now being pursued by the Natal Police. They were able to trap Bambata and his followers in the Mome Gorge on 10 June 1906. The slaughter lasted for sixteen hours. No opportunity was given for surrender and no prisoners were taken. Official records give the number of dead on Bambata's side as 600 which may be a conservative estimate. The freedom struggle continued for a while; 40,000 Zulu took part in the rebellion, 2,000 died, and 24 Europeans were killed.

This was the last major rising against colonial rule befor the Act of Union of 1910. It illustrates the strength of unity within the chieftaincy even at this late stage. There was a refusal to blindly accept domination by white colonial rule. There was a connection between Ethiopianism and armed resistance in Natal (at least 200 Ethiopian Christian converts died in the rising). Unfortunately for the African, armed resistance was futile at this time.

Urban Africans

Positive militant resistance was mainly an expression of the traditional African way of life. As such it was almost bound to fail in the rapidly changing economic and social life of South Africa. In the twentieth century two African groups have emerged who are important to the understanding of modern South Africa. They are the educated Christians and the growing working class in the main urban areas. The Christians are the 'progressives', they wanted improved education, a greater share in the South African economy and an expansion of political rights. In 1911 there were over 100,000 Africans in Johannesburg and about half a million in all the urban areas. The number of Africans working and living in the towns has increased so much that today over a third of all Africans are to be found there. It has been in the urban areas that the main racial conflict of the

twentieth century has taken place. Loss of land, increased poverty and the almost complete absence of political and economic rights in their own country have all been factors in the growth of a wider nationalism among African people in the twentieth century.

Summary of Chapter 10

Little African co-operation
Reasons:
  1 No nationalist feeling cutting across groupings.
  2 Great cultural differences between Nguni and Sotho.
  3 Resentment and suspicion after the Mfecane.
  4 Divisions produced by missions.
  5 Succession disputes.

Imperial protection preferred to colonial annexation
a) Khama III of Botswana.
b) Moshesh of Lesotho.

Armed resistance
Rarely successful: individual victories by the Zulu and Bapedi usually followed by ultimate defeat. 'War of the Guns' – only really successful African campaign.

Collaboration
a) Khama III with British South Africa Company against Ndebele.
b) Swazi with the Transvaal against the Bapedi.

Reaction after the establishment of European rule
Independency movement: Reaction against Christian missions. Sotho preacher Zachariah Magatho. 1906 Bambata Rising
Educated elite: Believed in improvement within the system through mission schools and overseas colleges – a gap developed between the educated and the masses.
Changing African life patterns: Employment in urban areas – brought poverty, insecurity and fear; meant a decline in standards associated with traditional way of life – one-third of all Africans living in urban areas.

Short questions on Chapter 10

1 Chief .... of the small .... clan gained protectorate status for Bechuanaland.
2 When did the War of the Guns take place?
3 Who led the Bapedi against the Transvaal in 1867?
4 What brought about the rise of the independency movements?
5 When did the Bambata Rising take place?
6 What drove thousands of Africans into the towns?
7 Which two African groups have emerged in the modern South African town setting?

Longer questions on Chapter 10

1 Describe the different African reactions to the imposition of colonial rule. The following headings are suggested to assist: militant resistance; lack of political unity; seeking protection; collaboration; independency movements; education and town life.
2 Write a brief paragraph on each of the following: a) Isandhlwana; b) independency movements; c) Bambata Rebellion.

Notes to Chapter 10

1 J. B. Webster and A. A. Boahen, *The Revolutionary Years: West Africa since 1800*, Longmans, 1967.
2 *ibid*.
3 Stuart, *A History of the Zulu Rebellion*, p. 103.
4 Binns, *Dinizulu*, Longman, p. 190.

11 Missionaries

In Chapter 4, mention was made of the impact of the missionaries on South Africa. It was an influence which was limited not merely to converting the African to Christianity. It had much wider implications: in attitudes towards the law, education and the development of a literate 'peasant' society. It influenced cultural values and standards. Undoubtedly missionaries undermined the traditional way of life and as a whole have made a great many enemies within African society. It has been suggested that the missionaries were actually agents of conquest. This opinion exists in spite of the many personal sacrifices made by individual missionaries like Van der Kemp, Moffatt, Casalis, Stewart, Brownlee and Livingstone. Such people were motivated by strongly held religious beliefs and not by any considerations of conquest.

Christianity and western culture

The missionaries, mostly British, were definitely men of their own time. As Victorians (nineteenth century British people were called by the name of their Queen), they had a proud and complete belief in the superiority of Western culture. It was this belief which persuaded the missionaries that they were doing the African a service by imposing their own standards of behaviour as well as preaching the gospel. Converts were expected to adopt Western dress, to settle in recognisable village patterns round the mission, to live in square houses rather than round, to reject traditional initiation ceremonies, and to have only one wife.

Early Christian missions

A very basic theme in the history of South Africa has been the mixing of different peoples and cultures. Religion has been a very important and early cause of this. The first missionary in South Africa was the Moravian, George Schmidt, who worked among the Khoikhoi from 1738 and with short interruptions until 1792. He developed a community based on the church and school in which the African converts learnt European farming methods, house building and crafts like carpentry and shoe-making. Another early missionary was the Dutchman, J. T. van der Kemp, who came to the Cape for the London Missionary Society in 1779. He devoted much of his time to working among the Khoikhoi and the Xhosa on the Eastern Frontier.

The early missionaries were motivated largely by the desire to preach the gospel to people, irrespective of colour, and van der Kemp set the pattern of mission work in South Africa by spending two years living with the Xhosa chief, Gaika, from 1799 to 1800. Later he established Bethelsdorp, a mission station where Xhosa and Khoikhoi were allowed to stay and where they learned to read and write, farm, and acquire a number of craft skills. Van der Kemp was frequently attacked by his political opponents at the Cape for encouraging idleness among the Khoikhoi, but he tried to instil among both the Khoikhoi and the Xhosa the value of hard work within the community. Van der Kemp's experiments were followed by others. Joseph Williams was the first missionary to establish a mission in Xhosa country. He was followed by John Brownlee and William Thompson. The Methodists built several mission stations, from Salem to Palmerston in East Pondoland. In each case it was necessary to learn the vernacular language and then to translate the gospels into that language. The next task was to teach the would-be convert how to read and write and this required printing presses and schools.

These early missions became centres of housing, learning and farming for converts

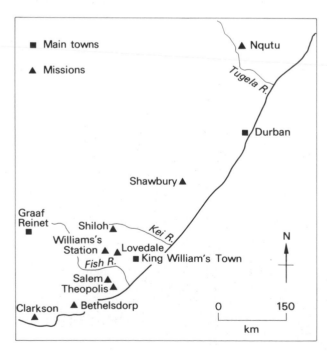

Fig. 31 *Christian missions among the Nguni*

Growth of an African peasant society

The missions gradually became a focal point of social life in the African areas, instead of the chief's great place. This was also true of the trading stations, and both the mission and the trading station became meeting places for people who had become separated from the traditional way of African life. It was through their influence that the African peasant farming economy developed.

The 'peasant' society differed from the traditional way of life in three ways. Firstly, the African peasants were settled farmers (cultivators) who had their own plots of land and who produced enough food to live on and usually a little for trading. The traditional African life was not based on a fixed plot of land owned by the individual. For the African a pattern of movement was more likely. Ownership of land was held by the clan and farming in order to trade was not important. Secondly, in the new peasant society there were the beginnings of

Tiyo Soga, an ordained minister of the Free Church of Scotland

farmer. With the new found faith, loyalty to the traditional chief became more difficult. The new loyalty was to the teachings of the Bible. The surplus food was sold to support the dominant white group.

Many Christian converts refused to fight for their own Xhosa chief during the Kaffir Wars and often had to take refuge in the missions. Tiyo Soga, a baptised Xhosa, refused to read messages found on white prisoners for his chief. In the 1850–53 wars, over a thousand converts refused to fight and went for safety to King William's Town.

Most of the missionaries accepted van der Kemp's ideas on 'work'. Stewart, the principal of Lovedale, a Free Church of Scotland mission in Natal, insisted on daily manual work on his mission. 'They are engaged in making roads, cutting water courses, constructing dams, or at work in the fields and gardens about the place. The object is ... the principle that Christianity and idleness are not compatible.'[1]

literacy and an awareness of a link with a way of life different from the traditional African one. This link was forged by the relationship with the whole culture and religious teaching of the Bible. The reading of the Bible was a daily happening and teaching people to read was the main purpose of the schools. Thirdly, there was the separation and division of political authority for the new peasant

School people and Red people

A division became apparent by the middle of the nineteenth century between the 'red' people, those who remained faithful to the old ways, and the

'School people', who attended mission schools and adopted European culture

'school-people', who were Christian converts and wore European clothes. Margery Perham, the colonialist scholar, writes of the contrast when she visited the Transkei in 1929. The Christian kraal was a good imitation of a European life style. Mud huts with windows, iron bedsteads, pictures on the walls, newspapers, a sewing machine and an old woman, a well-known midwife, reading a book in Xhosa. The 'red' kraal was very different. Women dressed in beautiful amber dresses embroidered with beads. They were unsure of themselves with the European. There was no furniture and only a few cooking pots in a hut with no windows which was full of smoke. Early converts were aware of the danger of changing to the new culture which meant giving up their old way of life. Christianity was one reason for justifying such a rejection. Another powerful argument was that education in its widest sense gave Africans their best possible chance of greater economic opportunity. Tiyo Soga saw that, without training, his people were doomed to

remain 'Grooms, drivers of wagons, hewers of wood or general servants.'[2] Colonialism emphasised the European way of life as the only way. Throughout colonised Africa there was a tendency for Africans to think that the lifestyle of the European was the only worthwhile one. Consequently, towards the end of the nineteenth century there were many qualified 'school-people', but too few who were content with the more humble but often more valuable status of peasant and artisan.

Political activities of the missionaries

Missionaries working in African areas often found themselves considered the 'men' of the local chief and were expected to work for the interests of the chief. At the same time the colonial government

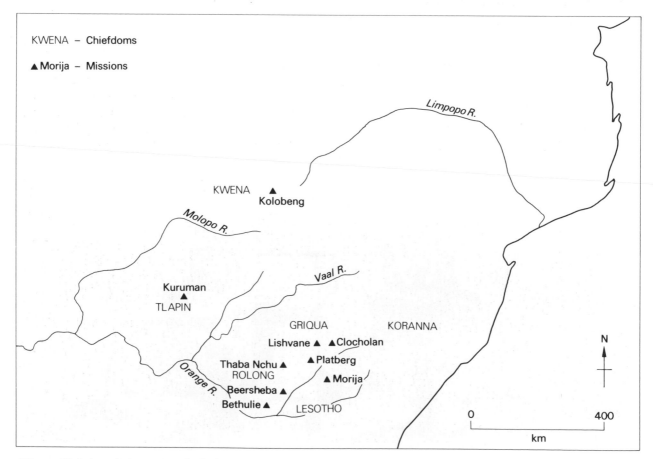

Fig. 32 Christian missions among the Sotho and Tswana

E. Casalis, who was a missionary to Moshesh

and Gosselin to work among the Basuto. Moshesh accepted them provided that they became 'his men'. Accordingly, Casalis and Arbousset became advisers to the King and found themselves in conflict with English missionaries who supported the interests of Moshesh's rivals, Chiefs Moroka and Sekonyela. After the passing of the Conventions of 1852 and 1854, Africans were not allowed to buy firearms legally, and missionaries started to play a more positive part in the struggle between the Boers and the Bantu. David Livingstone was suspected of supplying arms to African chiefs to protect them against the Transvaal and the Orange Free State. Two missionaries of the London Missionary Society, Edwards and Inglis, criticised the conduct of the Boer commandos sent out on a raid to punish the Rolong and the towns of Kwena and Ngwaketse. They were expelled from the Transvaal, and all London Missionary Society links with the Transvaal were cut.

Dr John Philip

often expected them to act as agents for the government. Many of them found themselves involved in political activities for the benefit of the chief. This was particularly true in Basutoland before Moshesh gained control over the neighbouring tribes. The Paris Evangelical Missionary Society sent three missionaries, Casalis, Arbousset

The career of Dr John Philip best illustrates how a missionary was able to work within the Cape Colony and influence political decisions in the colony. Van der Kemp had been despised by the Boer settlers but Dr Philip gained their undying hatred. Son of a Scottish weaver, Philip had a fine intellect linked to a powerful personality and he

Lovedale, a racially mixed mission school between 1841–1926

Kuruman, the mission station of Robert Moffat, Livingstone's father-in-law

gathered about him many devoted followers. He arrived at the Cape in 1819 and found the social situation of coloured slaves as a servant class, controlled by a privileged white class. This was against his religious principles, and he did his best to change the situation. His success can be gauged by the fact that he became the most hated man in the colony and that the Khoikhoi and eventually all the non-white people received greater freedom before the law in the Cape than elsewhere in South Africa. One of his great strengths was that, despite being hated in South Africa, he was admired and respected in England. He was employed from London and he was friendly with successive Colonial Secretaries. He used this connection to his advantage on many occasions.

Mission schools

Mission schools did invaluable work in not only providing education for African children but also in attempting to integrate the different racial groups. Lovedale started a racially mixed school in 1841, and it continued to be mixed until 1926. It was **non-sectarian** but was financed by the Free Church of Scotland. Lovedale was not unique in being open to all races. In 1891 a third of the European children attended such mixed schools, which were also mixed in that they were attended by girls as well as boys. It was the very high standard of the education provided at these schools which attracted many European parents. White Lovedale students later filled high ministerial posts. A student from Lovedale became Minister of Agriculture, two became Chief Justices and many others became doctors, teachers, pastors, nurses and administrators.

Reaction against the missions

Van der Kemp and other missionaries in the early nineteenth century were considered to be peculiar by other white people because they identified very closely with their African converts. They lived together, and often the missionaries would take African women as wives. They were following the principle of racial equality. They did not care about the other white people's political attitudes. At the end of the nineteenth century many missionaries and churchmen had withdrawn from the African communities. Their converts were confused and puzzled by a new attitude which interpreted 'rendering unto Caesar the things that are Caesar's' as an instruction not to meddle in African politics and not to oppose white policies. The Ethiopian Church, a separatist movement, was a reaction against the control of the white man and his Church. For a while in the early twentieth century it looked as if the Ethiopians would form an important element of African nationalism. But from the 1920s onwards they seem to have retreated more into the contemplation of the next life as compensation for the inequalities of the present. They took no more interest in political action.

The Church – a declining influence?

With regard to race relations, the missions sponsored by British societies followed a more liberal course than the Dutch Reformed Church. This is understandable when one remembers that the extension of equality before the law for all, and the abolition of slavery at the Cape, took place largely through the efforts of humanitarians in Britain. Their ideas were represented by missionaries sent from Britain. While the colonial and imperial link was maintained it was still possible for the British humanitarians to influence events. With Union and independence for a white controlled South Africa it has been much more difficult for churchmen to speak out positively and effectively against a government which is so well organised as South Africa's government is. The external link is broken and the Church relies for its existence and survival not on Britain, but on its own resources in South Africa. This may be the reason why in the last quarter of the twentieth century the Church is not as effective a curb on the extremism of the Government as people like Philip and van der Kemp were at the beginning of the nineteenth century. The Churches are in the same position as

other liberals in South Africa, who know that they have no political power to change the situation. Not only are they unwilling to upset their political masters but they are themselves afraid of what would happen if there was a revolution in South Africa and the white minority government was overthrown.

Dutch Reformed Church

The Dutch Reformed Church had decided on separate racial congregations by 1857. Today the Synod of the Dutch Reformed Church is the focal point of the Afrikaner community. It reflects Afrikaner attitudes as well as justifying from the Bible the present government policy of apartheid or separate development.

According to the Population Census figure for 1960, African membership of the various churches as a percentage is given as:

Dutch Reformed Church	5.1
Anglican	
Presbyterian	
Congregational	26.9
Methodist	
Lutheran	
Roman Catholic	7.0
Bantu Churches	20.0
Unspecified	33.5

The influence of the missionaries has been felt throughout the republic. Its overall importance has been that it has provided a cultural link with the world outside South Africa when all the pressures inside have been to reduce cultural mixing as much as possible. Its main contribution to the development of Africans has been in providing more education. An African nationalist movement could not have been developed without the two elements of an educated elite and the urbanised working Africans. An educated African elite would not have occurred had not the early missions held onto the ideal of equality.

Summary of Chapter 11

Christian missions and western culture
Objectives:
  1 Preaching the Christian gospel.

2 Imposing western standards and culture. This was often mistaken as being an intrinsic part of preaching the Christian gospel.

Early missions

Schmidt: 1738–92 – Moravian among the Khoikhoi.

Van der Kemp 1779 – LMS – among the Xhosa and the Khoikhoi; Bethelsdorp station – ideas followed by others.

African Peasant Society: Settled farmers – subsistence with surplus for trading. Beginnings of literacy. Divided loyalties – with the 'school' people and 'red' people.

Political activity of missionaries: Men of the Chief: Casalis, Arbousset, Moffatt. Livingstone suspected of gun-running for Africans. Missionaries – usually anti-Boer. Dr Philip – emphasised and worked for equality before the law – on close terms with Colonial Secretary – seemed to decide colonial policy – hated by the Boers.

Mission schools: Important as:

1 instruments of education.

2 agents of racial integration – Lovedale.

A declining influence? Modern Church not as outspoken or as influential as in early nineteenth century.

Short questions on Chapter 11

1 Who was the first missionary in South Africa and when did he arrive?

2 What did he teach the African converts?

3 Who was the first London Missionary Society missionary?

4 What was the name of the mission station he established?

5 Who was Tiyo Soga?

6 What was Stewart's attitude to manual work?

7 Who were the 'red people' and the 'school people'?

8 Who were the missionaries who were sent to Moshesh?

9 How was Dr John Philip able to influence affairs in South Africa?

10 What was the Ethiopian Church?

11 Why have the modern churches had less effect that the nineteenth century missionaries?

12 What has been the main contribution made by the missions in South Africa?

Longer questions on Chapter 11

1 In what ways can the missionaries be considered as agents of conquest?

2 Describe how the mission stations altered the traditional African way of life. Use the following headings as a guide: cultural meeting and mixing; peasant society; divided loyalties; manual work; education.

3 Write brief paragraphs on the following:
a) Dr John Philip; b) J. T. van der Kemp; c) Lovedale; d) the Dutch Reformed Church.

Notes to Chapter 11

1 J. Stewart, *African Papers 1*, General Missionary Conference, 1878.

2 J. A. Chalmers, *Tiyo Soga*, p. 288.

12 Afrikaner domination in the twentieth century

The Afrikaners established themselves very firmly in the government of South Africa after the Act of Union and throughout the present century. Succeeding governments have recognised the growing challenge of African nationalism. In 1948, the Nationalist Government of Dr Malan put into effect the policy of apartheid. The attitude behind apartheid was simply a reflection of conservative Boer thought for nearly three hundred years. To ensure the survival of the idea of separate development and the supremacy of the white man it had been necessary in the nineteenth century for the Afrikaners to remove themselves from British control. In the twentieth century government has been in the hands of Afrikaners. Halfway through the twentieth century the white communities moved closer together in their determination to withhold equal political rights from the non-European. As Joseph Chamberlain, the Colonial Secretary, said in 1903: 'It is necessary to make it plain to the natives that the war (Anglo-Boer War) altered the relations between the two white races, but not between the white and the coloured population of the country.'

Problems which existed before union did not disappear after the Act of Union had been passed. There have been two continuous problems for most of the present century. Firstly, that of a 'poor white' labour force which has demanded protection through the law. Secondly, the problem of a large African population which has become more aware of its rights and more articulate in its demands, but whose development has been held back because of the desire of the white minority to hold onto its privileges.

Afrikaans and schools

In the first Botha administration, places in the permanently all-white Cabinet were fairly evenly distributed among the provinces: four from the Cape, three from the Transvaal, and two each from the two smaller provinces. It was not long before the champion of Afrikaner nationalism, General Hertzog, who was Botha's Minister of Justice, began to support Afrikaans as the language of instruction for Afrikaner children. In the Act of Union it was agreed that English and Dutch were to be the national languages, and not Afrikaans. A Select Committee recommended that after Standard 4 in school, parents should have the right to choose the language of instruction. This was accepted in the Transvaal, Natal and the Cape, but only partly carried out in Hertzog's Orange Free State.

Formation of Nationalist Party by Hertzog 1912

The other major issue on which the cabinet was divided was Botha's friendly policy and attitude towards the English-speaking South Africans and the Imperial Government in London. Hertzog behaved as if he was still fighting the Boer War. He would not allow the ideals of Afrikanderdom to be submerged during this period of union. He advocated separate development for the two white peoples, with the government always in the hands of the Afrikaners. Botha asked for Hertzog's resignation as Minister of Justice but, when he refused, Botha was forced to resign and reform his cabinet without Hertzog. Hertzog then formed his own party, the Nationalist Party. It was not just chance that the formation of the Afrikaner Nationalist Party should coincide with the formation of the South African Native Congress (later

Hertzog, the founder of the Nationalist Party in 1912

named the African National Congress). The African nationalists were reacting in exactly the same way to European domination as Hertzog was to British domination. Both the Afrikaners and the Africans attached greater importance to progress by constitutional means (means which were considered to be legal) instead of fighting to solve their problems.

Economic rivalry between African and 'poor white'

The main problem throughout the twentieth century for the Europeans in South Africa has been the question of the non-white population in the country. The Bantu had ceased to be a military threat to the white communities by the end of the nineteenth century. They had become instead an economic rival to the lower paid European class which relied on the skilled and semi-skilled jobs in mining and industry. With an increasing number of poor whites leaving farming in the rural areas and looking for work in the industrial areas and the Bantu population increasing more rapidly than could be sustained in the reserve areas, the two groups were bound to meet in the white urban areas, looking for the same kinds of job.

Law-making in the present century has been concerned largely with protecting the poor whites at the expense of the non-Europeans. The Natives Land Act of 1913 was an attempt to provide a consistent land policy throughout the country. Inevitably it worked against the best interests of the Africans and can be considered a central pillar of white domination in South Africa.

The Land Act of 1913

The main purpose of the Act was the territorial separation or segregation of Europeans from Africans. The Act said that no African could buy or lease land from a European. This effectively reduced an African's opportunity to own land, to one-eighth of the country. The results of the Land Act have been bad for the African. In the African Reserves, overcrowding has resulted in landlessness, overgrazing by stock, soil erosion and reduced harvests. The landless African has been forced to drift into the European areas where **squatting** has been almost eliminated and where it is no longer possible to be a tenant. The African has become a labourer without grazing or sowing rights. The immediate effect was to make homeless thousands of Africans who previously had served as tenants on European farms outside the Reserves. The restrictions on the purchase and lease of land were only supposed to last until the Commission's report set out the limits of the European and African areas. When the report was made public, it was proposed that an extra seven million hectares should be set aside for the Africans. So far, only about a third of this amount has been acquired. In short, the Act legalised the possession of seven-eighths of the land by the white population, and gave the African the right to buy land in only one-eighth of the country. The only positive result for the Africans was that it led to considerable opposition to what was described as a 'confiscatory measure', and provoked a reaction which was both more united and more nationalist in character.

The Indian problem

The Indians, who at present number a little more than half a million, entered Natal from 1860 onwards in response to a demand for labour in the sugar and tea plantations. They came on contracts, first for three years and later for five years, with the choice at the end of the contract of either staying in South Africa or returning to India on a free passage.

By 1913 the Indian population in South Africa had reached 150,000. There were 133,000 in Natal, 11,000 in the Transvaal, 7,000 in the Cape, and 100 in the Orange Free State. The large number in Natal was causing concern as the Indians were outnumbering the European population which stood at just over 100,000. There were great demands to limit immigration, and by the terms of the 1913 Immigration Act it was possible to prevent the entry of anyone on social and economic grounds. The Indian lawyer, Mahatma Gandhi, then a young man, formed the Indian Congress in 1894. He was to play the leading role in the independence movement in India. Gandhi organised Indian reaction to the restrictions of the Immigration Act. He advised a policy of non-violent resistance against measures such as the pass laws, and was arrested and sentenced to a short prison sentence after a protest march. Although Gandhi was able to achieve the abolition of the £3 tax on all Indians and gain entry into South Africa for the first wife of an Indian, other restrictions were not lifted. As late as 1946 Gandhi was appealing to Prime Minister Smuts 'not to take the whites down the precipice that this artificial protection of races would lead to'.[1] The interests of the Europeans in Natal had greater influence on Smuts, and the Indians remained restricted to their own areas in the four provinces.

The 'poor white' labour problem

The movement of Africans into the urban areas was accompanied by a similar movement of poor

'Poor whites', the landless, unskilled whites who have been forced into the towns

whites. This immigration into the industrial areas was not welcomed by the local urban authorities. The Government from time to time attempted to reverse this movement and provide farming land for the poor whites to settle. This 'back to the land' policy was rarely successful and the poor whites, with no land, little education and few skills to offer, were forced onto an unskilled labour market in the towns. Here they were in direct competition for jobs with non-whites. Because of the basic wage policy of low wages for unskilled labour, the poor whites were an embarrassment to the governing authorities. Unfit for skilled work but opposed 'on principle' to menial work, the poor whites became an increasingly difficult problem. The Government passed a number of different acts which protected them, but by the early 1930s the problem had become one of growing unemployment for the poor whites. The Mines and Works Act of 1911 was an early attempt to reserve semi-skilled jobs for Europeans in the Transvaal and Orange Free State. In 1913 the Native Land and Labour Act stopped the recruitment of non-whites from beyond 22°S (the line of latitude just to the north of the Limpopo River).

From 1925 until 1939 the basis of economic policy was the employment of 'Civilised Labour'. Civilised Labour was defined as those people who drew wages which allowed them a European standard of living. In effect the legislation almost guaranteed that only white people could enjoy such a status. The Apprenticeship Act of 1922, enforced in 1925 decided that would-be apprentices should have reached Standard 7 in school. This measure effectively barred most Africans from apprenticeship schemes since they could not afford the extra education necessary to qualify. The Mines and Works Amendment Act of 1926 barred Africans and Indians from skilled mining work. The Native Administration Act of 1927 laid down that anyone found guilty of encouraging hostility between 'Natives' and Europeans was liable to be imprisoned or fined very severely. By the Wages Act of 1925, unorganised labour (mostly non-European) either lost the right to strike by registering under the Conciliation Act of 1924 or had to accept minimum rates of pay laid down by the Government.

Successive governments obsessed by the position of the poor white and concerned about giving massive protection, have failed to recognise or preferred to ignore the impact of this protection on African workers. Their indifference was rationalised in the belief that African workers thrown out of work could always return to the Reserve areas where a subsistence life was always possible. They ignored the increasing poverty and the growing population of these Reserve areas.

The African worker and the Industrial and Commercial Workers' Union

It is impossible to discuss the position of the African people in the 1920s in simple terms because there were at least three different groups, each with its own particular problems. There were:

(a) *Reserve Africans*
Living on the Reserve, this group existed in overcrowded, poor surroundings, often living on the verge of starvation. Many of the men were often away from the Reserves in search of work in the urban areas.

(b) *Urban dwellers*
These Africans had moved away from the Reserves and were living in poor conditions in the towns. They were frequently a frustrated group because, living close to the comfortable European areas, they saw living standards which they were unlikely to enjoy.

(c) *The educated African*
A small number of Africans had graduated from universities and had entered the professions only to find that their opportunities for advancement were sadly limited by the colour bar.

Industrial and Commercial Workers' Union

The greatest threat to the Europeans' position came from the last two groups, especially the town dwellers, since unskilled and semi-skilled African labour could be employed at cheaper rates than European. The Africans also had little or no voting or legal power to alter work conditions as most of them working in industrial areas would not have the vote. Therefore, there was a great temptation to employ African labour instead of European, where there was a choice.

There was considerable industrial unrest in the 1920s because of the uncertainty of job prospects for Europeans and the working and pay conditions of the non-Europeans. The Industrial and Commercial Workers' Union was formed by Clement Kadalie in 1919 and quickly gained ground in the Cape Province.

Kadalie was born in Northern Malawi in 1896. He was educated at the Livingstone Mission and for a time was employed as a teacher by the mission. In his search for wider experience he left his job and travelled first to Mozambique and then to Rhodesia (modern Zimbabwe) before reaching Cape Town in 1918. On the way south he worked in cotton in Mozambique and a mining office in Rhodesia. Soon after his arrival at the Cape he recognised the need for a trade union movement among African workers.

The union was mainly a protest movement against all forms of oppression, not just a trade union. It did give expression to protest within an industrial environment. In 1921, 71,000 Africans went on strike on the Rand. The workers only returned to work after a show of force by the authorities and after the police had isolated the

strikers into small groups. In Port Elizabeth twenty-four Africans were killed by unauthorised white civilians who took the law into their own hands at a peaceful demonstration against the detention of Masabula, the local secretary of the ICU.

Decline of Kadalie's ICU

Kadalie's ICU was unable to compete with such crushing legislation. Although the union had a membership of 200,000 in 1928 and had been successful in organising a number of impressive strikes, clashes in the leadership between George Champion and Kadalie weakened the impact of the movement when powerful leadership was most needed. In order to organise the disjointed and ill-disciplined movement, a British trade unionist, William Ballinger, was sent out from the United Kingdom. In 1929 Kadalie resigned his position and left Ballinger responsible for the effects of the movement.

The influence of Kadalie and the ICU spread northward into Zimbabwe, where it provided a fresh instrument of opposition to white policies. It was not as successful in gaining mass support as it had been in South Africa, but it did represent a real challenge to white supremacy based on a mass movement, the first of its kind and an example of what was to follow in the 1950s. The ICU could never make up its mind whether it wanted to be a protest movement against the whole political arrangement in Southern Africa or whether it was to be simply a trade union. This apparent indecision contributed to its downfall.

So ended the first and possibly the greatest example of a movement organised to break the Europeans' stranglehold on the lower levels of skilled and unskilled labour.

White South African Governments 1910–

Botha Ministry 1910–1919

The first Prime Minister after Union was Louis Botha, a Boer general who fought with distinction

Clement Kadalie, who was the leader of the ICU

Louis Botha

in the Anglo-Boer War. Together with Smuts, he recognised the need for partnership between Afrikaners and English-speaking South Africans after the war. The continuing undercurrent of hostility of the Boer for the British is illustrated by two events in the Botha Ministry. The formation of the Nationalist Party by Hertzog was one of these, showing as it did the desire to further the interests of the Afrikaner community along separate lines from the British. Hertzog gained considerable support from the rural Boers and made Botha's position much weaker. The second event was the First World War, 1914–18.

South Africa and the First World War 1914–18

Botha and Smuts had no hesitation in joining the war on Britain's side in 1914, but many Afrikaners did not share their feelings. Before entering the war, the Government had to put down a revolt led by Generals de Wet and Maritz who were keen to support the Germans against the British. South-West Africa, a German colony was invaded by Smuts and Botha and the Germans were forced to

surrender very quickly. South African troops later fought in Europe and in East Africa.

Both Botha and Smuts attended the Versailles Conference, and South Africa was granted control and administration of South-West Africa as a **Mandate** from the League of Nations. Subsequently, South-West Africa has been brought into a much closer association with the republic, with representatives for the area sitting in the Assembly. This development has taken place very much against the wishes and demands of the United Nations, and it remains to be seen how effective these demands will be with the inflexible South African Government.

Smuts Ministry 1919–24

Jan Smuts was the obvious successor to Botha when he died in 1919, but his period of office was made more difficult by the major problems discussed earlier, namely the poor whites and the position of the non-European in white South Africa. A slump in world trade made white workers on the Rand more insecure than ever, and constant demands were made to preserve a ratio of 1 European to 3.5 Africans in the minefields. The coalminers went on strike in January 1922 and were later joined by the gold workers. A General Strike on the Rand placed the area in rebel hands for a short time, before Smuts dealt ruthlessly with the strikers. The strike was over by March 1922, by which time over 200 workers had died.

Smuts's prospects of winning the next general election declined after the Strike, and disappeared almost altogether when Hertzog announced that the Nationalist Party would work closely with the Labour Party. The poor white worker could now count on the support of both these parties. In the election of April 1924, the pact of the Nationalist and Labour Parties was returned with a majority of twenty-seven seats in the Assembly.

The Pact Ministry 1924–33

The pact between the two parties was based on two fundamental principles:

a)   The need for independence from the British Commonwealth.

b)   The protection of 'white civilisation' in South Africa.

Imperial Conferences of 1926 and 1931 persuaded Hertzog that the independence of South Africa was not in question within the Commonwealth, and that the dominions (South Africa, Australia, Canada and New Zealand) were independent states and in no way subordinate to Britain.

Hertzog passed a series of laws (see p. 126) aimed at protecting the poor white community. Despite limiting African employment opportunities, the world trade depression of the late 1920s prevented any real advance for the poor whites. Support for the Pact fell and the chances of an election victory in 1933 dwindled. At this point Hertzog surprisingly joined Smuts in a coalition party. Smuts felt it was a time for national unity, and Hertzog declared that a refusal to join the coalition would have made the South African Party even more hostile to Afrikaner ideals.

There was an overwhelming victory for the coalition party in 1933. Dr D. K. Malan refused to accept that the interests of the Afrikaner people were best served by a coalition, and formed the 'Purified' Nationalist Party. This party only gained small support in the 1933 election but by 1948 was strong enough to win a general election.

The Fusion Ministry 1933–8

The prospects for the new Government were weakened by the obvious divisions within the party now known as the United Party. Many nationalists had definite sympathies with Malan's group and did not need much persuasion to join up with him. The 'Purified' Nationalist Party, although a small party, was beginning to influence people and events out of all proportion to its size. It had the support of and became the political organ of the Broeder-bond, a cultural secret society which wanted an independent and exclusive republic run by Afrikaners. Hertzog attacked the organisation but was unable to restrict its activities and influence as more and more of the leading Afrikaners joined its ranks.

The major pieces of legislation passed by the Fusion Ministry which affected the African population were:

a) 1936 Native Representation Act
b) 1936 Native Trust and Lands Act
c) 1937 Native Laws Amendment Act

Dr Malan, the leader of the 'Purified' Nationalist Party and the Prime Minister in 1948

When the Select Committee of both Houses reported on *Native Representation* in May 1935, Jan Hofmeyr and François Malan were opposed to the exclusion of Africans from the common parliamentary roll in the Cape. The more liberal Malan proposed instead that the vote should be given in the other provinces on the same civilisation basis as in the Cape Province. When the Bill came before Parliament, the Bantu in the Cape were to be entered on a separate roll, voting in three large constituencies for three Europeans who would represent their interests in Parliament. The Bill was passed by a majority of 169 votes to 11 with Hofmeyr and Malan voting against the Bill. The Africans who had lost the vote numbered only 10,000 but the passing of the Bill meant the end of the mixed voting in the Cape which had lasted for nearly a hundred years and the end of any opportunity for African advancement by constitutional means. From 1936 the constitution was virtually a monopoly of the Europeans in South Africa.

African opposition to the Bill

Opposition to the Bill was expressed throughout

the country but the African National Congress in the Cape, led by Dr Jabavu, was not prepared to follow a militant course of action. It satisfied itself with a deputation to the Prime Minister protesting at the contents of the Bill. There was a rumour that Jabavu and his delegation, instead of condemning the Bill outright, were on the point of suggesting a compromise. This apparent weakening in their resolve brought A. B. Xuma and James Moroka to Cape Town to persuade Jabavu that no such compromise should be considered. Instead of presenting a united front, the delegation argued amongst themselves and made no great impression on Hertzog. Eventually Moroka's advice prevailed: 'We must have nothing to do with it. If they are going to take our rights away let them do the dirty job themselves.'[2]

The *Native Trust and Lands Bill* followed the Representation Bill of 1936 and in Hertzog's opinion was the final solution to the land question. It increased the total amount of land in the Reserves to 15 million hectares out of a national total of 121 million hectares. The Bill also allowed for the control of squatters over the whole of the union. The *Native Laws Amendment Act* of 1937 enforced the Group Areas Act of 1923 which had divided the towns into racial districts. It gave powers to the local authorities to refuse entry to Africans for whom there was no work available. Africans could be refused entry if they could not prove they were just visitors, and Africans who were residents in a town could be returned to their Reserves if there was no work for them.

As a background to the passing of these Bills, there was an increasing amount of hostility and violence between Europeans and non-Europeans. Police were found to be inexperienced and too severe in their dealings with Africans. For their part, they claimed that their task was made almost impossible by the enormous amount of complicated legislation which had to be enforced against the Africans. Also, the sentences imposed on people varied, not only with the type of crime committed, but with the racial character of the defendant. These variations provided yet another grievance for the African. The Government was quick to accuse the communists of enflaming the situation. Liberals, communists, anyone who took the part of the non-European, were blamed rather than the inadequacies of government.

Added to the growing lack of security in the country was the increase in anti-coloured, anti-Indian and anti-Jewish propaganda which was put about by extremist Europeans. The Coloureds of the Cape who had previously enjoyed a relatively privileged position, began to realise that their status was likely to be more like that of the African than the European in the future. Dr Malan claimed that white society could not consider itself completely safe until the coloured population was also segregated.

The defeat of Hertzog

At the general election of 1938, the United Party was returned with a slightly reduced majority. One of the major considerations which troubled the new Government was South Africa's position as a result of the outbreak of war in Europe in 1939. By the end of 1938, Smuts was convinced that South Africa must stand by Britain, but Hertzog announced South African neutrality in 1939. He was supported by Havenga, Pirow and three other ministers. But in the debate which followed Hertzog was defeated by eighty votes to sixty-seven. His resignation was accepted by the Governor-General, Sir Patrick Duncan, and under the leadership of Smuts, South Africa joined the war on the side of the allies – Britain, France and later the USA.

1948 General Election

Support for Smuts began to dwindle in 1947 and the Dominion Party was also experiencing a slow death. A general election was called for 20 May 1948, and even the most enthusiastic supporters of Dr Malan were not very optimistic about the outcome. Malan entered the campaign introducing apartheid as his policy and using it as his election platform. Malan did not try to hide the fact that fear was the basis of the policy. He proposed as a start that all Bantu representation in Parliament and the Cape Provincial Council should cease. Very much to his surprise, Malan won the election by a small majority, although his party did not poll as many votes as their opponents.

The 1948 election was a turning point in white South African politics. It did not result in a completely new political programme. Dr Malan's

Government continued politics which developed easily from the discriminatory policies of the inter-war years. What was new after 1948 was the absolute dominance of the political scene by the Afrikaners and the Nationalist Party. The United Party has continued as the opposition party but the major decisions are taken by an all-Afrikaner cabinet, and the main interest centres around differences in the ranks of the Nationalist Party rather than in the Parliament. Radical change in governmental policy is only likely to result from pressure from within the Nationalist Party and in this respect the Government of South Africa is answerable more to the Afrikaner white majority group and less to the Parliament.

In the years since 1948, the Nationalists have gradually gained more power in South Africa and in the election of 1961 they gained their first clear majority under the leadership of Dr Verwoerd when they polled 53.5 per cent of the total vote. Dr Malan remained Prime Minister until 1954 when he gave way to Mr J. G. Strijdom, the leader of the Transvaal Nationalist Party, who led the country until his death in August 1958. His successor was the ex-Minister of Native Affairs, Dr Verwoerd, who survived one attempt on his life, only to be assassinated in 1966. His greatest contribution to Nationalist Government was that he made the policy of apartheid a reality with the establishment of the Transkei as the first Bantustan. It was Verwoerd also who led South Africa out of the Commonwealth in May 1961 and proclaimed a republic after the **referendum** of 1960 had given him a 52 per cent majority. The present Prime Minister is Mr Vorster who continues the inflexible policies of the Nationalist Party which has succeeded in achieving all the ambitions of the extreme Afrikaners who wished to be completely inde-

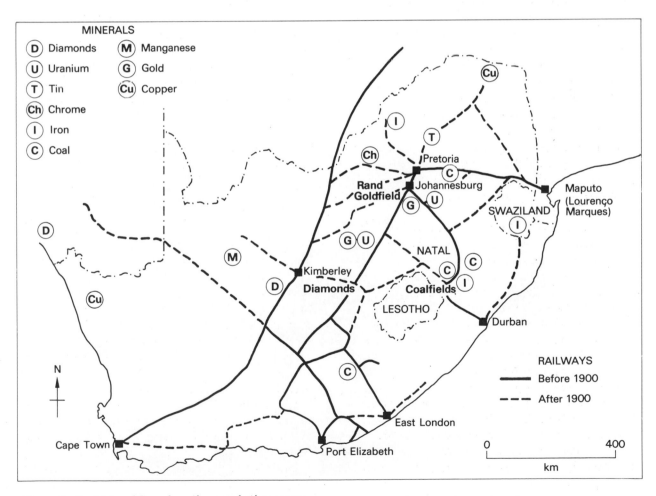

Fig. 33 South Africa: Minerals, railways and urban centres

pendent of any political influence from Britain. The aims of the Great Trek have been realised, although they have been achieved at the cost of isolating South Africa internationally. This situation was not unknown to the laager-conscious Voortrekker.

Economic development in the twentieth century

Economic development in the twentieth century has been closely related to the continued prosperity of the goldfields, the recent impressive growth of the manufacturing industries and a less spectacular increase in agricultural production. The crucial factor in the economic history of the last fifty years has been the determination of successive South African Governments to protect the interests of the white population, particularly the poor whites, against the increasing competition of the non-white population.

By 1913 the Africans had been deprived of much of the land which they considered their own and were limited to about 12 per cent of South African territory – the Reserves. Since 1913, the white South Africans have restricted African work opportunity in the four major industrial areas of South Africa – the Rand, Cape Town, Port Elizabeth and Durban.

The 'poor whites'

The emergence of the poor white group has much in common with the exodus from the Reserves of the poor blacks. Both existed in the nineteenth century in rural areas where the land had been allowed to deteriorate through over-cultivation, overstocking, soil erosion, drought and disease. Both had a system of inheritance by which the land was divided between the sons, a system which resulted in an enormous number of smallholdings, barely capable of supporting a family in a good year, let alone a year of drought. Poverty encouraged disease and certainly the poor whites of the late nineteenth century were stricken by disease far more often than their forebears, who lived in trek waggons and shot their own fresh meat. It was not even possible for the poor whites to surrender their land ownership and work as labourers for other farmers because of the presence of numerous Africans on these farms already. Also, there was no great enthusiasm amongst the poorest white to do

Johannesburg, the centre of the early gold-mining area and the second largest city in Africa

These migrant workers are temporary workers on the Rand who have come from all parts of Southern Africa

what they considered 'Kaffir work'. Possessing no particular skills which would be of value to industry, the poor whites who migrated to the towns found themselves thrown into an urban situation in which they qualified only for the lowest wages.

The African migration to the towns

The African Reserves also suffered from soil erosion, overcrowding and overstocking of cattle. The Africans were called upon to make a contribution to the South African economy through a Hut Tax which ranged from shs 20/- to 30/-. This may not seem much today, but at that time an African would have thought this a sizeable sum of money to pay. This tax was collected at a time when the more prosperous white South Africans were not even

paying income tax. The Glen Grey Act of 1894 had held out hopes of solving the problem of land ownership in the Reserves, but the Act did not justify the optimism of Cecil Rhodes who introduced it into the Cape Parliament. There was insufficient land available for individual land-holding and by 1929 there were over 11,000 families who had been made landless. The migration of the men to the towns left the land in the hands of the women and old people, who were unable to cope with all the work that had to be done. Ignorance, disease and drought increased the poverty of the Reserves until the only exportable commodity was poor black labour, expecting and accepting low wages in the industrial areas of South Africa. Africans began their migration into white South Africa at the time of the mineral discoveries of the nineteenth century. For nearly fifty years they had little competition for the unskilled jobs in the diamond fields and on the Rand.

The competition between poor whites and Africans grew in the early twentieth century. To begin with, the Africans were more favoured because they were prepared to accept very low wages. This meant that the poor white had the greatest difficulty finding employment. The major piece of legislation designed to help the white employee was the Mines and Works Act of 1911 which came into full operation in 1926 as the Colour Bar Act. This Act stated that certain positions of responsibility could only be held by white persons (see p. 126). For the second half of the nineteenth century, the Africans had filled the unskilled labour requirements. With the growing numbers of poor whites, the Government insisted on a policy of 'Civilised Labour'.

The role of gold 1918–65

Gold continues to play a dominant role in the South African economy. Despite warnings of decline from time to time, the industry has been able to sustain its growth. Gold mining holds a unique place in the economy because:

a) It is able to attract large amounts of capital.
b) It is able to attract large amounts of labour.
c) It is produced essentially for the export trade.

It was estimated in 1930 that one half of South Africa's total population was dependent directly or indirectly on the gold industry.

The search for new goldfields took place in this expansionist period of the 1930s and proved successful in three areas: the far West Rand; the Orange Free State – and the Vaal River. By 1964 the Orange Free State goldfields had become the major gold producing area in the country.

In 1910 gold contributed 80 per cent of the total export earnings and in 1965 gold and uranium were responsible for nearly 50 per cent of the total export earnings. South Africa supplies 70 per cent of the world's gold requirements. The other main contributors to the economy, manufacturing industry and agriculture, made progress during the present century, largely through investments raised from the profits of the goldfields. Since the war it

The gold mines are centres of attraction for African labour

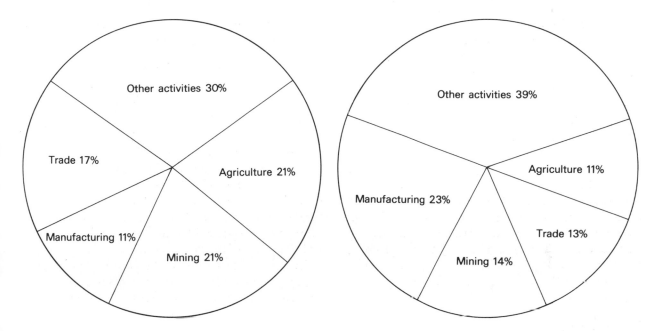

Fig. 34 *South Africa: Sources of national income, 1919–20*   Fig. 35 *South Africa: Sources of national income, 1959–60*

has been the manufacturing industries which have shown the greatest development. By 1960 these were producing a greater proportion of the national income than mining and agriculture combined.

The growth of secondary industry

The development of secondary (manufacturing) industry began in the second half of the nineteenth century. The first major stimulus for the growth of secondary industry came with the First World War of 1914–18 when imported manufactured articles were not easily available. After the war, conditions did not favour South African industry quite as much because of the relatively high labour costs for poorly trained white and non-white workers, and a very small domestic market for home produced goods. Despite the fact that South Africa lacked none of the industrial raw materials, the manufacturing industries were not secure. It was necessary for the state to provide them with protection against foreign manufacturers.

The kinds of industry set up after the war were mostly of the consumer type – footwear, clothing, flour milling, saw milling, motor assembly and tyre manufacture. This selection was to be found in the Port Elizabeth area and it attracted a great many poor whites from the surrounding countryside. The emphasis in the manufacturing industries was much more on white labour than was the case in the mining industries. The ratio in the newer industries of white to African labour was 1:3, whereas in the mining industry it was 1:9.

One industry which enjoyed considerable protection was iron and steel. This industry became a public corporation in 1929 when the private company failed to raise enough capital to run. To begin with, the new corporation had to be run with high labour costs for the white workers, but from 1936 onwards many Europeans left to go and work in other industries. Their places were taken by Africans and this resulted in a considerable saving in labour costs.

Just as the First World War led to greater interest in the manufacturing industries, so did the Second World War from 1939 to 1945. Not only was there increased productivity because of the shortage of imports but also there was a major change in the organisation of industry. Coloureds, Asians and some Africans filled the posts of whites who had left to fight in the war. At the end of the war it had to be decided whether this change would remain or whether the white South Africans would go back to the labour structure of the pre-war years.

Iron and steel works are the basis of secondary industry in South Africa. This is a view over the ISCOR works at Pretoria

Agriculture

One important report which was published during the war was the *Van Eck Report* of 1941. It made valuable comments on the state of agriculture in which it emphasised the poverty of the land. It said that at the very most only 15 per cent of the land could be cultivated and that South Africa should concentrate mainly on livestock farming. It pointed out the rapid deterioration of the land due to soil erosion and bad management. Although two-thirds of the working population was still dependent on agriculture, it produced only one-eighth of the national income. The report suggested a more planned approach to farming and suggested that if manufacturing industries were to be successful, more attention should be paid to the domestic market, with particular reference to the lower income groups.

Agriculture in the Reserves

In the 1830s, the Basuto were producing and storing large surpluses of grain which were exported in time of drought and shortage. This continued until the end of the century when it was probably true that most African farmers were producing at least enough for subsistence. In the Victoria East district 6,000 Africans sold £19,000 of produce in 1875. Fifty years later, 12,000 Africans could only sell £10,000 of produce. The situation was changed by the sharp increase in population growth in the twentieth century.

Greater pressure was placed on the land to produce more food, land was in short supply, a shifting form of cultivation was no longer possible, and landlessness increased. Landlessness was made worse by the legislation of 1913 and 1936 which further restricted African opportunity to settle and purchase land. The re-settlement schemes have had an even more depressing effect on land availability. Those incapable of working in the white areas – the very old and the very young – have been sent back to the 'homelands' where there is no work and little land. There has been a general trend for more and more men to leave the Reserves and gain work in the towns. The least able are left to look after the land. It is thought that a reduced African population in the Reserves is the surest way to development in African agriculture. But the insecurity of housing and employment in the towns sometimes discourages the move to the town.

It is considered that Reserve Africans are less well fed than previously and university research indicates that well over a million young Africans are suffering from malnutrition. This is not so surprising when one realises that so far over a million Africans have been moved out of the white areas and re-settled in the already poverty stricken 'homelands'. More people to support has meant overcropping and over-grazing. This in turn leads to soil erosion and lower crop yields.

The post war period

It became clear, soon after the Nationalist Party's election victory in 1948, that the new Government was opposed to any change which would alter the set relationship between white and black South Africans.

In the last twenty-five years the South African economy has shown impressive growth. Agriculture has become more commercialised and competitive than ever before. It has been assisted by guaranteed domestic markets in which the bulk food buying by the Government has played an important part. The growth of export products such as wool illustrates a similar development; from R8.5 million (equivalent to about £16 million in 1977) in 1939 to R14.5 million (£28 million in 1977) in 1947, to an all-time peak in 1961 of R91 million

(equivalent of £174 million in 1977 money). Agriculture, despite improvements and a more scientific approach is making a declining contribution to the national income. This is quite a natural trend in a country whose most spectacular progress has been in manufacturing.

South Africa was self-sufficient in nearly all types of plant and machinery by 1965. This had been achieved mainly by guaranteed domestic markets for home producers through tariff protection and limited imports. Electric locomotives, rolling stock, machinery, power stations, mining equipment are all made locally. The rise in the use of tractors demonstrates not only the growth of a manufacturing industry but also the increased mechanisation in South African agriculture. There were 6,000 tractors in 1937, 22,000 in 1947, and 100,000 in 1957. The growth of the Iron and Steel

The Paarl Valley is the centre of the Cape's wine industry. It was settled by French Huguenots in the late seventeenth century

Corporation (ISCOR) indicates the general expansion rate of the manufacturing industries; in 1945 output was 500,000 ingot tonnes, in 1951 1,000,000 and in 1960 2,350,000; the target for 1969 was 4,500,000 ingot tonnes. In 1939 manufactured goods constituted 3 per cent of the total South African exports. In 1966 this figure had been raised to nearly 40 per cent.

Summary of Chapter 12

Afrikaner domination in the twentieth century
1910 *Act of Union* All white franchise except for the Cape. Triumph for Boer individualism.
1912 *Hertzog forms the Afrikaner Nationalist Party*
1924 Nationalist Government with Hertzog as Prime Minister.
1926 Full sovereign rights for a dominion within Commonwealth. Afrikaans becomes the official language instead of Dutch.
1936 *Africans lose the vote in the Cape Province* 'Purified' Nationalist Party led by Dr Malan.
1948 *Election victory for Malan*
1959 *Apartheid Policy* – Dr Verwoerd the chief architect.
1961 South Africa becomes a republic outside Commonwealth.

Economic development in the twentieth century
Poor whites and African migration to the towns: 'Civilised Labour' policy.
Expansion of gold: role of gold
Growth of secondary industry: need for protection – spectacular expansion.
Agriculture: decline in the Reserves – more commercialised and competitive in white areas.

Short questions on Chapter 12

1 What was the main result of the 1913 Land Act?
2 Why did the Indians come to South Africa?
3 Where do most of the Indians live?
4 What did the Mines and Works Act of 1911 attempt to do?
5 When did South Africa take responsibility for South-West Africa?
6 What was the ICU?

7 Which party was formed when Hertzog and Smuts entered into a Coalition Government in 1933?
8 What was 'Civilised Labour'?
9 Name three pieces of legislation aimed at favouring the Europeans.
10 What did the Native Laws Amendment Act of 1937 achieve?
11 Name the four Nationalist Prime Ministers of South Africa since 1948.
12 When did South Africa leave the Commonwealth?

Longer questions on Chapter 12

1 In what ways is it true to say that 'Britain won the war, but the Afrikaners won the peace'?
2 What were the main problems facing the Botha Government of 1910–19?
3 What caused Hertzog to form the Afrikaner Nationalist Party in 1912?
4 Describe the main features of the 1913 Land Act. What were the results of this measure?
5 Explain the contribution and influence of Clement Kadalie in the awakening of African nationalism in South Africa.
6 What was the result of the passing of the Native Representation Bill of 1936?
7 If mining and industry are prospering, the same cannot be said of agriculture. Explain some of the problems of agriculture in the African Reserves.

Notes to Chapter 12

1 *Harijan*, 24 March 1946.
2 M. Benson, *The Struggle for a Birthright*, Penguin, 1966, p. 68.

13 The growth of apartheid

During the twentieth century the white minority in South Africa has gradually increased its control over the rest of the country's population. Starting with military domination, successive white governments have built up a political, economic and social system aimed at guaranteeing white control and political security from a 'black threat'. As has been seen, this has involved a great many laws being passed which limit African opportunity in the major aspects of life: land ownership, employment, political representation and education. The restriction on educational opportunity is the policy which affects Africans most. An inferior education system condemns the mass of the African population to the status of second or third class citizens in their own country. They have little chance of improvement in the near future. The attack on this policy has always been the most important part of any campaign organised by African nationalist leaders.

This complete white control did not happen overnight, 1948 is considered to be an important stage in the gradual move towards white control. The Nationalist Government of Dr Malan enjoyed a greater political freedom than any previous government. Smuts in 1919 was under considerable pressure from Hertzog and his newly formed Nationalist Party. Hertzog himself found it impossible to rule without the support of other parties, first of all with the Labour Party in the Pact Ministry and later with Smuts's South African Party. Dr Malan had no need to rely on the support of any other party, and since 1948 the Nationalist Party has dominated white South African politics. As a result the Nationalist Party has been able to determine the political development of the whole country.

By 1948, working class whites in South Africa found themselves among Africans who were not only more educated and better paid than before, but who were more aware of their grievances. Moreover, their leaders were generally as well-informed on political matters as the white leaders. The white South African had two ways of dealing with this: either to accept complete economic and political integration between the different peoples or to impose white control. When they chose the latter it was inevitable that the white South Africans would have to introduce new laws to maintain their privileged position at the expense of about 80 per cent of the population.

Jan Smuts, surprisingly defeated by Dr Malan in the 1948 General Election

What is apartheid?

Despite the great many laws needed to establish white control, it is not easy to find a clear definition of the apartheid policy. The Bureau of Racial Affairs defines apartheid as the 'territorial separation of European and Bantu, and the provision of areas which must serve as national and political homes for the different Bantu communities and as a permanent residential area for the Bantu population or the major part of it.'[1]

In a rather blunter but perhaps more honest fashion, Mr J. J. Strijdom, Prime Minister of the Union from 1955–8 said, 'Call it paramountcy, "boss-ship" or what you will, it is still domination. I am being as blunt as I can. I am making no excuses. The only way the European can maintain supremacy is by domination.'[2]

The development of white domination in South Africa since the Act of Union has been achieved by a deliberate limitation of opportunity for non-whites in all aspects of life. Policies have been followed which have had several results: non-whites now have very few political rights; whites and non-whites are not allowed to mix socially; non-whites have to live in areas set aside for them; poorer educational facilities are provided for them and they do not have the same employment opportunities as whites. Associated with these measures has been the policy of setting up Bantustans. This policy aims at reducing the amount of national feeling among Africans by creating 'tribal homelands'. This is a clever extension of the Government's old 'divide and rule' maxim, the idea being that the Government can have more control over separate, small units than over one large region.

Political suppression

In the Cape the Africans had direct representation at Parliamentary level in the past and then only for about 10,000 of them. This right to direct representation was given some protection in the Act of Union but other parts of the Union were not given the same right. Its precarious existence was ended in 1936 when the Representation of Natives Act was passed. Qualified Africans from the Cape were placed on a separate voting register or roll. They were allowed to vote for representation by three Europeans in the House of Assembly. Africans throughout South Africa were represented in the Senate, by four European Senators. A Native Representative Council was formed at the same time. It consisted of twelve elected and four nominated Africans and five European officials with the Secretary for Native Affairs as chairman. It never fulfilled the more optimistic hopes that it would be a valuable advisory council for the Government. In 1946 the Council decided to suspend itself in token protest against the Government's policies.

Thus, having got rid of the African's right to direct representation in Parliament the Government had to make sure that they had adequate means for dealing with any political opposition outside Parliament. The ideal test measure for such control was the Suppression of Communism Act of 1950. This gave the Minister of Justice sweeping powers to deal with supposed communists, a name which has been loosely used to describe anyone who is acting against the best interests of white South Africa. Bans on individuals and prison sentences of up to ten years proved effective in reducing political activity among all but the most dedicated nationalists. Many student leaders, politicians and church leaders have been prosecuted as a result of this act.

All African representation in the South African Parliament was removed by the 1959 Bantu Self-Government Act. The Act got rid of the three elected members of the Assembly for Africans in favour of direct representation by Africans in their own Bantustan parliaments. The Act ignored the fact that nearly half the African population was living and working outside the African Reserve areas. By 1959 the South African Government had successfully got rid of all African representatives in Parliament. It had begun the next phase to divert African political ambition away from South Africa as a whole to the smaller Bantustans.

Loss of land

In 1913, the first Union Government had passed the Land Act. This created a land division wholly to the advantage of the whites. The 1936 Native Trusts and Lands Act was considered by Prime Minister Hertzog to be the final solution to the land problem. Provision was made for the handing over

Detention camps are the centres where convicted opponents of the South African Government are sent. This is the Stofberg Camp

of a further 6 million hectares to the African Reserves. Today, Africans have acquired 14 million hectares instead of the 15 million hectares due. As the total acreage of South Africa is just over 120 million hectares, the 1936 Act may be considered 'the final solution' by the whites but is the basis of a huge problem in the African areas. These make up about one-eighth of the total area of South Africa but have to support half the African population directly and be considered as a homeland for the other half. In other words, all the Africans, comprising 65 per cent of the total population are supposed to fit into 13 per cent of South Africa, while the whites, comprising 19 per cent, have the other 87 per cent.

The South African Government has been able to enforce this division of the country by a series of laws which have made it easier for Africans to live permanently in white areas, but this is mainly for those who are able to provide a source of labour for the white economy. The Native (Urban Areas) Act of 1923 provided the first framework to control the number of Africans entering the white areas and this Act has been altered on numerous occasions since. The 1935 Native (Urban Areas) Amendment Act gave local authorities powers to force an African to leave a white area if his presence was considered a threat to peace and order. The 1937 Native Laws Amendment Act said that African visitors to white areas in which they are not resident or employed can only stay for up to seventy-two hours without a permit, after which their presence is considered a criminal offence. The result of these Acts controlling the movement of Africans into white areas has been to produce a contracted labour force for the white areas, a contract usually of up to a year before the worker returns to the Reserve. Such a contracted worker would not qualify to have his wife and family with him and this has had a divisive effect on African family life.

Re-settlement

The Government is making the situation worse by re-settling Africans in the Bantustans from the white urban areas. The argument used in favour of re-settlement is that the people are too old, unproductive, unfit, or are women with dependent children. People in these categories are ordered out to the Bantustans. Here many live in appalling

Welcome Valley; this is the halfway stage to re-settlement in the Bantustans

conditions with poor health, outbreaks of lawlessness among the young and despair among the older people. It is worth noting that members of the Fingo community near Grahamstown have been forced out. Land was given to them in recognition of help given to the British against the Xhosa. In 1970 as Grahamstown celebrated the 150th anniversary of the settlers' arrival, descendants of the settlers' old allies were being forced out of their village on the outskirts of the town.

The plight of the resettled people is told by Father Cosmas Desmond in his book. *The Discarded People*. He writes in the early part of the book: 'The poverty, suffering and broken families caused by the re-settlement schemes are not accidental. They are allowed to happen because they are part of the price of white wealth.'

Law enforcement – Pass Laws

The laws restricting African movement and residents in white areas have been enforced through a whole range of Pass Laws, which mean constant checks for the Africans. It is the Pass Laws which arouse the greatest resentment and anger among Africans. They are a symbol of oppression and slavery. Every African over the age of sixteen, male or female, has to carry a 'reference' or 'pass book'. This combines up to a dozen passes, a certificate from an employer that has to be signed by him every month, a residential pass, a tax receipt and a curfew pass. Failure to produce a pass book on demand is a criminal offence and it is an offence if any one of the relevant passes is not in order.

Passes restrict African movement

Africans have many descriptions of the pass – 'badge of slavery' and the 'dompass, the verlande, or accursed pass'.

A quotation from *The Rand Daily Mail* of 25 February 1960 gives some indication of the working of the Pass Laws. A certain Simon Legodi was fined for non-possession of a pass book. In a statement he told the court: 'About lunchtime I decided to cross the road to go to the butcher's shop to buy some food for lunch. I was stopped by a non-European constable who asked for my pass. I pointed to my place of work and told him my pass was in my jacket pocket. I was not given a chance to get my pass.' Later a friend showed the magistrate a letter with Legodi's pass. 'The magistrate read the letter in my presence, but a few days later I was put into a truck and I was told I would have to work for a certain European on his farm.'

Employment

From the earliest periods of white settlement the white settler had always considered unskilled manual labour beneath his dignity and had relied on non-white labour for the unskilled work. In the twentieth century the white governments have always been under pressure. They have been under pressure not only to maintain this work relationship of the master and servant, but to protect and reinforce the poor whites position. Many measures were passed in support of the poor whites and 'Civilised Labour' to limit non-white opportunities. The Mines and Works Act of 1911 restricted Africans to unskilled mine work. The Colour Bar Act of 1926 prevented Africans working at a wide variety of skilled and semi-skilled work. The Industrial and Conciliation Act of 1924 excluded African workers from organised consultation with employers. The labour laws follow very closely the land and franchise laws. In all cases the non-white is discriminated against. He is forced into the powerless position of finding work in the white areas where the range of work will be determined by the whites. He will have no rights of land ownership and no political rights.

Education

The Education Acts have provoked great African hostility, second only to the Pass Laws.

A Bantu school in Soweto

Schoolchildren protest in Soweto in 1976

The two significant Education Acts are the Bantu Education Act of 1953 and the Extension of Universities Act of 1959. The aim of the 1953 Education Act is that Africans should be made aware from childhood that equality is not for them. They should be prepared for the opportunities which will be made available to them in either the 'homeland' or the 'white' areas. Obviously the work in the urban areas intended for them does not demand a highly technical or academic education. In fact the Government would suggest that an educated African was a positive danger, since 'knowledge is power'. Dr Verwoerd, who was mainly responsible for the Act, said that the standards of the Reserve areas were lower in terms of educational levels. There was no point in educating Africans to a level which was not needed in the reserve areas and which could not be used by Africans in white areas.

The Government took over from the missions the responsibility for African education. It decided who should be taught, who should teach and what they should teach. In this way, the Government was able to control the direction of education and through this the degree of African advancement. Education has always been considered as a means of improvement. The thought that this advancement could be controlled or hindered by a people who had consistently shown that African interests were always at the bottom of their list of priorities angered Africans more than any other single issue, excluding the Pass Laws. One means of advancement in modern South Africa had been the knowledge of English, but the new act made English only a second language, the main language of instruction being the particular Bantu language of the area. There are obvious disadvantages in emphasising the value of Bantu languages and traditions, although these are worthwhile in themselves. Africans were not slow to recognise this distinct limit on opportunities. African nationalism had always struggled because of the lack of unity among Africans. The Bantu Education Act would only serve to reinforce these divisions and make a strong and united nationalist movement even more difficult to organise.

The ever-widening gap in educational opportunity can be seen in the different costs per student in a year between white and black.

1953　White : £50
　　　　Black : £6
1963　White : £70
　　　　Black : £6.25
1969　White : £100
　　　　Black : £6.50

The teacher/student ratio in African schools is very revealing also:
1949 – 1:42
1968 – 1:72

When one considers that the secondary school population is only 5 per cent of the total black population it is obvious that the Government is being ruthlessly effective in carrying out its policy of non-advancement for the African.

By the Universities Act of 1959, separate universities were set up for the different races. The open universities which had previously admitted students of all races had their doors closed to all except Europeans. Africans resent these acts because they feel that the acts are establishing a mass of second class citizens. The educational system prepares Africans for a social and economic role which is little better than that of unskilled or semi-skilled labourers. The 1976 riots in Soweto and other urban centres started as a reaction against these rules by African high school students.

The first Bantustan

The policy of self-development and the introduction of Bantustans was just one more method of maintaining white control in South Africa. Supporters of Dr Verwoerd, who introduced the Promotion of Bantu Self-Government Act of 1959 would claim that the new policy was the final answer to the black problem. When the Plan for Separate Development was presented to Parliament in January 1959, Dr Verwoerd concentrated on a number of main points.

a) He did not believe in complete racial separation on a territorial basis as he realised that the majority of Africans would continue to work in white areas. In fact, white South Africa is getting 'blacker' all the time. Despite rigorous apartheid legislation, over a million Africans moved into the white urban areas in the years 1950 to 1960.

b) Africans will have no political rights in the white areas, but they will have rights which they can exercise through the Bantustan of their ethnic grouping. This involved the repeal of the Native Representation Act of 1936 which provided African representation through three European members of the Assembly and four European senators.

c) Verwoerd proposed to solve the problem of unemployment in the Bantustans by encouraging white industry on the white side of the Bantustan border, and by building African townships on the Bantustan side, thus providing labour for European industry.

d) The Government feels that the Bantu peoples of South Africa do not constitute a homogenous people, that is, they are not all of the same kind but form separate national units based on language and culture, and because of this, the Bantustan units bear a strong resemblance to 'tribal' divisions. The ethnic units are: North Sotho, South Sotho, Swazi, Tsonga, Tswana, Venda, Xhosa, Zulu and Ndebele.

In these Bantustans, the idea is to develop a system of local government organised by the Africans in the territory, although the Government of the Republic reserves the right to overrule any decision taken by the Legislative Assembly of the Bantustan. The Bantustan does not have control over military forces, the manufacture of arms and ammunition, foreign affairs and the right of entry or the presence of police forces from the Republic. It does not control post offices, railways and harbours, national roads, civil aviation, the entry of aliens, currency and public loans, customs and excise.

The Transkei

The first Bantustan to be developed was the Transkei, the home of the Xhosa. Among the reasons why the Transkei was chosen for an experiment in separate development are that the Transkei provides a fairly homogenous ethnic unit with a long experience of advisory bodies which

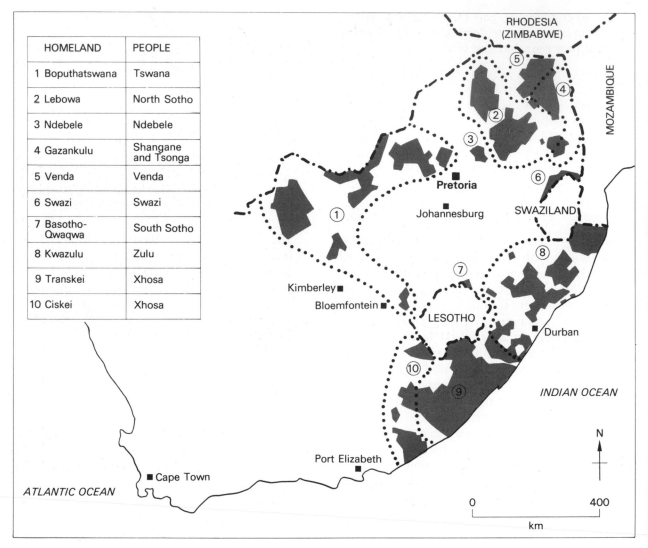

HOMELAND	PEOPLE
1 Boputhatswana	Tswana
2 Lebowa	North Sotho
3 Ndebele	Ndebele
4 Gazankulu	Shangane and Tsonga
5 Venda	Venda
6 Swazi	Swazi
7 Basotho-Qwaqwa	South Sotho
8 Kwazulu	Zulu
9 Transkei	Xhosa
10 Ciskei	Xhosa

Fig. 36 The Bantustans

could easily be transformed into governing assemblies. The Transkei is also a united area, whereas the other projected Bantustans are on the whole broken up, with the possible exceptions of the Ciskei and Zululand. A further reason is that 60 per cent of the Xhosa people live in the Transkei, a figure which is way above the average of 37 per cent for ethnic groups in other Reserves.

Setting up the first Bantustan

The steps toward the setting up of the Transkei Bantustan can only be understood with reference to the general political scene in South Africa, from 1948 onwards. Between 1948 and 1952 the more militant sections of the ANC started the Defiance Campaign of 1952 in the urban areas. This protest was supported by the Bunga, an advisory council in the Transkei made up of chiefs and headmen. It rejected the principles of the 1951 Bantu Authorities Act which hoped to increase the power of the chiefs at the expense of the democratic principle. The Bunga opposed political inequality and called for more authority in the Transkei. The Bunga accepted the Bantu Authorities Act of 1951 expecting that it would provide the hoped for authority within the Transkei. Perhaps at this stage also there was a feeling that it was useless to try to oppose the Government.

The detailed legislation for the Bantustans was laid down in the Promotion of Bantu Self-

The Transkei; this was the first of South Africa's Bantu Homelands

Government Act of 1959. It was the logical successor to the earlier Bantu Authorities Act. This had talked in general terms of the restoration of the prestige and authority of 'native' laws and customs, eventually leading to territorial authorities under African control. During the debate on the bill, the leader of the United Party, Sir de Villiers Graaf, had this comment to make: 'Will permanently urbanised Africans be satisfied with political rights in the Bantu areas where they have never lived, which they have probably never visited, and about which they possibly have no knowledge?' The answer to this question indicated the gamble the South African Government is taking in trying to make the Bantustans into a political magnet which will attract the politically minded Africans. It is hoped that this will distract them from the political demands they are making on the whole country.

Transkei constituency

By 1960, the confidence of white South Africans had been shaken by a series of events culminating

with Sharpeville. One of the results of this was that Verwoerd announced an acceleration in the timetable of the development in the Transkei. The main provisions of the 1963 Constitution of the Transkei were:

a) A separate flag and anthem.
b) A franchise open to all Transkei citizens over the age of twenty-one, both men and women.
c) A Legislative Assembly consisting of four Paramount Chiefs, a maximum of sixty additional chiefs and forty-five elected members.

Transkei elections 1963, 1968

The results of the election of 20 November 1963 proved that the supporters of Chief Victor Poto were more popular than those of Chief Kaiser Matanzima. Of the forty-five successful candidates no less than thirty-five could be counted as pro-Poto. When it came to the selection of Chief Minister, the appointed chiefs supported Matanzima rather than Poto and Chief Kaiser Matanzima was elected as a result of their vote in

The Bunga Parliament and buildings in Umtata, the Transkei capital

his favour. Chief Poto, instead of serving with Matanzima, formed the opposition Democratic Party. In the following election in 1968 however, Matanzima's party won with an overwhelming majority. The major difference between the two parties is over the race question. Poto stood for a multi-racial society, whilst Matanzima supported the principle of separation, demanding early independence for the Transkei.

How independent can the Bantustans be?

The success or failure of the Transkei experiment is of real importance in considering the eventual success of the apartheid policy. The *Tomlinson Report* (issued as a White Paper in May 1956) speaking of all the Reserves, first of all stated bluntly that these territories were very poor. The most important economic facts to be gained from the report were:

a) 30 per cent of the land was badly eroded.
b) 44 per cent of the land was moderately eroded.
c) Since 1936 the real income (or the money with which they actually buy things), of Africans in the Reserves had remained unchanged.
d) 50,000 new jobs a year would be required over the next five years. Related to this, the report states, 'As far as industries are concerned, the Bantu areas are a desert.'
e) A hundred urban townships would need to be established.
f) £25 million would be needed in the first five years.
g) The overall cost of the scheme would be well over £100 million.

It was thought that with this kind of expenditure, the Reserves would be able to support about seven million Africans – still only about 60 per cent of the total African population. The Government has not been over-generous in the money it has placed at the disposal of the Transkei and the other Reserves. In the first five years, 1956–61, only £8 million was spent, and in the five year period 1961–6, the expenditure was £157 million, two-thirds of which was spent on building new townships. As for attracting new industries to the border areas, the Government found that industrialists prefer established industrial areas, despite the financial incentives offered to them to set up factories near the border. There has been an increasing demand for these industries to be established inside the territory and not on the other side of the border.

Transkei independence

Chief Matanzima has never disguised his aim to gain self-government for the Transkei first of all, and then from this slightly stronger position hope to wrest more concessions from the South African Government. He had an overwhelming victory in the general election prior to Independence Day of 26 October 1976. Only four Opposition candidates were elected to the seventy-five seats and with seventy-two out of the seventy-five nominated chiefs supporting his party, the Transkei National Independence Party, Matanzima has all but ten of the total number of seats. The turnout of the electorate of 66 per cent was higher than the figures for the two previous elections.

Transkei was granted 'independence' by South Africa on 26 October 1976 but it was something of a hollow victory for Matanzima since there was neither international representation nor recognition for the new state at its independence celebrations. Although admitting that the former High Commission Territory of Lesotho may be no more economically self-supporting than the Transkei, critics of the new Transkei status insist that recognition of independence might be equivalent to a recognition of apartheid.

The first major issue to be raised between the Transkei and the South African Government concerns the political and citizenship rights of over a million Xhosa living in the white areas. Matanzima hopes to persuade South Africa that these urban African need not take out Transkei citizenship but should retain South African citizenship instead. It remains to be seen who gives way, for a concession by South Africa on this issue might lead to the collapse of the apartheid policy, which relies on all Africans having citizenship rights only in their own 'homelands'.

Afrikaner opinion on apartheid

Afrikaners feel that if everyone was to have the right to vote for members of the South African Parliament this would mean the end of a culture and civilisation which has lasted for over three hundred years in South Africa. The Afrikaner is not prepared to see the non-white population invade and swamp modern South Africa, which is what he expects to happen if national decisions and policies fall into the hands of the majority of the non-white population.

The only apparent alternative is to separate the races territorially and allow the non-white people to develop within their own culture in their own areas. It is the intention that Africans should be cheated out of a greater South Africa into the poverty and landlessness of the Bantustans where they are to have a false independence.

Views of the opponents of apartheid

The argument most frequently used against apartheid is that differences in cultural background are not necessarily determined by a difference in race. The opponents of the system point out that many non-Europeans in the country show that cultural development along western lines is not the privilege and monopoly of the white person alone. It has been suggested by some reformers that a civilisation level rather than colour should determine social divisions, if these divisions are in fact necessary. But strong African and world opinion now holds that since Africans are human beings just as much as the whites, the walls of apartheid should be pulled down so that everyone lives as an equal in South Africa.

The proportion of non-whites in the population has not been used as the basis for the division of the country into racial areas. The African population

Chief Gatsha Buthelezi, Prime Minister of Kwazulu and an opponent of apartheid

comprising 65 per cent of the total population, is expected to support itself on about 13 per cent of the land, leaving the rest of the country to the Europeans. This seems to the opponent of apartheid not only unreasonable, but, in the long run, impractical also. The division of the Reserves into ethnic areas seems to prevent any development towards a national society rather than a society which is made up of many different ethnic groups. The Bantustans, with the exception of the Transkei and the Ciskei, are fragmentary and small. Any attempts at creation of independent states will fail because they are unable, because of size, to develop self-supporting economies.

The Bantustans are unlikely to support the whole of the African population. Some six million

Africans are expected to live in European areas, in which they will have no political or civil rights but in which they will be supplying most of the labour force. The Bantustans, although on the eastern and more favoured side of the country, are among the poorest. They are still expected to support the highest densities of population. It has been suggested that about £100 million needs to be spent very quickly to offset the effects of bad farming, soil erosion and soil exhaustion. The amount of money being invested in these areas at the moment does not seem enough for there to be any reason to hope they can develop their own self-supporting economies. Yet even if all that money was put in, it would not reduce the right of Africans to claim the whole of South Africa as their home.

The point is that everyone – Bantu, Boer or Briton – ought to have equal access to all the land in South Africa.

The separate areas policy applies only to the Africans. The Coloureds and Asians are not to be allocated their own land. The argument of the need for cultural self-determination does not appear too consistent in the case of the Coloureds, who have in the past been accepted as part of the Europeans' culture. Through legislation, they are being driven away from a society of which they have always been a recognised part.

Attitude of English-speaking South Africans to apartheid

The English-speaking section of the country comprises 39 per cent of the white population but English-speaking members of Parliament hold less than a quarter of the total seats. This apparent political disinterest disguises a very strong economic position. English-speaking South Africans control almost completely the mining, financial and industrial wealth of the country, and this strong interest determines the attitude of many South Africans of English origin to the Government. Although most English-speaking South Africans agree with the need for a segregationist policy, many are irritated by the inflexible nature of the apartheid system. They feel that the way it is being enforced is too rigid, is harmful to the economy, will eventually prove unworkable and will also increase the isolation of South Africa from the rest of the world. It is important to stress this: as owners of the wealth of the country, they could bring about significant changes if they really wanted to. This they have so far not done.

It must be understood that the English-speaking South Africans are about as far removed from the 'mother country' as the Americans are from Britain. They are first and foremost South Africans and it is not surprising that most of them agree with the Afrikaner's point of view. They also enjoy the privileges of apartheid. There are exceptions to this general acceptance, and they are found in small minority groups who are more radical in outlook. In literary circles, a few people such as Alan Paton and Dan Jacobsen make the voice of protest heard abroad. Journalists in South Africa also keep the public informed of events which would not normally be given space in government journals. Some of the most outspoken centres of protest are in the universities, particularly among the National Union of South African Students (NUSAS), which was described by Mr Vorster when he was Minister of Justice, as a 'cancer to be eradicated.'[3] In the second half of 1968, Mr Vorster once again met strong opposition from NUSAS over the cancellation of an African lecturer's appointment to Cape Town University. And since then, NUSAS leaders have been subjected to harassment as have been the leaders of the black South African Students Organisation (SASO).

Until recently the political expression of radical opinion was through the Progressive and Liberal Parties, but in 1968, the Liberal Party, which had Alan Paton as its President, was disbanded when the Government decided that multi-racial political associations were illegal. The Progressive Party was founded in 1959 when eleven MPs broke away from the United Party. This number was reduced to one in the 1961 election. The one member was Mrs Helen Suzman, who has been quoted as saying, in 1963, 'Dr Verwoerd says we would rather be poor and white than rich and mixed. I believe that most South Africans will opt for the latter once the time of decision comes.' The Progressive Party has a programme of a qualified non-white franchise, a Bill of Rights, and a Senate membership of all races which could only be achieved through support from all the racial groups. The Liberal Party was in favour of universal suffrage, that is votes for everyone.

All these white organisations have not achieved much. Given the context in which they are operating, this is not surprising. They have called for reform, and yet the South African situation calls for more than just reform of aspects of apartheid. For real change to come about the whole apparatus of apartheid has to be got rid of. This means no more or less than a revolution in South African society.

Many opponents of apartheid would like to substitute full integration for separate development, but as the years go by there is a growing number of people who feel that 'South Africa for the Africans' should be the watchword of the African nationalist campaign, and the chances of a solution through integration seem less and less likely. At present the Government is determined to crush any opposition in the country. Reasonable people all over the world are wondering just how long it is possible to suppress every sign of African opposition without retaliation from these same Africans. People are also aware that Africans have liberated themselves in Angola and Mozambique so increasingly people are now asking: 'Why not South Africa?'

Changing pattern of African life

In the first half of the nineteenth century few people in South Africa either white or non-white, worked within a money economy. Most people followed a subsistence type of life, mainly hunting and pastoralism. There was considerable competition for land between the Boers and the Bantu. The population was mainly rural. The whites were establishing their control over a larger proportion of land at the expense of the non-whites. Many of the Africans were forced, through loss of land, to search for work in the white areas, at first on farms and later in the towns. By 1960 all Africans were involved in South Africa's modern cash economy, and the rural economy was in a state of decline.

Loss of traditional standards and values

Nearly half of all Africans live in urban areas today. It is the half of the population which is the most able-bodied, the most vital and includes most of the better educated Africans. It is not surprising that the rural areas stagnate and decline. Despite having experience of town life for two or three generations, Africans are not allowed to settle permanently in towns although they have lost contact with the Reserves. Many of the traditional social controls such as the unity of the family, the authority of the elders, the importance of kinship, and the security of land tenure are absent in the town areas and one cannot say that the alternatives have improved the situation. Employment in the towns is of a temporary contract type and involves many of the men living apart from their basic family of wives and children, as well as being separated from other kinsfolk in the town. The role of women has altered

in the towns also. Greater independence through separate incomes has made it almost impossible for educated and independent African women to be absorbed into the old traditional Reserve areas.

African wages in South Africa

The breakdown of traditional values has led to confusion. This is reinforced by the attitude of the white authorities. They insist on enforcing a whole range of legislation intent on emphasising African inferiority. Africans provide two thirds of the work force in South Africa but the reward for this contribution is not equal to the effort. Government spokesmen point out that Africans in South Africa are wealthier than anywhere else in Africa. Wage rates appear high when compared to other African states but they disguise two factors which need consideration. Firstly, in most parts of Africa, landlessness has not reached the state it has in South Africa and consequently cash income can be used to pay for taxes, school fees and other requirements, but does not need to provide for basic living expenses which are supplied from the family land. In South Africa, for many of the urban labourers their wages are their only source of wealth and must cover all expenses. Secondly, Africans have never had the power to negotiate wage rates with their employers. Because of this serious limitation it is reasonable to suggest that wage rates are the lowest needed to support the African labour force. Today, average earnings for whites are about £1,000, for Africans just under £200 a year. The minority white population controls the South African economy and most of the wealth of the country is in the hands of the few.

The economy is growing at a rate of 5 per cent per year. If this encouraging rate is maintained it is estimated that the average income per head of population in the year 2,000 will be the same as that for Britain in 1960. Unfortunately for the African in South Africa, income is not evenly distributed between the races. The white population enjoys an average income at least five times better than anyone else, and the gap is widening all the time. The African has not enjoyed the benefits of this economic expansion. The unrest in the African townships suggests that Africans in the urban areas are far from satisfied with this. The Government's policy of limiting African opportunity also restricts

Soweto (South-Western Townships), an outskirt of Johannesburg. This is the second largest settlement in South Africa, with a population of 1.3 million Africans

the size of the domestic market (the people who buy things within South Africa). The domestic market would be much bigger if there was to be a significant rise in the incomes of the non-white population. This rise in the domestic market would increase the possibilities for further economic expansion.

The problem of the urban African

The competition for land that began in 1795 is temporarily over. The Europeans now control the whole country, and have specific rights and privileges in seven-eighths of the country. Two-

thirds of the population – the Africans – are expected to consider the Bantustans – or 13 per cent of the land – as their homes, despite the fact that through living in the urban areas many Africans have become totally urbanised in culture. Nat Nakasa, a journalist living in Johannesburg, commented on the problem of the urban African: 'I am supposed to be a Pondo, but I don't even know the language of that tribe. I was brought up in a Zulu-speaking home, my mother being a Zulu. Yet I can no longer think in Zulu because that language cannot cope with the demands of our day . . . I have never owned an assegai or any of those magnificent shields. I am just not a tribesman. I am, inescapably, a part of the city slums, the factory machines and our beloved shebeens.'[4]

The development of the modern South African economy has involved the co-operation of all races. Although complete integration has not taken place undoubtedly many Africans have developed and acquired a new culture which is similar to that of the European. It is estimated that the population of South Africa by 2000 will be about forty-two million, of which only seven million will be European. At a time when these figures seem overwhelming, the white South Africans have closed ranks. Within the House of Assembly only a handful of MPs stand for a multi-racial society.

The present political situation in South Africa is based on a belief that economic growth should not be allowed to change the traditional economic and social relationship between black and white. Will economic reason defeat this political idea or will the solution to South Africa's difficulties be found in more extreme methods?

Summary of Chapter 13

Definition of apartheid
a) 'Territorial separation of European and Bantu.'
b) 'Baaskap' – white domination.

Apartheid legislation
Political:
  1936 Representation of Natives Act
  1950 Suppression of Communism Act.
  1959 Bantu Self-Government Act.
Land:
  1913 Land Act.
  1936 Native Trusts and Lands Act.
  1923 Native (Urban Areas) Act.
  1955 Native (Urban Areas) Amendment Act.
  1957 Native Laws Amendment Act.
Employment:
  1911 Mines and Works Act.
  1926 Colour Bar Act.
  1924 Industrial Conciliation Act.
Education:
  1953 Bantu Education Act.
  1959 Extension of Universities Act.

The Transkei
1963 *Constitution:* Legislative Assembly –
  4 Paramount Chiefs.
  60 Chiefs.
  45 Elected members.
1963 *Election:* Chief Matanzima – Chief Minister despite Chief Poto's greater support among elected members.
1968 *Election:* overwhelming majority for Chief Matanzima.
1976 *Independence for the Transkei.*

Results of homelands policy
Too large a population dependent on too small an area. Able-bodied men and women in towns – older people and children on Reserve land – has led to overgrazing, overcropping and soil erosion. Poorer yields from farming units – no cash for development and investment has led to increased poverty and a state of decline.

Urban Africans
No permanent settlement in white towns.
Employment – temporary contract type.
Men separated from wives and families.
Breakdown of traditional values.
No power to negotiate wages – little above subsistence level after deductions for food, rent and school fees.

Attitude of English-speaking South Africans
Economic investment – identity with Government.
Journalists and writers.
Liberals and Progressives.

Short questions on Chapter 13

1 Give two definitions of apartheid.
2 In what five spheres have the Europeans passed laws to guarantee their continued domination of the African?
3 Name the two Parliamentary Acts which determine land ownership in South Africa.
4 What are the Pass Laws?
5 Name three pieces of legislation restricting African opportunity in employment.
6 Name the two main Education Acts affecting the African population.
7 How many Bantustans are there and what are they?
8 What do the Bantustans not have control over?
9 Who is the Chief Minister of the Transkei?
10 Who is the Chief Minister of Kwazulu?

Longer questions on Chapter 13

1 Describe the way the South African Government has applied its apartheid policy to land ownership, education and employment.
2 Why has the South African Government created the Bantustans and why was the Transkei chosen as the first?
3 Describe the steps taken to set up the Transkei Bantustan, giving an outline of its constitution and its political development since 1963.
4 What changes in traditional African life have been brought about by the growth of industrial towns and the imposition of apartheid?

Notes to Chapter 13

1 Oliver & Atmore, *Africa since 1800*, Cambridge University Press, 1967, p. 258.
2 *ibid.*
3 *Johannesburg Sunday Times*, 29 September 1963.
4 Wilson & Thompson, (eds.), *Oxford History of South Africa*, Vol. I, Oxford University Press, 1969, p. 209.

14 African nationalism

Opposition to European domination in South Africa existed before the nineteenth and twentieth centuries. As the European settlers moved further away from the Cape more frequent contacts were made with an increasing number of ethnic groups. Invariably wars between the races revolved round the critical problem of land ownership. Generally, the Europeans were too powerful for the poorly-equipped African societies. By the end of the nineteenth century military opposition to European domination was virtually over. With the exception of the success of Moshesh in moulding Basutoland from a number of different groups, and the development of the Zulu nation during the time of Cetshwayo, few alliances were made among the Bantu speaking communities to obstruct European advances. In most cases opposition was from one group rather than a national movement. The African leaders in the twentieth century have been concerned to make the nationalist movement one which is truly national in character and not representing the opinions of one particular ethnic group only.

Early twentieth century nationalism

The two outstanding leaders early in the present century were John Tengo Jabavu, the editor of *Imvo Zabantsundu* (African Opinion), and Dr Pixley Ka Isaka Seme. Both were in favour of racial equality rather than black domination in place of white domination.

The twentieth century opened with serious disappointments for the Africans. They were excluded from the National Convention of 1908 which decided that the Union constitution would not extend the non-white franchise of the Cape to the other three provinces.

Attitude of Africans and Coloureds to the Act of Union

The few educated Africans who had gained the vote at the Cape were prepared to leave the future franchise of their people to the Cape's white delegation to the 1908 Convention. Leading newspapers such as J. T. Jabavu's '*Imvo*' advised Africans to trust the white delegates. This can be interpreted as self-interest in that they were protecting what little advantage they had gained from the vote. Perhaps they were not prepared to risk losing their privileged position by indicating their suspicions about being represented by white politicians.

The Coloured Association, African Political Organisation and the Transvaal National Natives Union petitioned the Convention to include a non-racial franchise in the Union constitution. This they failed to achieve. Despite denouncements by African clergy, journalists and the leaders of all Protestant churches except the Dutch Reformed Church, the draft document for a Union constitution was sent to the British Government in London. A deputation led by Schreiner, a respected white Cape politician, and including J. T. Jabavu; Dr Aburahman, President of the African Political Organisation and the Rev W. Rubusana did its best to persuade the British Government to revise the franchise arrangements. They failed because the Government considered it ill-advised to alter the unanimous recommendations of the four self-governing colonies. It was more concerned with bringing Boer and British closer together, and less concerned with the fate of the non-whites. Africans and Coloureds in South Africa felt betrayed by the British and this was in fact the very last occasion when the British could have intervened on their behalf.

One of the first pieces of legislation passed by the new Union Parliament was the Land Act of 1913. This Act limited property ownership for the Africans to one-eighth of the country. On 12 January 1912 (the same year as the formation of Hertzog's Nationalist Party) the South African Native Congress was formed. In 1935 this organisation was renamed the African National Congress. The aims of the Congress were to break down ethnic differences, to encourage joint action, to remove racial prejudice and to win the vote and civil rights for all people. The early movement was led by mission converts from Natal and Cape Province, John Tengo Jabavu and Dr Pixley Seme (both emphasised racial partnership).

12 January 1912:
South African Native Congress formed (later renamed African National Congress).

Aims:
1 To remove racial prejudice.
2 To achieve civil rights for all people.
3 To achieve the unification of the various ethnic groups.

Grievances:
1 Land question.
2 Pass Laws.
3 Masters and Servants Act.

Tactics:
1 Non-violent resistance inspired by Mahatma Gandhi.
2 Petitions and delegations.

Dr Pixley Ka Isaka Seme

Seme was educated through mission school to university level in the USA and Britain. When he returned to South Africa he was exposed again to the humiliations heaped on his fellow Africans. He abandoned a dream to rebuild the Zulu nation in favour of an African nationalism which cut across all existing difficulties.

It was Seme along with three other African lawyers who called the conference of all chiefs and leaders in January 1912 which marked the beginning of the South African Native Congress. In the same year, Seme began the first national African newspaper, the *Abantu-Bathu* ('People') which was published in English and three Bantu languages. On a more practical level, he bought land in the Eastern Transvaal and set up the African Farmers' Association in an attempt to introduce modern farming methods and to encourage Africans to buy more farm land. The 1913 Land Act ended all these hopes.

After a bright beginning, Seme's leadership proved something of a disaster. His newspaper was forced to close down. He had difficulty working with others, always demanding full control of the organisation. He opposed more militant action such as boycotts and strikes, and in 1935 when Hertzog was threatening to remove the African voters at the Cape from the common roll (the list of voters), he was unable to give the lead many Africans wanted. He so misread the situation that he welcomed the alliance between Smuts and Hertzog as a 'rare combination of the most powerful and capable people'. By the 1940s the leadership of the ANC had been taken over by Dr A. B. Xuma and Dr Seme died in 1951. The African National Congress is a fitting symbol of his contribution to twentieth century African politics.

The methods of protest, petitions, delegations and representations used by the Congress between 1912 and 1946 brought no great success. If anything the Congress was weakened by a lack of support from the mass of the people. They were either living in the Reserves with the problems resulting from the breakdown of the traditional way of life, or were too busy discovering the excitement and advantage of city life to be worried about such things as civil rights. This complaint of 'being motivated too much by material things' was to be levelled at many Africans by a somewhat disappointed Chief Albert Luthuli during the late 1950s.

Developments after the Second World War

At the end of the Second World War, Africans had a claim in the developing prosperity of the country.

Nelson Mandela

Walter Sisulu

They were better educated, their leaders were articulate in modern political thought and were providing more of a challenge to the European than at any previous time. The obvious conflict in the aims of the different races produced apartheid, and the Government reacted violently to any kind of resistance.

Youth Wing of ANC

In the late 1940s young men like Oliver Tambo, Nelson Mandela and Walter Sisulu were recruited to the ranks of the African National Congress. They were mainly well-educated professionals working in the urban areas who maintained a close contact with the rural areas. The more conservative, older members of the African National Congress had difficulty in coming to terms with the more dynamic approach of the new men, who formed a Youth Wing. The Youth Wing produced all the more worthwhile suggestions for future action. By 1949 most of its proposals had been

accepted by the African National Congress. The leadership passed to the younger members. The new young leadership ran the risk of losing the support of the more conservative members and were fortunate in finding a man who was sufficiently popular and respected to encourage co-operation between the different groups. This man was Albert Luthuli. Before dealing with Luthuli's career in more detail it is worthwhile considering the main trends of African nationalist activity from 1950.

Defiance campaign 1952

The Defiance Campaign of 1952 was one of the first concerted attempts by the African National Congress to activate protest and demonstration. The campaign was against the more obvious examples of segregation. Park benches marked 'Whites Only', offices, buses, bridges and restaurants, were the targets for token demonstrations. The effect on the Government was minimal but it did prove valuable for the growth of the African

National Congress. It promoted a great deal of inter-racial co-operation, an attitude which was to typify the middle 1950s. It attracted attention to the Congress as an organisation not prepared just to be overtaken by events, and it gained considerable mass support. It also highlighted the emergence of Luthuli as a significant figure.

Freedom charter

In the mid-1950s there was an expansion of this attitude of inter-racial co-operation which culminated in the Congress of the People. Attended by the African National Congress, the Indians, Coloured and Trades Union organisations near Johannesberg in 1955, it proclaimed that 'South Africa belonged to all who lived in it, Black or White.' The Freedom Charter which was produced by the Congress outlined its aims for a 'free' South Africa based on political equality, and a moderate programme which looked forward to power-sharing between the different races. This modest and reasonable approach was not to the liking of all

Africans and was the reason for a later division. The Congress of the People and the Congress Alliance had little chance to develop since the Government arrested 156 leaders and held Treason Trials which lasted for four years. Although the accused were later released the Government had successfully detained every potential leader and prevented the Alliance from working effectively. The African National Congress was seen to have no well organised nation-wide structure and seemed incapable of providing the necessary organisation to unite the rural and urban Africans.

Pan African Congress 1959

Complaints about the lack of organisation of the African National Congress and its ill-informed and misdirected alliance with other non-white organisations were heightened by the late 1950s and led to the formation of the Pan African Congress by Robert Sobukwe in 1959. The main difference between the African National Congress and the Pan African Congress centres on the

A bridge in Cape Town divided into two gangways, one for whites, the other for non-whites

attitude towards the future government of South Africa. The Pan African Congress is more Africanist and claims South Africa for the Africans while the African National Congress has always considered a multi-racial society in South Africa to be inevitable. The Africanists had been critical of the African National Congress's failures to provide a nation-wide organisation but they themselves were no more successful. Resistance to the Government was limited to local outbursts and demonstrations against education policies in the Eastern Cape and against the prevailing political policies in the Transkei. These resulted in violent protest in Pondoland as well as similar protests in the Transvaal. The two major organisations were never able to co-ordinate their activities to the point where they became more than a temporary embarrassment to the Government.

Anti-pass campaign 1960

It was obvious that both the African National Congress and the Pan African Congress required a campaign which would both regain lost ground and boost morale. They both chose an Anti-Pass Campaign for March 1960. The response was good and the campaign was carried out by Africans in a disciplined, sensible way, and with no violence. The stage was set for a massive confrontation with the Government. The result was the indiscriminate shooting of Africans at Sharpeville and Langa. The Government was probably more worried than it had ever been before and immediately banned both the Pan African Congress and the African National Congress.

Underground movements

The latest stage in African nationalism revolves around the activities of the two underground movements – the Spear of the Nation and the Poqo. After the banning of the Pan African Congress and the African National Congress, since peaceful resistance had failed completely, African leaders resorted to acts of sabotage and violence. The formation of the sabotage groups reflected their feelings of desperation. Nelson Mandela was closely associated with the Spear of the Nation but with his detention after the Rivonia Trial (see p.

Demonstrators burning their pass books

164) the organisation has lost its way. The urban African seems almost resigned to his fate and without adequate leadership of the stature of Mandela or Sobukwe, African nationalism concerned with the whole of South Africa lacks organisation and direction. More attention is paid to leadership in the various Bantustans where men such as Matanzima and Buthelezi appear to be developing nationalism based on the ethnic regions. It could be that the Nationalist Government is more than content with such a development in which South Africa's Africans are divided on the old ethnic lines. The changing attitudes of African nationalism can be seen clearly through the careers of three outstanding African leaders – Albert Luthuli, Robert Sobukwe and Nelson Mandela.

Chief Albert Luthuli 1898–1967

Luthuli spent most of his early life on the mission at Groutville in Natal after his family had moved

Chief Albert Luthuli

southwards from Zimbabwe. He taught at Adams College from 1920 to 1935 where he appears to have been extremely happy. In 1935 he was offered the Umvoti chieftaincy with responsibility for 5,000 of his fellow Zulu. Despite being happy at Adams, he felt it was his Christian duty to accept this new responsibility.

For perhaps the first time, he became aware of the problems facing his own people. There was a shortage of land. Each African family was restricted to about 1.6 hectares because of overcrowding in the Reserves, while the Europeans enjoyed an average of nearly 160 hectares per person. The other major problem was the breakdown of African families, and traditional ethnic groups when the men were encouraged to move to the towns in search of high wages. For some time Luthuli did not realise the need for political action to improve matters. Until 1945, when he joined the African National Congress, he had spent much of his time reorganising the traditional groupings of his people and serving on multi-racial organisations like the South African Christian Council and the Durban Joint Council of Europeans and

Africans. In 1946 he became a member of the Native Representative Council, a body set up by the Government to advise it on African affairs. The Council adjourned in protest after the stern measures taken by Smuts to deal with Asian and African matters and since 1946 it has never met.

Gradually Luthuli became more popular in Natal. When in 1952 the Government, growing more concerned about his Congress activities, gave him the ultimatum of resigning either from the Congress or from his chieftainship, he refused to do either, and was immediately removed from his position among the Zulu. From 1944 to 1953, the ANC had been led by Dr Moroka, the successor to Dr Xuma. For a time Moroka had led the movement with vitality, but when he was arrested and tried under the Suppression of Communism Act in 1952, he engaged a defence counsel independently and alone decided to take the witness stand. These moves lost him a great deal of support from his colleagues, Sisulu and Mandela, who had also been arrested. Luthuli was elected to the post of president in place of Moroka by the conference of 1953.

Luthuli's policy was one of non-violent resistance. The Government's reaction was to ban him from attending or addressing public meetings. Undeterred, Luthuli continued to protest against the system. He organized boycotts against the Bantu Education Act and other demonstrations attempting to undermine the Government's authority. After his term of restriction had ended in 1954, he was served with a further two year restriction, this time on his farm at Groutville. In 1956, his second ban completed, he and his family took a holiday in Swaziland, 'a shake in the air of freedom' as he called it. Soon after his return he was arrested for high treason. The trial of 156 men and women dragged on for years. Luthuli was released soon after the trial began and was recognised as their leader by people from different political parties who were all involved in the civil rights struggle.

The Congress organised various boycotts at this time, some being more successful than others. The Alexandra Township Bus Boycott was a protest against a penny rise in bus fares on certain routes. It lasted three months and in spite of massive action by the Government, the walking Africans, 5,000 of them, succeeded in having the fare reduced. The Potato Boycott was organised in protest against the

Demonstrators being closely watched by the police

working and living conditions on some of the European farms. On many farms, cheap labour was contracted out to farmers, who locked their workers up in 'filthy, vermin-infested quarters'. They were forced to work from dawn to dusk on a very basic diet of mealie (maize) meal and were given sacking for a uniform. The worst cases were found in East Transvaal. Despite the success of the campaign, the practice still persists in some areas, although to a minor degree.

With the growing popularity of Luthuli, in 1959 the Government once again imposed a further restriction on his activities, this time for five years. On 5 December 1961, Luthuli received the Nobel Peace Prize for 1960. In the opening of his address he spoke of the three-fold significance of the award – the honour granted to him for his contribution towards finding a peaceful solution to the race problem; the recognition and support of the world's progressive governments for Africans' desire for political freedom and a 'welcome recognition of the role played by African people during the last fifty years to establish peacefully a society in which merit, and not race, would fix the position of the individual in the life of the nation'. In making its award the Nobel Committee was obviously considering the growing impatience of

African nationalists, and the tendency towards the use of violence and sabotage which began to grow steadily after 1960.

With this account of Luthuli we leave the era of non-violent resistance which stamped the activities of the Congress while under his leadership and turn to the different approach used from 1960 onwards when more radical nationalists such as Robert Sobukwe and Nelson Mandela exerted their authority.

Robert M. Sobukwe 1924–78

Robert Sobukwe became a Languages Assistant at the University of Witwatersrand after being educated at Lovedale Mission and Fort Hare University College. He held this position until he resigned in 1960. In 1957 he became the editor of *The Africanist*, a paper which promoted radical articles and editorials. In March 1959 he formed the Pan African Congress, an organisation which advocated black African militancy rather than the non-violent multi-racial policies of the ANC. In the early part of 1960 both congresses prepared for an

Robert Sobukwe

anti-pass campaign but it was the PAC which forestalled the ANC by starting its own campaigns on 21 March. The campaign led to the shootings at Sharpeville on the same day.

Sharpeville March 1960

Numbers of Africans proceeded to police stations at Langa in Cape Town and Sharpeville in the Transvaal where they invited arrest for non-possession of passes. The crowd at Sharpeville was estimated by the Department of External Affairs as being 20,000 while members of the press gave the number of 3,000. The police seem to have been intimidated by the huge numbers, and nervousness gave way to careless shooting. The crowd dispersed very quickly leaving sixty-two dead Africans behind.

Sobukwe was arrested, charged with incitement and destruction of pass books and sentenced to three years imprisonment. On 1 May, a second General Law Amendment Act was passed which gave power to detain persons after they had served their sentences. Sobukwe was not released on 3 May 1963 when his term expired, but instead was transported to detention on Robben Island, a flat, bleak island off Table Bay which has been a prison for many years. Sobukwe's detention was renewed every year from 1965 until 1969 when it was decided that he could be detained in his home area instead of on Robben Island.

After the Sharpeville incident African leaders began to have doubts about the success of non-violent resistance. Luthuli was once again in restriction and overtaken by ill health. The ANC and the PAC were banned by the Government in April 1961 and any recognition of Luthuli could mean three years imprisonment under the Sabotage Act. Nelson Mandela then became the virtual leader of the ANC.

Nelson Mandela

Born at Umtata in the Transkei in 1918, the eldest son of a Tembu chief, Nelson Mandela was also educated at Fort Hare University College. After graduating, he practised law in Johannesberg with Oliver Tambo, another influential Congress leader who now represents the interests of the Congress outside the Republic.

Mandela organised the general strike in protest against the white referendum on republican status for South Africa. To do this he had to leave his home, his family and his office and travel around the country encouraging and exhorting his fellow Africans to support the strike. Living the life of a political outlaw, evading arrest and assuming various disguises, Mandela led a charmed life and gained for himself the title of the Black Pimpernel. 'But there comes a time when a man is denied the right to live a normal life, when he can only live the life of an outlaw because the Government has so decreed to use the law to impose a state of outlawry on him.'[1]

Mandela and his colleagues formed the *Umkonto We Sizwe* (Spear of the Nation) in June 1961, the same time as the founding of the Republic. Mandela believed that the Congress's policy of non-violence was meaningless and unrealistic in the face of growing violence from the Government. Umkonto set out to disrupt the life of the country by attacks on government installations and all other establishments which were expressions of apart-

Sharpeville, some of the dead and wounded

heid. It was to be controlled violence rather than terrorism. The introduction of this movement marks the end of non-violent African resistance and the beginning of a more militant approach by African leaders.

Mandela was imprisoned for five years for incitement to strike and for leaving South Africa without a valid passport, but in October 1963 he was brought from prison to faces charges with eight other defendants concerned with the organisation of Umkonto. In the trial, which is known as the Rivonia Trial because most of the accused had been arrested in the Rivonia suburb of Johannesburg, Mandela was accused of sabotage and conspiracy to overthrow the Government by revolution. In the closing speech in his defence he said: 'During my lifetime I have dedicated myself to this struggle of the African people. I have fought against white domination and I have fought against black domination. I have cherished the idea of a democratic and free society in which all persons live together in harmony and with equal opportunities. It is an ideal which I hope to live for and achieve. But if needs be, it is an ideal for which I am prepared to die.'[2] Mandela was sentenced to life imprisonment on Robben Island, where he joined Robert Sobukwe.

Umkonto We Sizwe and Poqo

Umkonto has concerned itself with acts of sabotage which, where possible, have avoided injury to civilians. By May 1963 there had been some two hundred acts of sabotage committed. On the other hand, Poqo, a branch of the Pan African Congress activated by despair perhaps, directed its attacks from 1962 primarily against the white community. According to an acting leader of the PAC, P. K. Leballo, Poqo in 1963 consisted of an army of 150,000 men preparing for a final attack on white supremacy. The organisation has been held responsible for outbreaks of violence in Cape Town, Paarl and the Transkei in which over twenty people were killed. The reaction of the South African Government has been to pass the General Law Amendment Act to combat the violence. Under the Act people can be detained after completing a prison sentence if it is thought in the interests of the state. In addition, anyone advocating, encouraging or defending revolution by violence is liable to five years imprisonment. The Acts also allows for a detention of ninety days for anyone on suspicion without necessarily being brought to court. Over 3,000 Poqo members had been arrested by June 1963.

Republic of South Africa 1963

By 1963, South Africa had become a republic outside the Commonwealth and it might be fairly said that the aims of the Great Trek had been achieved. The country had become completely independent of British influence, and the Afrikaner brand of nationalism had triumphed over a more liberal policy. In May 1968 the multi-racial Liberal Party led by Alan Paton was disbanded: by then it was illegal for people of different races to associate in the same political party.

Summary of Chapter 14

New challenge of African nationalism
Africans in 1945 were better educated, more highly paid, more skilled as leaders.
European answer: apartheid introduced in 1948.
1952 *Defiance campaign:* Inspired by ANC: 8,000 arrests, harsher measures by South African Government. Boycotts of buses, potatoes, South African goods.
Albert Luthuli 1899–1967: Sincere Christian teacher (Adams College).
  1953 Chief President of ANC.
  1954–67 restriction and detention.
  1961 Nobel Peace Prize, advocated a policy of non-violent resistance; his ambition was racial partnership in South Africa.
Robert Sobukwe 1924–78: Founder of the PAC 'South Africa for the Africans', organised Pass Laws Campaign which ended with Sharpeville, 1960. April 1960 ANC and PAC banned. Sobukwe arrested and sent to Robben Island.
After Sharpeville: More violent African reaction.
Nelson Mandela: Virtual leader of the ANC after Luthuli's last detention, advocated sabotage as a way of undermining the Government's au-

thority. Founded *Umkonto We Sizwe* (Spear of the Nation), arrested 1961, Rivonia Trial, imprisoned on Robben Island.

Short questions on Chapter 14

1   Who were the two leading African leaders of the early twentieth century?
2   What were the four main aims of the South African Native Congress?
3   What tactics were used to further these aims in the first thirty years of the Congress?
4   Name three leaders of the Congress Youth Wing.
5   What was the Defiance Campaign of 1952?
6   What was the Freedom Charter?
7   What do you understand by the term 'Africanist'?
8   When were the ANC and PAC banned by the Government?
9   What was the Rivonia Trial?
10 What are the names of the two underground African nationalist movements?

Longer questions on Chapter 14

1   Outline the development of the ANC up to 1948 with reference to leadership, aims and tactics.
2   Assess the contributions made by the following African leaders: Albert Luthuli, Robert Sobukwe, Nelson Mandela.
3   In what ways can the shooting at Sharpeville be considered a moment of crisis for both Europeans and Africans in South Africa?

Notes to Chapter 14

1   Nelson Mandela, *No Easy Walk to Freedom*, Heinemann, 1965, p. 157.
2   *ibid.*, p. 189.

15 Swaziland, Lesotho and Botswana in the twentieth century

Political and economic stagnation

Although the British had taken responsibility for all three of these territories by the beginning of the twentieth century, their lack of interest in the areas from then on resulted in fifty years of neglect. This neglect could be seen in the political sphere where little attempt was made to modernise the traditional African form of government. In the economic field there was no significant development aid or investment made until after the Second World War. Successive British Governments attempted to run the areas as cheaply as possible either by employing South Africans in the administration or second rate civil servants. These had difficulty dealing with talented African leaders like Tshekedi Khama in Bechuanaland (Botswana).

This kind of administration can be loosely described as 'parallel rule' in which the chiefs ran the 'tribes' and the administration collected the taxes. As long as there were no obvious difficulties the British were relatively content with the continuation of the nineteenth century model of traditional rule by the chiefs. There was always the likelihood of the incorporation of the territories in the Union of South Africa at a later date despite the opposition of various British politicians, and it was thought that there was little point in spending huge sums of money on development.

The territories were never really economically developed, as this would have produced an alternative source of employment to the mining industries of the Union. British money had developed these mines and Britain had a special interest in maintaining the supply of cheap labour from the High Commission Territories.

The Second World War gave a much needed stimulus to political and economic activity in the areas. The Colonial and Welfare Fund of 1945 began to make important investments, and after the 1948 Nationalist Party election victory in South Africa, the British began to think and speak in terms of eventual political independence for all three countries. Before independence, all three territories had become recognised as safe places for political refugees from South Africa, but Britain prevented the protectorates from becoming bases for possible guerilla activity against the Republic. Independent governments have tended to follow much the same line of policy, recognising their very precarious relationship with the vastly more powerful Republic.

Relations of the High Commission Territories with South Africa

It was seen in Chapter 8 how all three countries avoided being swallowed up by either the Boer republics or the Cape Colony, and accepted protectorate status under the British Crown. At the Peace of Vereeniging which brought the Anglo-Boer War to an end, reference was made to the incorporation of at least two of the areas in either the Transvaal or the Orange Free State. As at future conferences between white South Africans there was a difference of opinion about the proposed future treatment of non-white inhabitants. To avoid delaying a conclusion of the Veereeniging talks, the whole matter of incorporation of the High Commission Territories was deferred.

In 1906, with the granting of responsible government to the Transvaal and the Orange Free State, the question of the territories was once again put on one side, although the British Government was a little more definite when it said 'that pending any grant of representation to natives, no territories administered by the Governor or the High Commissioner would be placed under the control of the new Responsible Governments.'

All three states remained at the centre of a controversy as to their future status after the Act of Union. In the Act, although not stated definitely, there was a general understanding that they would all become part of the Union of South Africa if political conditions were right. Since union, there have been no signs that the rights of the African would be protected and developed. In fact, the tendency has been in exactly the opposite direction.

Attempts at incorporation 1905–55

The attitude of the British Government towards the incorporation of the territories in South Africa has gone through two major phases. Firstly, immediately after the Act of Union, there was a genuine feeling that the more liberal policies of the Cape would overcome the less progressive ideas of the old Boer republics. Accordingly, there seems to have been a positive desire to meet the demands of the Union. This positive desire quickly disappeared, as it became more and more obvious that the Union was unlikely to help the Africans in South Africa.

The second phase was when it was emphasised that prior consultation within the territories was necessary before any transfer could take place. This meant that the British Government did not have to condemn the racial policies of the South African Government outright.

General Botha made the first approach to Britain in 1913. He suggested that Swaziland and Bechuanaland should be transferred to the Union at the earliest possible date. He was told that the transfer would be considered but that it would not be possible to transfer Bechuanaland in the near future. After the First World War in Europe, (1914–18), Premier Smuts found himself confronted with a variety of problems in the Union which prevented any action over the High Commission territories. General Hertzog, taking over the premiership in 1924, concentrated his attention on establishing a 'White South Africa', and this obviously involved dealing with native

legislation. The Native Land Bill of 1913 had been concerned with providing separate areas for the Bantu. It was agreed that only by the incorporation of the three areas could enough land be made available.

Mr Amery, the British Colonial Secretary, replied to Hertzog's demands mainly by answering Botha's queries on the transfer of Swaziland. He said the chief concern of the British Government was for the Africans rather than for the white population. In High Commissioner Lord Athlone's letter to Hertzog outlining the proposals about the transfer of Swaziland, he concerned himself with questioning the strength of the safeguards for Swazi rights after transfer.

Thus began a long series of exchanges between Hertzog and succeeding Secretaries of State, Amery, Thomas and MacDonald – which completely exasperated Hertzog. He said, 'If the Natives do not want to come in . . . (but) to hold themselves apart, then they must realise that the markets of the Union will no longer be open to them. . . . The longer they try to remain outside the more they will have to pay the penalty for it.'[1]

There was little activity about the territories during the Second World War, but after 1945, the South African Government protested about the course taken by certain Bechuana chiefs led by Tshekedi Khama who were supporting the demand of the Herero people of South West Africa to be transferred as a mandated territory to Britain. This was considered as interference in the internal affairs of South Africa, which in no way concerned Bechuanaland despite the fact that Bechuanaland shared 800 kilometres of boundary with South-West Africa.

The second event which affected relations between South Africa and the territories also concerned Bechuanaland. Seretse Khama, Ruling Chief Designate of the Bamangwato tribe married an English girl while at Oxford in 1948. This caused consternation among his own people. The effect on South Africa was amazing. As General Smuts remarked: 'White South Africans were hardly sane about the subject of miscegenation.' In 1949, the Mixed Marriages Act was passed, followed by the Immorality Act of 1950. It was a dangerous period in which a blockade of the territories as well as the incorporation of Bechuanaland were considered in the Union. The British Labour Government gave in to external pressures:

Seretse Khama was not allowed to return to Bechuanaland but was forced to spend his time in exile in London.

Dr Malan outlined a further argument for the inclusion of the territories in the Union. He said: 'Constitutionally (the Union) stands on a footing of equality with other members of the Commonwealth. . . . But in one vital respect she differs from them all, and that is, within her embrace, and even within her borders, she is compelled to harbour territories entirely dependent on her economically, and largely also for their defence, but belonging to and governed by another country. . . . And so long as this is tolerated . . . there can be no real equality nor ever full independence for her.'[2]

Malan was succeeded by Strijdom in 1954. The following year the *Tomlinson Report* (the plan for the development of the Bantustans) was published. This report noted the desirability of the territories being within the Union so that they could form three of the eight Reserves for the Bantu people. Dr Verwoerd emphasised that although not essential for the plan, it was in the best interests of the people in these territories to join the Union. The British Government was not prepared to change its position, which had been clearly described by Sir Winston Churchill in 1954 when he said that he hoped that the Union Ministers would 'not needlessly press an issue on which we could not fall in with their views without failing in our trust.'

Political development in Swaziland up to independence

During most of the protectorate period, the traditional Swazi administration, headed by the King, carried out its functions separately from the central governing body of the High Commission. Traditionally the King was unable to act without the approval of two councils. The Liqoqo was smaller and contained the more influential advisers and members of the royal lineage. The Libandla was the largest council of which every adult male was a member. This council met about once a year. It had to agree to any change in legislation considered necessary by the Liqoqo. Communication between the central government and the main council was through a standing committee called the Swazi National Council.

From 1928 regular meetings were arranged between the Resident Commissioner and the Ngwenyama, the King, and between local district officers and chiefs. These meetings did not affect the main emphasis, which was still of a traditional system working parallel with the Commissioner's officials. In Swaziland, legislation affecting many routine African affairs was still in Swazi hands. It must be said that the King, Sobhuza II, exerted tremendous influence on all deliberations of the councils.

Sobhuza was born in 1899 of the Swazi ruling family, the Dlamini, and he became Paramount Chief in 1921. He is a traditionalist and pays great attention to his responsibilities and traditional duties. Yet he was enough of a realist to form his own political party and win the first election in 1964. The Native Administrative Proclamation of 1944 tried to promote the status of the King to that of being the native authority in Swaziland but it met with so much opposition that it was replaced in 1950 by a system which gave some expression to the growing demand for a more modern approach to government. The 1950 proclamation dealt with the form of the Swazi courts and the creation of a

King Sobhuza II of Swaziland

Swazi National Treasury, both important elements of the present Swazi administrative system.

Swazi political parties

The Swaziland Progressive Party was the country's first political party. It was formed in 1960 by John Nquku, a qualified schoolmaster and schools' inspector who had had experience of editing newspapers in the local languages. He had travelled widely through Europe and America. The aims of his party were: internal self-government leading to independence and the rejection of any incorporation in the Republic. A serious split divided the party and it was never able to benefit fully from being the first party. In 1964 the royalist Mbokodvo National Movement was formed, with the full support of Sobhuza, to fight the first election. All twenty-seven seats in the Legislative Council were won by the MNM and in 1967 the party won all the seats again with Prince Makhosini Jameson Dlamini becoming the country's first Prime Minister.

Prince Makhosini Jameson Dlamini

The Prince was educated in Swaziland and trained to be a teacher in South Africa. From 1947 he took an active part in the affairs of the Swazi National Council. He returned home after a course in public and social administration in Britain and re-entered Swazi political life, returning to Britain in 1963 as leader of the Swazi delegation on constitutional proposals. In 1964 he became leader of the Mbokodvo National Movement, and in April 1967 he became Swaziland's first Prime Minister.

Constitutional development in Swaziland

It was King Sobhuza who took the initiative to introduce constitutional reform and in a statement in 1960 he suggested that a Legislative Council of both Europeans and Africans should be formed, with the Europeans electing their representatives and the Swazi appointing their members in the traditional way. This automatically meant that all the King's nominees would be appointed and the

suggestion was opposed by the Swaziland Progressive Party.

The constitutional talks in London in 1963 produced a constitution which involved a Legislative Council and an Executive Council. The Legislative Council was composed of four official members, up to three nominated members and twenty-four elected members. The Executive Council included an unofficial majority with all the members associated with government departments.

Prince Makhosini, on being elected to the Legislative Council pressed for a fresh constitution, recommendations were passed on to the British Government and a committee was appointed to review the existing constitution. Under the new constitution, dated 25 April 1967, Britain retained responsibility for defence, external affairs and internal security. The constitution consisted of a House of Assembly with twenty-four elected members; six members appointed by the King and an Attorney-General, and a Senate which had six members elected by the House of Assembly and six members nominated by the King. Passage through both Houses is necessary for a Bill to become legal. The House of Assembly has the sole right to initiate finance Bills but no power to legislate on matters governed by Swazi law and custom.

Swaziland independence

The first House of Assembly election of April 1967 resulted in the Mbokodvo National Movement Party winning all the seats. It immediately requested independence which was granted on 6 September 1968.

Political development in Lesotho before 1950

The main pattern of government after 1884 was a form of 'indirect rule' by the British. The Resident Commissioner was aided by a small number of assistant commissioners but the local chiefs were the main agents of the administration. They were given wide judicial powers and were expected to carry out traditional Basuto law. The traditional meeting of the pitso was incorporated into a National Council, the first of which was held in 1903. The Council consisted of the President (Resident Commissioner), the Paramount Chief and ninety-nine nominated Lesotho members.

There was considerable criticism of the chiefs' power during the 1920s and 1930s, and there was a move to involve people other than chiefs in the administration, and in 1937 the National Council included twenty-two nominated commoners. Between 1944 and 1945 nine district councils with a partially elected membership were set up and they were able to propose motions in the National Council and send representatives to that body. The elected representation on the National Council was increased to forty-two in 1950, and in 1945 a standing committee was set up to deal with matters between council sessions. A further development of a more national character was the establishment of the National Treasury in 1946 and the reduction in the number of courts from 1,340 to 107 by 1949. Fines and fees from these courts went to the Treasury.

Constitutional change after 1950

The first Basuto constitution was introduced in 1960. The National Council had eighty seats, half being indirectly elected by universal franchise, twenty-two principal chiefs, fourteen members nominated by the Paramount Chief and four senior officials. An Executive Council was created with equal official and unofficial membership. Its function was to act in an advisory capacity to the High Commissioners and the Paramount Chief. A Constitution Committee was set up to review the 1960 constitution with a view to producing a pre-independence constitution. In its report the commission suggested that independence should take place a year after the new constitution had been introduced.

Pre-independence constitution 1965

The British retained responsibility for internal security and defence, and for foreign affairs. Apart from this the constitution was almost the same as that adopted by the 1966 independence constitution. In the 1966 constitution the Paramount Chief

was given the position of a constitutional monarch. The Parliament consists of the King, the Senate with its twenty-two chiefs and eleven members nominated by the King, and a National Assembly of sixty members elected by universal suffrage.

Political parties

The Basutoland Congress Party was founded in 1952 by Ntsu Mokhehle. He attended Fort Hare University College in South Africa for two years. He returned to Lesotho in 1942 and joined the first modern Basuto national movement – the League of the Common Man. In 1944 he went back to South Africa to complete his studies for a Masters degree and joined the Youth Wing of the African National Congress.

In the 1960 elections to district councils the BCP won 73 seats out of 162, and in the indirect elections to the National Council the party won 29 out of the 40 elected seats. This was to be the best performance by the party for afterwards internal disputes, ending in expulsions and resignations, seriously weakened the party to the point that the BCP obtained only 25 out of 60 seats at the National Council in 1965.

Basutoland National Party (BNP)

The National Party was founded by Chief Jonathan in 1959. Chief Jonathan was born in 1914 and was educated at the local mission school. He had a number of jobs in a minor administrative capacity until he was elected to the Leriba District Council, the National Council, and became one of four advisers to the Paramount Chief. In the 1965 election the BNP gained thirty-one of the National Council seats and Chief Jonathan became Prime Minister after winning a by-election to the National Council.

Speaking at the end of the independence conference Chief Jonathan recognised Lesotho's special position in relation to South Africa, and was adamant that Lesotho 'should not become a political football in an international power struggle. We will not interfere with South Africa and we do not expect South Africa to interfere with us but no less important is our determination to ensure that Basutoland is not used as a pawn in the

Chief Jonathan, Prime Minister of Lesotho

hands of those who have interests to secure other than the immediate interests of Basutoland. This is no parochialism; this is elementary commensense.'

King Motlotlehi Moshoeshoe II

The King is the eldest son of the late Paramount Chief, Simeon Seeise Griffith and is directly descended from the great Chief Moshesh. He was born in 1938 and educated at Roma College, Ampleforth College (Yorkshire) and Corpus Christi College, Oxford, and he was installed as Paramount Chief in 1960. The constitutional status of the King was probably in no small way decided by the action of the King in April 1966. The resolution of Parliament asking for an early independence was delayed when the King dismissed five senators because they had voted contrary to his wishes. It was later decided that the King had no power in law to revoke the appointment of a senator.

Political development in Botswana before 1966

Political progress was slow in Botswana as in the other two territories. Botswana has no Paramount Chief as do Swaziland and Lesotho, but instead there were eight separate chiefs who were allowed a fairly free hand in their own ethnic areas. Botswana rarely made world news and when it did it was because of an incident involving the extraordinary Tshekedi Khama, son of the great Khama.

Tshekedi became Regent of the Bamangwato at the age of twenty-one in 1926. The heir apparent was the four-year-old Seretse Khama, son of Khama's successor, Sekgoma. Tshekedi was an immensely strong character, scrupulously honest, very autocratic but prepared to accept change when it was in the interests of his people. A man of tremendous vitality, Tshekedi was never content to wait for decisions, he went looking for them, frequently exhausting officials who were often incapable of matching his energy or his intelligence. Like his father he was always prepared to go to London if the solutions to his problems were not readily available in Africa.

Problems: mining concessions

A first major clash with the administration was over mining concessions granted to the British South Africa Company by his father. Tshekedi had seen what mining had done for the Africans in South Africa and wanted to avoid a similar situation in his own country. He had the support of various ethnic groups to cancel his father's agreement but it required a long campaign before London agreed that he was entitled to cancel. He negotiated a new agreement, more favourable to the Bamangwato which included extra land as compensation. This land still came to the people even though the Company decided that the terms of the new agreement were not advantageous enough for them to start mining operations.

Hut burning incidents

In 1931 a dissident Bamangwato faction, the Ratshosa, were punished by Tshekedi and according to custom their huts were burned. The Ratshosa claimed and won damages, but Tshekedi appealed to the Privy Council in London and had the earlier decision reversed. This was a test case as to whether traditional law and custom were to prevail in the territory.

Whipping incident

Two years later in 1933, Tshekedi was at the centre of another political storm, this time over his sentencing of a white youth to be whipped for assaulting an African girl. This created a great stir and a Royal Naval detachment of 200 marines were rushed to Serowe to show that Tshekedi had overreached his responsibilities. In a very badly handled affair the administration suspended Tshekedi from the regency. Tshekedi obviously had great support among both black and white communities in Botswana and his people would not appoint a successor. Two weeks later, Tshekedi was reinstated.

Seretse's marriage

The last serious incident revolved around Seretse Khama's marriage to London-born Ruth Williams. Tshekedi took a characteristically strong line against the marriage as he felt it would permanently damage his people for the chief to be married to a white woman. The two men were on bad terms for many years and both were banned from living in the protectorate. Eventually in 1956 both men returned to Botswana as private citizens to work for political change in the country. Tshekedi died in June 1959, soon after the British Government had agreed to set up a Legislative Council.

Constitutional change in Botswana

In 1920 the European and African Advisory Councils were formed and began to meet once or twice a year. The establishment of a Joint Advisory Council in 1950 was a step in the right direction, although the legislative responsibility still lay with the High Commissioner.

The territory's first constitution of 1960, included a Legislative Council, an advisory

Tshekedi Khama, outstanding Regent of Botswana

Executive Council and an African Council. Internal self-government was granted in the 1965 constitution, the Executive Council was replaced by a Cabinet and Seretse Khama, as leader of the Bechuanaland Democratic Party, was appointed the country's first Prime Minister. The independence constitution which took effect from 30 September 1966 was prepared for the Republic of Botswana whose Head of State would be responsible for exercising the executive power of the republic. The legislative power is vested in the President and the National Assembly, and on occasions with the House of Chiefs. The National Assembly consists of a Speaker, thirty-one elected members and four specially appointed members.

Botswana political parties

The Bechuanaland Protectorate Federal Party was the first political party founded in Botswana in 1959. It was a conservative party supporting the power of the chiefs and opposing the call for a black majority in the administration as being against the best interests of a multi-racial society. It was never very influential and was overtaken by the Bechuanaland People's Party formed in December 1960 by K. T. Motsete. BPP was the first of the modern parties to be critical of the way the country was organised on ethnic lines and the dominant status of the chiefs. Motsete was born in about 1900 at Serowe and completed his education at London University where he gained four degrees. His party made spectacular progress and gained strength from contact with the South African Congress Alliance. But by June 1962 divisions occurred in the party and Philip Matante emerged as the most powerful figure in the BPP. In the 1965 election the BPP was opposed by the Bechuanaland Democratic Party.

Bechuanaland Democratic Party

Seretse Khama showed a shrewd political insight when he formed the BDP at the end of 1961. He gained support from the moderates in the country. They had become alarmed by the militant demands of the BPP. He was assured of support by the Bamangwato because of his royal background.

Sir Seretse Khama, President of Botswana

Since he was already a member of the Executive Council in 1962 his party assumed a powerful position before the elections. In the 1965 election the BDP won twenty-eight of the thirty-one seats and the BPP led by Matante won the remaining three seats.

Sir Seretse Khama

A son of the chief of the Bamangwato people, Seretse Khama became chief-designate at the age of four and his uncle Tshekedi Khama ruled as Regent. In the course of his extended education, he went to Lovedale College, Fort Hare University College, the University of Witwatersrand, Balliol College, Oxford, and the Middle Temple, London.

After his controversial marriage to his English wife, Ruth, in 1948, he returned from exile, surrendering all claims to the chieftaincy. He became secretary to the Bamangwato Council in 1959, and he founded the Bechuanaland Democratic Party. On independence he was elected the first President of Botswana.

Political developments since independence

The immediate post-independence period in the three countries has not been without incident. Botswana appears to be more stable than either Lesotho or Swaziland. Seretse Khama has maintained his position without much difficulty. Swaziland's experiment with a parliamentary form of government was brought to a halt when King Sobhuza repealed the constitution in 1972, and in Lesotho, Chief Jonathan suspended the constitution in 1970 after his defeat in the elections.

Botswana

1969 Election:

A third party fought the 1969 election. It was the Botswana National Front Party led by ex-chief Bathoen Goseitsiwe, and its main election platform was the demand for closer and more friendly relations with South Africa and white Rhodesia. It won three seats, one of the successful candidates defeating the Vice-President, Dr Quett Masire. Matante's party kept their three seats and the governing party, BDP, won twenty-one seats. Only 39 per cent of the electorate voted.

1974 Election:

At the 1974 election only 33 per cent of the electorate voted. At this election the President's party gained seats at the expense of both the opposition parties. However the fact that few people had voted seemed to show that there was no great enthusiasm for the Government, but no great desire for change through the opposition parties.

Seretse Khama's foreign policy has been restrained by Botswana's position relative to the Republic. He has maintained fairly distant relations with the Republic, emphasising the value of an integrated multi-racial society. Khama has always recognised that *sanctions* would inevitably produce harmful effects in Botswana but that has not prevented him putting into practice many of the UN decisions. Full diplomatic relations have yet to be set up with the Republic, but Khama insists that Botswana must not become a launching pad for attacks against her neighbours. He has been involved in conversations with the Republic's Prime Minister, Vorster, about the future of Zimbabwe and Namibia, together with other African Presidents.

Lesotho

Lesotho's development is typified by an internal struggle between the ruling party, the BNP led by Chief Jonathan, and the main opposition party led by Ntsu Mokhehle, the BCP.

1970 Election:

The election in January 1970 resulted in a defeat for Chief Jonathan and a substantial victory for the BCP (thirty-three seats for BCP – twenty-three seats for BNP). Before the final results were checked, Chief Jonathan declared a state of emergency, suspended the constitution and arrested and imprisoned Mokhehle. He was released in June 1971 and in July 1973 the state of emergency was lifted. Every indication was given that Lesotho was to be a one-party state. The possibility of a one-party state perhaps motivated the anti-government revolt organised by the BCP in 1974. Government

forces smashed the revolt but Mokhehle escaped to Zambia via Botswana. Retaliatory attacks were made against BCP villages and twenty-five people died. Chief Jonathan has always followed a policy of good neighbourliness towards South Africa, a factor which probably contributed to his defeat in the elections, but this relationship was weakened when South Africa released nine BCP refugees instead of returning them to Lesotho.

At a trial of BCP supporters in 1974, the Chief Justice accepted that BCP supporters had a real grievance in the banning of any political activity since 1970. He agreed that the police had misused their powers, and stated that the Government had ignored its function of the maintenance of law and order and protection of life and property.

In the meantime the country is governed by Chief Jonathan with the support of an interim National Assembly of nominated members corresponding to the membership of the earlier assembly. This assembly is expected to produce a new constitution which is likely to support the continuation of a one-party state in Lesotho.

Swaziland

1972 Election:

This provided three seats for the National Liberatory Congress Party led by Dr Zwane, formerly a leader of the Progressive Party. The ruling Mbokodvo National Movement Party won twenty-one seats. Later, in April 1973 King Sobhuza dissolved the Dlamini Cabinet. He repealed the independence constitution, banned political meetings and reverted to rule by royal decree. The Prime Minister, Ministers and state officials continued in office at his discretion. There was no doubt that the King had decided that parliamentary government on the Westminster pattern allowed too many dangerous activities against the interests of the Swazi nation.

Dr Zwane wrote in protest to the OAU and various heads of state. He was then detained under a sixty-day detention order. Dr Zwane has suffered three periods of detention since 1973. Colonel Maphevu Dlamini, the commander of the Swazi army, replaced Prime Minister Makhosini Dlamini who resigned for health reasons.

Summary of political development

Political development in all three states is complicated by relations with the Republic and by particular internal interests and conflicts. Before independence most of the new political parties were influenced by the opinions and policies of either the ANC or the PAC in the Republic. This was understandable when one remembers that the founders of these parties had gained their political education in South Africa. Since independence, conservative governments have gained control in all three countries, and the more militant approach of the ANC or the PAC has been silenced. Local politicians have become more involved in internal problems, such as the role of traditional authority in both Swaziland and Lesotho, the need to be less dependent economically on South Africa, and the desirability of a more radical approach to relations with South Africa. It is possible that in the long term the three states will call for improved living conditions for their people working in the Republic. It may be truer to say that the militant support for Black South Africa will come not from the former High Commission Territories, but from the states further north, who are not so closely linked with the South African economy.

Economic development

All three countries reflect to a greater or lesser extent a reliance on South Africa. Of the three, Swaziland is more likely to achieve economic independence. Both Botswana and Lesotho are more likely to follow the pattern of development as found in the Transkei.

Botswana

Botswana, whose population is increasing every year at a rate of more than $3\frac{1}{2}$ per cent, has severe problems in achieving economic independence of South Africa. The climate, with its small and irregular rainfall, makes farming very difficult. In the past, drought and harvest failure were checks on population growth but imports of food have allowed a population increase which the country has difficulty in supporting.

The cattle-rearing industry remains the main source of income but it will be overtaken in the next year or so by mining. There are over two million cattle and nearly half a million sheep in the country. They produced over 60 per cent of exports in 1974. The imports of food and manufacturing goods are paid for mainly by the earnings of migrant labourers working in South Africa. Nearly half of the able-bodied men of Botswana are working in this way.

The recent expansion in Botswana's economy is the result of mining of Botswana's new found minerals – diamonds, nickel and copper. The Orapa Diamond Mines, first developed in 1971, now produce more than three million carats of gem and industrial diamonds. This places Botswana among the world's top diamond producers. The mining of copper/nickel ore at Selebi-Pikwe, 160 kilometres south of Francistown turned a trade deficit (which occurs when more goods are imported into a country than are exported from that country) into a surplus in 1974. Eighteen billion tonnes of nickel and seventeen billion tonnes of copper ore were produced and exported to the United States.

This spectacular expansion has meant that the average income per person in Botswana has doubled in less than five years. This improvement has not made a great difference to the rural areas, and it is one of the Government's top priorities to see that these areas receive a reasonable proportion of the new income.

Lesotho

Lesotho's development is limited by a lack of good farmland (only 10 per cent of the country is suitable for farming). There are few prospects for mining and industry. Major obstacles to progress are poor roads and a fast rate of population growth. Two-thirds of the country's internal wealth is produced from agriculture which is mainly from subsistence farming. The main sources of export products are wool and mohair.

Lesotho is not self-supporting and imports food mainly from the Republic. The country pays for the imports through the earnings of migrant labourers in the Republic's mines, factories and farms. Earnings of Lesotho miners in 1974 amounted to £43 million and are likely to rise substantially in the next few years. Ninety-seven per cent of Lesotho's imports come from South Africa, and 53 per cent of her exports reach the Republic, emphasising once again the strong dependence on South Africa. Limitation on migrant labour from outside the Republic could have a disastrous effect on Lesotho as over 40 per cent of adults work as migrant labourers.

Swaziland

Swaziland is more fortunate than either of her African neighbours. Her economy is much more diversified, but it must be emphasised that 90 per cent of the population is still engaged in subsistence farming and only 35 per cent are in paid employment of any sort.

Europeans continue to play an important part in the Swazi economy. European-owned farms are interspersed between African farms; South Africans tend to control the wholesale and retail trade, and mining and manufacturing concerns have been administered by European and South African-based companies.

The asbestos mine at Havelock, which has recently taken second place in the economy after the iron-ore mine at Ngwenya, and the coal field at Mpaka, is a good example of Swaziland's rich mineral resources. Swaziland has also a developed timber industry, a developing tourist industry and large potential as a producer of hydro-electric power. An outline of Swaziland's domestic production indicates how diverse her economy is, for agriculture and forestry account for 29 per cent of domestic production, mining for 20 per cent and the manufacturing industries for 13 per cent.

The fact that the United Kingdom and Japan come before South Africa as the main destinations for exports suggests that Swaziland is less dependent on South Africa than either Lesotho or Botswana. Swaziland relies less on migrant labourers since only a quarter of her male population seeks employment in the Republic

Summary of Chapter 15

Political and economic stagnation before 1945
Political: indirect or parallel rule.
Economic: source of cheap labour for South Africa.
   No incorporation in the Republic despite

repeated attempts by South Africa.

Swaziland independence
   1960 First political party – Swaziland Progressive Party – John Nquku.
   1964 Royalist party – MNM – supported by King Sobhuza II – won all 27 seats in the Legislative Council.
   1967 Prince Makhosini Dlamini – first Prime Minister.
   1973 Sobhuza dissolved cabinet – rule by royal decree.

Lesotho independence
   1952 Basutoland Congress Party – Ntsu Mokhehle.
   1959 Basutoland National Party – Chief Jonathan.
   1965 Chief Jonathan – first Prime Minister.
   1970 Defeat for Government at polls – state of emergency – Chief Jonathan supported by nominated National Assembly.

Botswana independence
Tshekedi Khama: mining concessions – hut burning incident – whipping incident – Seretse Khama's marriage.
   1960 Bechuanaland People's Party – Motsete and later Matante.
   1961 Bechuanaland Democratic Party – Seretse Khama.
   1965 Electoral victory for BDP. Seretse Khama – first President.

Economic development
Swaziland: most diverse economy – rich minerals, developed forests, potential HEP producer, only $\frac{1}{4}$ of male population in Republic.
Botswana: closely bound up with Republic. $\frac{1}{2}$ of male population in Republic – cattle and sheep rearing – recent mining (diamonds, copper and nickel) – average income doubled in 5 years.
Lesotho: lack of good farmland – mainly subsistence farming; wool and mohair – main exports; $\frac{1}{2}$ of male population work in Republic; very reliant on South Africa.

Short questions on Chapter 15

1 What do you understand by 'parallel rule'?
2 Which two incidents affected relations between the protectorates and South Africa?

3 What are the names of the two traditional Swazi councils?

4 What changes did the 1950 Proclamation make in Swaziland?

5 What was the first Swazi political party, who formed it and when? What is the ruling Swazi political party?

6 When was the Basuto National Council formed, and what was its composition?

7 What changes took place in 1946 and 1949 in Lesotho?

8 What was the first political party in Lesotho, when was it formed and by whom?

9 By whom and when was the Basutoland National Party formed?

10 What was the result of the 1965 election in Lesotho?

11 List three incidents involving Tshekedi and the administration.

12 What was the result of the 1965 election in Botswana?

Longer questions on Chapter 15.

1 What attempts have been made to incorporate the ex-High Commission Territories in South Africa, and why have they failed?

2 Describe the constitutional changes towards independence in each of the three areas.

3 Describe the contribution of Tshekedi Khama to the development of Botswana.

4 Describe political developments and changes in each of the three states since independence.

5 To what extent can the three states be considered economically viable?

Notes to Chapter 15

1 Hailey, *The Republic of South Africa and the High Commission Territories*, Oxford University Press, 1963.

2 *ibid.*

16 Namibia (South-West Africa)

Three main African groups live in Namibia:

(a) The Ovambo

These are a Bantu-speaking people living in the north of the country, occupying both sides of the border with Angola. They make up about one half of the total African population and are an agricultural people relying on the annual flooding of dried-up water courses called 'oshanas'. The farming is barely subsistence and famine has occurred frequently in times of prolonged drought. The Ovambo have not experienced invasion or conquest as have other groups. Until recently they were thought to be satisfied with existing conditions. From 1971 onwards, labour disputes have disturbed the peace and in 1972 a state of emergency was declared over the Ovambo area.

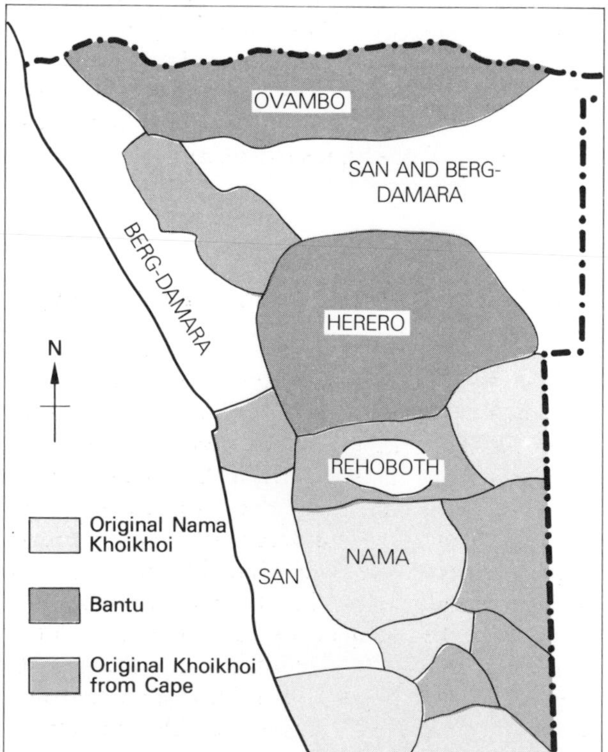

(b) The Herero

These are another Bantu-speaking people and they live in the central part of the country and have followed a pastoral way of life. They have always been in the forefront of the fight for independence, both against the Germans at the beginning of the present century and against the South Africans today.

(c) The Nama

Like the Herero, the Nama are cattle-keepers but they are nomadic Khoikhoi rather than Bantu. They have been the enemies of the Herero in the past when shortage of good grazing land and the expansion of the Boers from the Cape made conflict between the two groups inevitable. The Nama also resisted German rule and are closely connected with the present independence struggle.

There are other smaller non-white groups. The San live either in isolation in the desert areas or work on farms in the north-east on a seasonal basis. The Berg-Damara have lived for generations among the Nama and the Herero as servants. The Rehobothers are a people of mixed race who like the Coloureds in South Africa have been rejected by the Afrikaner community. Of the total population of 750,000 only 90,000 are white, which is only 12 per cent of the population; but they have access to 60 per cent of the land.

Fig. 37 Namibia: Ethnic areas 1800

German colonisation of Namibia 1884

The nineteenth century history of Namibia is largely a record of conflict between the Nama and the Herero. To begin with the Herero had the upper hand until the Nama were joined by Jonker Afrikaner, who had led a group of mixed blood people from the Orange River into Namibia. The joint forces defeated the Herero led by Chief Kamaherero. Revenge was not gained until 1864 when Kamaherero defeated the Nama and Jonker's son, Jan Jonker. These were not entirely African affairs. European traders and missionaries were on the scene from 1821, and more permanently from 1840 when the Rhenish Mission Society took over from the London Missionary Society. They frequently intervened on one side or the other in those disputes.

Complaints about the instability of the area were sent by German missionaries to the King of Prussia in 1868. Requests for protection were also sent to the administration at the Cape. Kamaherero also asked the Cape for protection and Special Commissioner Palgrave spent four years producing a document which would have placed the Herero under Cape control. The Nama would have nothing to do with Palgrave's mission and the Commissioner advised that Namaland should be invaded. It was the possible cost of invading Namaland which persuaded the Cape not to extend its influence there. The mission plea for German protection although not immediately successful eventually produced a positive response. The area was made a German colony in 1884.

Bismarck, the German Chancellor, sent an Imperial Commissioner, Goring, to organise the new colony. His first job was to persuade the Africans to accept German 'protection'. Kamaherero signed an agreement first of all and then tried to reject it in 1888, threatening to kill the German party if they remained in Namibia. The Germans returned in 1889 with an increased military force. The Nama had refused to sign any agreement but suspected that the Herero had agreed to fight for the Germans against the Nama. The Germans attacked Hendrik Witbooi, the Nama leader, in April 1893 and a peace treaty was not concluded until September 1894. Although able to retain his weapons and much of his power, Witbooi had become an ally of the Germans, and five times in the next ten years the Nama fought with the Germans against various other African groups.

Kamaherero died in 1890 and was succeeded by his son Samuel Maherero, who also became an ally of the Germans. This did not make him very popular with his people. Therefore before 1897 there was an uneasy alliance between the Germans and the two major African leaders. White settlement was being encouraged by the Germans but suitable land was not readily available. The Herero were opposed to selling land until 1897 when a great outbreak of rinderpest (cattle plague) killed off most of their cattle. Maherero began to sell land to farmers at a reckless rate, and the number of German settlers grew spectacularly from 310 in 1891 to 3,000 in 1903. With this increase in white settlement there was a growth of conflict between the races. The Africans realised that almost without noticing, they had lost much of their land, their cattle had died and their chiefs had lost a great deal of independence. There were a number of isolated uprisings among the Nama and the Herero in the last years of the nineteenth century. These were put down by the Germans with the help of Maherero and Witbooi, but in January 1904, the first serious rising against the Germans took place.

The Herero Rising January 1904

The Herero were united in their rising against the Germans but it cannot be said that the revolt was well-organised. The Germans were aware of the uprising almost as soon as it had begun and were able to concentrate their forces in their garrisons. About one hundred settlers and traders were less fortunate and were killed by the Herero. The Herero did not try to storm the garrisons and neither were the German forces strong enough to defeat the Herero immediately, and it was not until June 1904 and the arrival of reinforcements from Germany that the Africans were defeated. Over 15,000 German troops were involved; 1,000 of them died but the new German strategy of enormous military strength was aimed at exterminating the Herero. General von Trotha devised a plan in which the Herero were to be encircled at Waterberg. As many as possible were to be killed, the remainder were to be forced into the desert, where they would eventually die. This tactic was put into operation at the two-day battle of Waterberg on 11 August. It was estimated that three-quarters of the Herero died in the short war, leaving only 16,000 survivors. Just before the start of the rising Samuel Maherero had sent an invitation to Hendrik Witbooi to join the revolt. The letter was given to a Rehoboth chief to deliver but the Germans and not the Nama leader were given the letter. Maherero wrote: 'Rather let us die together and not die as the result of ill-treatment, prison or all the other ways.' Witbooi sent a hundred soldiers to fight for the Germans at Waterberg. In almost all respects this very able, ambitious leader had compromised his own principles and thrown in his lot with the Germans. He had been converted to Christianity, he spoke German and had fought in German wars. In October 1904, he followed the Herero's example and possibly as a means of atonement he led a rising against the Germans.

The Nama Rising 1904–07

Unlike the Herero Rising there was a religious element in the Nama Rising of 1904. The 'Prophet' Sturman arrived in Namaqualand from the Cape a few months before the outbreak of the war. The Nama had taken part in the Independency movement of the Ethiopian Church which had separated itself from the missions and government influence in the 1880s. Witbooi probably used the prophet to bind people to him as the political and religious leader of the Nama people. The prophet offered the hope of victory but he did not cause the rising. He only helped to create the possibility of such a rising. Witbooi's move against the Germans was dictated more by the likelihood of the Germans disarming his people.

He had about 1,500 men fighting for him but was no more successful than the Herero in dislodging the Germans from their garrisons. Witbooi's capital and cattle were captured and the Nama were forced to use guerilla tactics for the next three years. Witbooi had realised too late what German control meant: 'Peace means my death and the death of my nation, for I know that there is no refuge for me under you.'[1] He was mortally wounded in October 1905 and the fight was carried on by Simon Cooper and Jakob Morenga. Morenga gave himself up to the British, was released a year later and had a price of 20,000 marks put on his head by the Germans. In September 1907 he was shot by the British police on the Cape border. The rising was virtually over at that point but it was not until early 1909 that Cooper agreed to remain in Botswana rather than stay in Namibia.

After the Risings

Namibia became completely dominated by the Germans. The Herero and Nama were barred from owning land or cattle. Everyone over the age of eight had to carry a pass. Traditional forms of authority such as chiefdoms were banned and the 25,000 Herero and Nama survivors were forced into labouring jobs mostly on European farms. In 1914 there were only 200 men from the two communities who were not in paid employment. This shattering change in circumstances has not been forgotten and the loss of land, cattle and personal dignity are all contributary factors to a fierce nationalism which has developed during the twentieth century. Before the First World War, the European population in Namibia had grown from 4,600 in 1905 to 15,000 in 1913.

Defeat of the Germans

The Germans were easily defeated in 1915, as part of the First World War, by a South African army 46,000 strong, and led by General Botha. The main German Army surrendered to Botha at Tsumeb in the north. The South Africans had not come to help the local people but the Herero and Nama felt that they ought to benefit from the liberation of Namibia from German rule. They were to be bitterly disappointed. The British and South Africans were only concerned with showing the rest of the world how bad German rule had been. They had no intention of supporting the African cause.

Granting of the Mandate to South Africa, December 1920

Writing about Mandates General Smuts said: 'The mandatory state should look upon its position as a great trust and honour, not as an office of profit or a position of private advantage for it or its nationals.' Namibia was classed as a 'C' type Mandate which could be administered as an integral portion of the mandatory power subject to safeguards in the interests of the native population. South Africa was expected to make annual reports on the territory to a Permanent Mandates Commission set up by the League of Nations. To the more cynical observers at the Versailles Conference which ended the First World War, the way in which a territory became a Mandate was little more than a carefully disguised attempt at further annexation.

Chief Hosea Kutako, leader of the Herero

The years of the Mandate 1920–45

The introduction of South African rule made life even more difficult for the Namibian people despite the words of Article 22 of the League of Nations Convenant in which 'the well-being and development of the people' were given emphasis. Instead of the land being returned to the African, the Herero and Nama saw more and more land being given to Afrikaners from the Union. The white population had risen to 28,000 by 1928, double the 1915 figure, despite the loss of 6,000 Germans through repatriation. The Herero were given 800,000 hectares of land in the sandveld on the margins of the Kalahari Desert. Chief Hosea Kutako's reaction to the new Reserve was: 'In fact it . is a desert where no human being ever lived before. It is not healthy for people or cattle. Only one farm can depend on borehole water. It is no use for a whole nation.'[2]

The South Africans have maintained the German division of the country. In simple terms the northern section, which is less than a third of the country contains most of the African Reserves and accommodates about half the African population. In the remaining two-thirds is the Police Zone or the White Areas where the richest farming and mineral areas are located. In the Police Zone are separated Reserve areas for the Damara, Herero and Nama groups. The groups of migrant labour that work in the various white enterprises live in these areas.

Repressive measures

Soon after the South Africans took over Namibia there was a request from a young Ovambo chief, Manduma. He claimed that he was being attacked by the Portuguese from across the Angolan border. The South African commander was not sympathetic. When further incidents took place on the border, a force was sent north to punish Manduma and he and many of his followers were killed.

The second incident – the Bondelswarts Bombing – is comparable to the Sharpeville Shooting in 1960. The Bondelswarts had a history of resistance to European rule from the 1896 Witbooi war to the 1904 rising. South African rule had made life difficult. They had not recovered their land after the German withdrawal and there were many irritating taxes and regulations which had to be endured. Non-payment of taxes became more frequent by the beginning of 1922 and fines and terms of imprisonment were imposed. At this moment a certain Abraham Morris, who had led the Bondels in the 1904 war, returned from South Africa. Through a series of mistakes by minor officials, Morris became unwittingly the centre of an incident which ended with the Administrator attacking the Bondelswart community with sixteen bombs and killing one hundred men, women and children in the process.

Despite these incidents and other discriminating laws and regulations the Mandates Commission seemed powerless to intervene in Namibian affairs and when the League of Nations collapsed at the beginning of the Second World War the question arose: who was now responsible for the old mandated territories?

Namibia after the Second World War

Three themes dominate the post-1945 history of Namibia. They are:

a) The legal and international status of the country with regard to the United Nations (UN).
b) The gradual introduction of apartheid policies in Namibia by South Africa.
c) The development of political and militant activity among African nationalists in the country.

Namibia and the United Nations

The UN, formed in 1945, agreed that the old mandated territories should become Trust Territories of the UN. South Africa demanded the annexation of Namibia to the Union. She was the only mandate power not to recognise the UN's responsibility for the mandated areas. Smuts was able to block a General Assembly resolution that Namibia should be placed under **trusteeship**. Smuts's successor, Dr Malan, refused to continue to submit annual reports on the area. The South African opinions on Namibia were opposed for the first time by Namibian representatives, the Rev Michael Scott and Mburumbi Kerina at the Fourth (Trusteeship) Committee.

The International Court of Justice, another organisation set up by the UN, gave the first of a number of rulings on the legal position of Namibia. It decided in 1950 that South Africa still had international responsibility for the area and that annual reports should be submitted. Surprisingly, the Court decided that South Africa had no legal obligation to place Namibia under trusteeship.

Throughout the 1950s the UN was kept in touch with conditions in Namibia by a whole series of petitioners. For many years the Rev Scott had been the solitary representative for an isolated people but in the late 1950s he was joined by Hans Boukes, the Rehoboth leader, Oliver Tambo, the eminent leader of the South African ANC, and Jariretundu Kozonguizi, chosen by the Herero to be a spokesman, alongside Scott.

In 1962 Ethiopia and Liberia brought a resolution to the International Court on the Namibian issue but the Court could only decide that the two countries were not competent to bring the case before the court. A later decision in 1966 caused considerable surprise and disappointment when the Court decided that it had no power to decide whether South Africa was guilty of changing the conditions of the Mandate without the consent of the UN. This decision was greeted with satisfaction by the South Africans, but in October 1966 the General Assembly withdrew South Africa's right to administer the territory. A Council of Namibia was set up to administer the area but it has no real power and no real support from any of the major world powers. The final judgement of the International Court was made in 1971. It states that South Africa should withdraw from Namibia and members of the UN should refrain from any action which implies recognition of the South African administration.

With all its resolutions and judgements the UN has failed to force South Africa's withdrawal from Namibia, and perhaps the fault for this lies with the major powers who have not been prepared to risk a confrontation with South Africa on this issue. Opinion in Namibia had realised that the UN would be incapable of imposing its resolutions and this allowed South Africa time to go ahead with the policies of apartheid in the area and to arrange for the inclusion of the territory as a fifth province of the Union.

South African policies in Namibia

The South African Government has steadily extended its policies of separate development into Namibia. As in South Africa, apartheid relies on separating non-whites from whites on the basis of land, labour, education and political power. The South Africans had during the mandate era imposed a land division in which the whites, with 12 per cent of the population, were left with 60 per cent of the land, the rest being given to the Africans as Reserve areas. A dangerous situation developed at Windhoek in 1958 when 30,000 Africans were required to move from the 'Old Location' of the town to Katutura, a town 8 kilometres away which had nothing to recommend it. The UN were informed of the re-settlement by Chief Hosea Kutako, Chief Samuel Witbooi and Sam Nujoma, later President of the South-West Africa People's Organisation (SWAPO). A boycott of municipal services was organised but this did not stop the relocations going ahead. One crowd of demonstrators was fired on by the police, resulting in the deaths of eleven and the wounding of forty-four people.

Employment in Namibia is organised in much the same way as in the Republic. Africans provide a source of cheap labour which is of a short-term

Sam Nujoma, President of SWAPO

migrant form. They are never allowed to stay permanently in 'white areas'. Job discrimination in favour of the whites is widespread and reinforced by law. Unskilled or semi-skilled work is usually the most that Africans can expect. Although trades unions are not illegal, strike action is forbidden. Forbidden or not, about 20,000 African workers withdrew their labour in December 1971 as a protest against the contract labour system. This prevents workers from choosing and changing their jobs freely. The protest only gained small benefits for the workers but it did demonstrate that resistance to the South African presence is not limited to guerilla activity or petitioning at the UN.

An inferior educational service prevents any appreciable advance by Africans on a wide front. Most Africans do not move beyond the lower primary levels and although there are usually three times as many African students in school, four times as much money is spent on white students.

The basis of the modern apartheid system has been the formation of Bantustans in the Reserve areas where Africans have nominal self-government, and the setting up of these Bantustans on ethnic lines has been established in Namibia as well as South Africa. In 1968 the South African

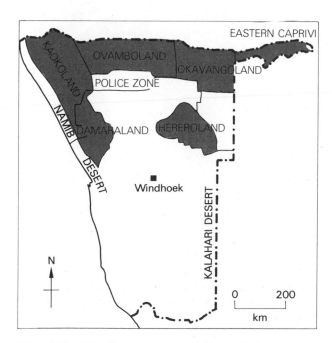

Fig. 38 Namibia: Bantustans proposed by 1968 Act

Parliament, through the Development of Native Nations in South-West Africa Act, provided for the creation of six Bantustans – Ovamboland, Damaraland, Hereroland, Kaokoland, Okavangoland and Eastern Caprivi. Ovamboland held elections on 1 August 1973 to fill fifty-six seats, thirty-six of which were already appointed and only six were contested. A successful boycott of the election was organised and only 1.6 per cent of the 50,000 electors voted.

The enforcement of these policies is achieved by the same legal machinery as in the Republic. The Suppression of Communism Act, the Immorality Act, Terrorism Act, curfew arrangements and the Pass Laws are all meant to suppress any opposition to government policy. The effect of these laws, the dismemberment of the country, the limited opportunities in education and employment and the reduction of political power have all contributed to a growth in locally organised nationalist groups. They are intent on gaining independence and preventing the inclusion of Namibia in the Republic.

African resistance movements

Chief Hosea Kutako of the Herero symbolises African reaction to European rule in the first half of the twentieth century. He was wounded in the Herero Rising of 1904. He was eventually asked to lead the Herero in Namibia. The real chief, Samuel

SWAPO guerillas

Maherero had had to flee to Botswana after the battle at Waterberg in 1904. It was Hosea Kutako who complained bitterly about the resettlement of the Hereros in the 1920s and who enlisted the support of the Rev Michael Scott to petition the UN on behalf of the Namibians. He died in 1970 and throughout his life had been an inspiration and a rallying point for his people.

Before Hosea Kutako died it was clear that support in the UN was not going to bring independence and that the South Africans were never going to withdraw as a result of peaceful petitioning. This realisation coincided with the formation in April 1959 of the Ovamboland Peoples Organisation by Sam Nujoma and Jacob Kahange. A year later, at the request of Kerina, the Namibian representative at the UN, the organisation became the South-West African Peoples Organisation (SWAPO) which is the movement officially recognised by the UN and the OAU. In 1971 the National Convention was set up and included a number of political groups such as SWAPO and SWANU (South-West African National Union). The difference between these two is partly one of emphasis and partly one of ethnic origin. SWANU has always emphasised the need for self-help and considers that SWAPO has put too much energy into petitioning at the UN.

The first armed clash between SWAPO and South African forces was in August 1960 and since then there have been periods of guerilla activity which has tied down thousands of South African troops. The guerilla groups face fearful odds against the better-armed South Africans but the accounts of the Treason Trial of thirty-seven Namibians in 1968 show a clear, undivided affirmation of faith and loyalty to the cause of independence. One of the founder members of SWAPO, Toiro Hermann Ja Toivo (now serving a twenty-year sentence on Robben Island), concluded in a statement to the court in Pretoria: 'Only when we are granted our independence will the struggle stop. Only when our human dignity is restored to us, as equals of the whites, will there be peace between us.'[3]

The Namibians have tried peaceful, legal methods of gaining independence. They have been forced to try more militant methods. It is still not clear what formula will eventually produce a South African withdrawal from Namibia.

Summary of Chapter 16

Main African groups in Namibia
a) *Ovambo:* Bantu – bordering Angola – half of African population in Namibia – subsistence farming – did not suffer conquest.
b) *Herero:* Bantu – central Namibia – led fight against Germans and South Africans.
c) *Nama:* Khoikhoi cattle-keepers – closely associated with freedom struggle – traditionally enemies of the Herero.

1884 German colonisation
Request for protection from the Rhenish Missions to King of Prussia (Germany).

Serious African resistance
Delayed until 1904:
1904 *Herero Rising:* Herero nearly exterminated – only 16,000 survivors.
1904–07 *Nama Rising:* struggled on as a guerilla campaign after early German successes. Both people barred from owning land or cattle by German authorities.

Developments during the Second World War
1915 Germans defeated by General Botha.
1920 South African Mandate Granted.
1922 Bondelswart Bombing.
League of Nations powerless to intervene.

After the Second World War
Relations with UN – Rev Michael Scott – failure to force South African withdrawal.
Introduction of apartheid policies.
Political and militant action of SWAPO and SWANU.

Short questions on Chapter 16

1 What are the three main African groups in Namibia?
2 When did the Germans colonise Namibia?
3 Who were the leaders of the Herero and Nama people at the end of the nineteenth century?
4 How many Herero survived the war?
5 What was the religious element of the Nama Rising of 1904?
6 What happened to the Herero and Nama after the risings?
7 What is the Police Zone?
8 What was the 'Bondelswart Bombing'?

9 What are the three themes to dominate
Namibia since World War II?
10 Give the dates and judgements of the three
decisions made by the International Court
which have concerned Namibia?
11 What was the 'Windhoek Incident' of 1958?
12 How many Bantustans are planned for
Namibia?
13 Which two people have represented Namibia
at the United Nations?
14 Who is Toivo Hermann Ja Toivo and where is
he now?

Longer questions on Chapter 16

1 Describe the circumstances in which Germany
colonised Namibia. (You will need to use
information from Chapter 8 as well as this
chapter.)
2 How did South Africa gain the Mandate over
Namibia and what changes have resulted?
3 Outline the different attempts made to gain
independence for Namibia.
4 Why has independence been so difficult to attain
in the case of Namibia?

Notes to Chapter 16

1 J. Iliffe, *Aspects of South African History*,
University of Dar-es-Salaam, p. 103.
2 Ruth First, *South-West Africa*, Penguin African
Library, 1963.
3 R. Vigne, *A Dwelling Place of Our Own*,
International Defence and Aid Fund, 1973, p. 30.

17 South Africa in the modern world

At the end of the First World War in 1918, South Africa had a good reputation among the Great Powers of the world. This was partly due to her close relationship with Britain in the Commonwealth, the speed with which South Africa had entered the war on the allies' side, and to the strong influence of Jan Smuts abroad. Smuts was treated abroad with greater respect as a soldier, statesman and philosopher than ever he was in South Africa. South Africa was considered responsible enough to be granted the Mandate over the ex-German territory of South-West Africa by the League of Nations, an international organisation formed after the war. It must be remembered that 1918 was still the era of the imperialist powers with most of what is now termed the 'developing world' still under the control of one European country or another.

When Dr Malan came to power in South Africa in 1948, circumstances had changed considerably. Smuts had been defeated at the 1948 election and in fact was to die only two years later. The British Labour Government had begun its de-colonising programme with its granting of independence to the Indian sub-continent. There was a growing feeling among Afrikaners in South Africa that the link with Britain ought really to be broken. A new international Body, the United Nations Organisation, had taken the place of the old League of Nations.

South African foreign policy

From 1948 onwards the policies of apartheid within South Africa have come under ever-increasing attack from a growing number of countries who have recently achieved independence. The South African Government and the vast majority of white South Africans think that the only policy is complete resistance to any radical change. Because of this inflexible attitude, South Africa's internal affairs have dictated both her foreign policy and the relationship of the rest of the world to the Republic. South Africa's foreign policy is based consequently on the following broad ideas:

a) Trying to defend South African internal policies to the rest of the world.
b) Guaranteeing the survival of the white minority in South Africa.
c) Identification with the West against a supposed communist threat to Southern Africa.
d) Improving her relations with African states.

Most of these ideas are inter-related but it is worthwhile looking at each one in turn in a little more detail.

Defence of South African policies

The administration of Malan and Strijdom made little attempt to defend South Africa's policies. They tended to isolate themselves or to criticise every other country with racial problems, for example the Americans and their negro population. Instead of trying to gain approval from other countries, the South Africans flaunted their own independence by taking over responsibility for South-West Africa, against the wishes of the UN.

Dr Verwoerd tried harder to defend South Africa's internal policies, and the Bantustan solution was meant to sound like an improvement on the old 'basskap' (boss-ship) way of thinking of the earlier Government. The benefits of developing separately were argued at great length at every level. The South African Government has maintained a very large staff operating overseas whose first job is to promote interest and sympathy for South Africa's policies. South African embassies have been and still are great sources of propaganda for the home country.

Survival for white South Africa

South Africa continually points out that white settlement in South Africa is 300 years old, that 90 per cent of white South Africans were born there, and know and recognise no other country as their mother country. The Government insists that to guarantee the continuance of what they call 'civilised settlement' the present apartheid policies have to be rigidly enforced and any threat to white control has to be suppressed. Internally South Africa has made anti-government activity both difficult and dangerous but the threat of rebels moving into South Africa from outside remains.

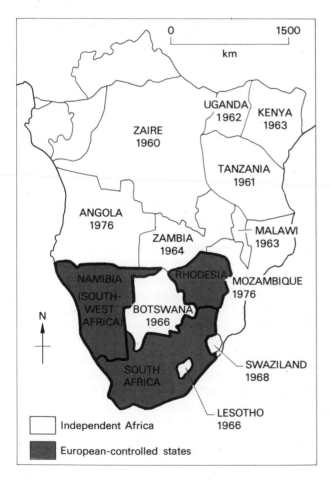

Fig. 39 Central and Southern Africa: Moves towards independence

South Africa has spent a great deal on defence and is now spending £1,000 million a year, and has a total armed force of 50,000 men with 27,000 Reservists and 75,000 Commandos in the para-military forces.

Relations with neighbouring countries are affected by South Africa's need to control the numbers of African nationalists entering South Africa. South Africa has a considerable hold over Lesotho and Swaziland in this respect. Both countries gain much of their revenue from their people working in the mines of the Republic. Sheltering nationalists could result in South Africa turning against Swaziland and Lesotho. Since the 1960s, South Africa has been assisting the Rhodesian Government in its fight against guerilla groups. Recently it has become clear that Mr Vorster would be more than happy if a political settlement could take place between the Rhodesian Government and African nationalists to replace the present uncertainty and instability. He is probably hopeful that he can maintain a good working relationship with a black government in Zimbabwe as he has done in the case of Mozambique. It remains to be seen how long South Africa will insist on Namibia remaining part of the Republic or whether the Government will be prepared to allow it independence. South Africa's intervention in the Angolan Civil War was the opposite of its conciliatory approach to Mozambique. It needs to be considered in the light of the third part of South African policy.

Recognition of a communist threat

For thirty years now, any opposition to government policies at home has been labelled 'communist inspired'. Many South Africans have been detained under the Suppression of Communism Act. In the same way South Africa has tended to identify threats to her survival as communist supported. In many respects the communist support for nationalist groups is a very real one. The training and provision of equipment for guerillas is being supplied from China, Russia, Cuba, Bulgaria and Algeria. For some observers this bears out what President Nyerere said in May 1969: 'Only the western world can help solve the problem of South Africa with the minimum of violence. We still appeal for that. If all this fails we shall be compelled

Julius Nyerere, President of Tanzania, a front-line president

Detente with Africa

Since 1967 South Africa has entered a new phase in her relations with neighbouring states. From being very much on the defensive, in the words of Vorster, the Prime Minister: 'South Africa was on the threshold of moving out into the world'. This involved the promise of economic and military aid to any African state prepared to ignore the political situation in South Africa. This policy aims at producing a series of states which will form a buffer between the Republic and the rest of the continent. The greatest single encouragement for this policy has so far come from Dr Banda's administration in Malawi. Thousands of Malawian immigrant labourers depend on South Africa for work. Her most accessible seaport is on the Mozambique coast and imported goods are cheaper from the Republic. All these factors persuaded Banda that his country cannot afford poor relations with the South Africans.

Following the withdrawal of the Portuguese from Mozambique and Angola, Mr Vorster stressed the desire of South Africa to live in peaceful co-existence with whatever government came into being and emphasised the need for political stability in the area. This early recognition of the Frelimo-based government did not conceal the warning that South Africa would deal very severely with any guerilla activity originating from Mozambique. In 1975 Vorster started consultations with President Kaunda in an attempt to provide the basis for a fresh series of talks on the future of Zimbabwe. The failure of this attempt does not disguise the fact that he was concerned with solving the problem as soon as possible, although South Africa's action in invading Angola may have risked this new attitude of trying to reach agreements as far as the rest of Africa is concerned.

to take arms from the East and we shall be accused of being communists.'[1] Nyerere refers to the inability of the British Government to bring down the Smith regime in Rhodesia, the refusal of Western Powers to finance the Tanzam Railway, the continued sale of arms to South Africa and the large scale financial investment in South Africa which makes the overthrow of the present Government through Western support, almost unthinkable. When the Chinese took on the building of the railway they brought with them the idea, 'Finish the railway in five years; finish the guerilla war in twenty.' The railway is now finished. Western governments have undoubtedly been embarrassed by South Africa's insistence that she is the last barrier to a communist takeover in Southern Africa and that as a defender of 'western civilisation' she deserves to have western support. In the Angolan civil war of 1976 it has been abundantly clear thàt western countries have not felt inclined to intervene while at the same time criticising the Russian and Cuban support of the victorious MPLA side.

South Africa and the United Nations

Despite efforts to gain approval from the rest of the world, South Africa is becoming more and more isolated. The major areas of conflict between the Republic and most UN members are apartheid and the issue of South-West Africa. In the early years of

The Vorster-Kaunda meeting at Victoria Falls is an example of South African 'detente' policy

the UN, South Africa was bitterly attacked by Indian and Soviet delegates for its Indian policy. As more and more countries gained independence and membership of the UN, strong criticism of South Africa was heard more often in the General Assembly.

The Sharpeville shootings of 1960 persuaded the USA to vote against South African policies in the Security Council and Britain to vote against South Africa in the General Assembly. This was the first occasion that Britain had voted on what had been considered previously as an internal South African concern. Up until that point the UN had only passed condemnatory resolutions. From 1962 there have been repeated attempts to make economic and diplomatic sanctions compulsory against South Africa. In 1964, the Security Council, supported on this occasion by Britain and the USA, called for a ban on the sale of arms to South Africa, but over the years France and Italy have ignored the ban. Britain and the USA have sold military equipment to the Republic claiming that they could not be used against nationalist groups in South Africa.

South-West Africa has been a great source of conflict between South Africa and the rest of the world. The deliberations and decisions of the International Court of Justice have been outlined in the chapter on Namibia (South-West Africa). South Africa seemed to gain the greater benefit from the 1966 judgement. Despite the General Assembly's resolution ending the Mandate in 1966, South Africa continues to govern the area as an integral part of the Republic.

The Afro-Asian countries in the UN have been more successful in their bid to expel South Africa from the Specialised Agencies attached to the UN. Over the years South Africa has been forced to withdraw from the World Health Organisation (WHO), the International Labour Organisation (ILO) and the Food and Agricultural Organisation (FAO).

Despite the very great hostility of the Afro-Asian countries and even the somewhat weaker hostility of the Western Powers, South Africa remains a member of the UN. The South African Government considers the General Assembly perhaps its last world platform from which to defend and excuse its policies. Continued attacks at the UN have helped to increase white support for the Government's domestic policies.

South Africa and the West

The West's relations with South Africa seem to be dictated by economic and defence interests rather than by any great sympathy with her apartheid policies. The West has large economic investments in South Africa and is very reliant on South African minerals. British companies, for example, hold direct investments amounting to some £1,550 millions. In recent years there has been a significant build-up of Soviet naval power in the South Atlantic and the Indian Ocean, and South Africa has been able to use this Russian presence to her advantage. The North Atlantic Treaty Organisation (NATO), set up by the Western Allies after the Second World War against possible Soviet expansion in Europe and the North Atlantic areas, is having to look beyond its original area and is finding that South Africa could be an ally in a defensive arrangement in the South Atlantic. South

Simonstown, a naval dockyard. There was military collaboration between South Africa and Britain until 1975

Africa is continually emphasising her role as a defender of 'western civilisation'. Formal treaty agreements have not been made between South Africa and NATO, but the West is likely to be increasingly dependent on South Africa in defence arrangements. This could prevent the West from supporting compulsory resolutions in the UN against South Africa.

Indeed the Western countries have tended to suggest that South Africa is not a threat to international peace and security. They have resisted attempts at the UN to introduce compulsory sanctions on such things as arms sales. Because of the supposed importance of the Cape route to the West and her own obvious economic interest in South Africa, the West has blocked more positive resolutions at the UN to the point where action has been impossible by the world body. To many world observers the West appears to be more closely identified with the white South African Government than with the African nationalist movement. This in itself could be dangerous for both the West and South Africa since the obvious support for African nationalism will come from the

East. This could eventually destroy the present regime in South Africa and seriously affect Western interests in the country. By avoiding a confrontation with South Africa, the West may be encouraging international conflict in the area at a later date. The reluctance of the USA to get involved in the Angolan civil war must also be a signal to the South Africans that she cannot necessarily count on external support should a massive increase in internal guerilla activity occur.

South Africa and the Organisation of African Unity

The Organisation of African Unity (OAU), has not been successful in promoting a united front against South Africa. Many of the member states think understandably of their own national interest first and when this interest seems best served by co-existence with South Africa then there is unlikely to be any unified action. Countries close to South

Africa – Lesotho, Swaziland and Malawi – consider that they have no choice but to keep up relations with South Africa, whereas countries such as Zambia and Tanzania have allowed guerilla groups to use them as a base and have never disguised their contempt for the policies of white South Africa. However divided the OAU may be, Mr Vorster has found it worthwhile to try and improve relations with African leaders most closely concerned with Southern African affairs by discussion and consultation. It may well be that he is trying to provide a basis for a peaceful transfer of power in neighbouring white-controlled areas (Zimbabwe and Namibia) and thereby giving South Africa a breathing space in which to develop her Bantustan policies more fully. It is strange that South Africa is embarking on, for her, a liberal foreign policy whilst maintaining a repressive policy at home. It could be that 'liberalism' has arrived too late in the day to provide a sound basis for white South African security.

Summary of Chapter 17

Foreign policy
1 Self-justification of internal policies.
2 Ally of the West in opposition to communist threat.
3 Detente.

South Africa and the UN
Isolated within UN over (a) apartheid, (b) Namibia.
International Court of Justice decisions.
Withdrawal from WHO, ILO, FAO.

South Africa and the West
Defender of 'western civilisation' in South Atlantic.
Resolutions against South Africa in UN blocked by Western countries.
Continued supply of arms to South Africa.
Massive economic investment from the West in South Africa.

South Africa and the OAU
No united front against South Africa.
Detente aimed at providing breathing space for South Africa to develop Bantustan policies.

Short questions on Chapter 17

1 With what argument did Dr Verwoerd try to defend and excuse 'apartheid'?
2 How else does South Africa defend the policies that she follows at home?
3 Describe the South African defence commitment.
4 What is Mr Vorster's attitude to white Rhodesia?
5 Which countries have supplied African nationalists with military equipment and training?
6 Which country financed the building of the Tanzam Railway?
7 How have Western countries failed to satisfy African expectations?
8 Which African country has opened up diplomatic relations with South Africa?
9 Which sanctions have been proposed against South Africa in the UN?
10 Why do you think South Africa remains a member of the UN?
11 Why does the West appear to sympathise with white rather than black South Africa?
12 Why has it been difficult to produce a united OAU policy for South Africa?

Longer questions on Chapter 17

1 Describe South Africa's attitude to her neighbours since 1967 and assess how successful the new policy has been.
2 What has been the policy of nationalist movements in Southern Africa since 1960?
3 'The solution to the problem of South Africa lies largely outside the African continent.' In what ways can this statement be justified?

Notes to Chapter 17
1 *Guardian*, July 18, 1969.

Major events in Modern South African History

1779 First Kaffir War	
1780 Eastern Frontier of the Cape at Fish River	1834 Freedom for slaves
	Sixth Kaffir War
	1835 Great Trek begins
	1836 Vegkop
1789 ⎫	
⎬ Second Kaffir War	1838 Death of Piet Retief
1793 ⎭	Blood River
1795 Revolts at Graaf-Reinet and Swellendam	1846 Seventh Kaffir War
First British occupation	
	1848 British Kaffraria
1799 ⎫	1850 Eighth Kaffir War begins
⎬ Third Kaffir War	
1803 ⎭ Batavian Administration	1852 Sand River Convention
	1853 Eighth Kaffir War ends
1806 Second British occupation	1854 Bloemfontein Convention
	Sir George Grey – Governor
1811 ⎫	
⎬ Fourth Kaffir War	
1812 ⎭	1865 Kaffraria annexed to Cape
	Treaty of Thaba Bosiu
1815 Slachter's Nek	
	1870 Death of Moshesh
1819 Fifth Kaffir War	
1820 5 000 Albany Settlers	1877 Transvaal annexed
	1879 Zulu victory at Isandhlwana
	1880 War of the Guns
	First Anglo-Boer War begins
1828 Death of Shaka	1881 Majuba Hill
50th Ordinance	Pretoria Convention – war ends

1884	Basutoland Protectorate		
	German colonisation of Namibia (South-West Africa)		
1885	Gold on the Rand	1933	Fusion Ministry
	Bechuanaland Protectorate		
		1936	Native Representation Act
		1938	Fusion Ministry ends
			Smuts becomes Prime Minister
1895	Jameson Raid		
1899	Anglo-Boer War begins		
1902	Peace of Vereeniging		
	Swaziland Protectorate	1948	Malan Government
1904	Herero Rising		
	Nama Rising begins		
1906	Bambata Rising	1952	Defiance Campaign
1907	Nama Rising collapses	1953	Bantu Education Act
1908	National Convention	1954	Strijdom Government
1910	Act of Union – South Africa independent of Britain	1958	Voerwoerd Government
	Botha Ministry	1959	Bantu Self-Government Act
1912	South African Native Congress	1960	Sharpeville
	Hertzog forms Nationalist Party		ANC and PAC banned
1913	Land Act	1961	South Africa leaves Commonwealth
		1963	Transkei becomes the first Bantustan
1919	Smuts Ministry		
	ICU Kadalie	1966	Vorster Government
1920	Namibia (South-West Africa) – granting of mandate to South Africa		Lesotho and Botswana independent
		1968	Swaziland independent
			Matanzima Chief Minister of the Transkei
1924	Pact Ministry		
	Hertzog Prime Minister		
1926	Colour Bar Act	1976	Transkei 'independent'

Bibliography

Books

ANENE, J. & BROWN, G., (eds.), *Africa in the Nineteenth and Twentieth Centuries*, Nelson, 1967

BARBARY, J., *The Boer War*, Victor Gollancz, 1971

BENSON, M., *Albert Luthuli: A Biography*, Oxford University Press, 1963

BENSON, M., *The Struggle for a Birthright*, Penguin, 1966

BORER, M. C., *Short History of the Peoples of Africa*, Museum Press, 1963

BRYANT, A. T., *History of the Zulu*, C. Stuick, 1964

BUNTING, B., *The Rise of the South African Reich*, Penguin, 1964

CARTER, KARLS & STULTZ, *South Africa's Transkei: The Politics of Domestic Colonialism*, Heinemann, 1967

CLINTON, D. K., *South African Melting Pot*, Longmans, 1937

DE KIEWET, *A History of South Africa*, Oxford University Press, 1941

DE KOCK, M. H., *The Economic Development of South Africa*, P. S. King, 1936

DENOON, D., *South Africa since 1800*, Longman, 1972

FAGE, B., *Southern Africa*, Thames & Hudson, 1965

FIRST, R., *South-West Africa*, Penguin African Library, 1963

GLUCKMAN, M., 'The Zulu Kingdom' in *African Political Systems*, Fortes, M. & Evans-Pritchard, E., (eds.), Oxford University Press, 1940

HALPERN, J., *South Africa's Hostages*, Penguin African Library, 1965

LORD HAILEY, *The Republic of South Africa and the High Commission Territories*, Oxford University Press, 1965

HOFMEYR, J. H., *South Africa*, 2nd edn., Ernest Benn, 1952

HORWITZ-WEIDENFELD, R., *The Political Economy of South Africa*, Nicolson, 1967

LEGUM, C. & M., *South Africa: Crisis for the West*, Pall Mall Pres, 1964

LUTHULI, A., *Let My People Go*, Fontana, 1966

MACMILLAN, W. M., *Bantu, Boer and Briton*, Oxford University Press, 1964

MANDELA, N., *No Easy Walk to Freedom*, Heinemann, 1965

MARQUARD, LEO, *The Story of South Africa*, Faber, 1963

MORRIS, D. R., *The Washing of the Spears*, Jonathan Cape Ltd., 1972

OLIVER, R. & FAGE, J. D., *A Short History of Africa*, Penguin, 1962

OMER-COOPER, J., *The Zulu Aftermath*, Longmans, 1966

PERHAM, M., *African Apprenticeship*, Faber, 1974

POLLOCK, N. C. & AGNEW, S., *An Historical Geography of South Africa*, Longmans, 1963

RANGER, T. O., *Aspects of Central African History*, Heinemann, 1968

ROBINS, E., *White Queen in Africa*, Robert Hale Ltd., 1967

SHEPHERD, R., *Lovedale 1841–1941*, Lovedale Press

TINDALL, P. E. N., *History of Central Africa*, Longmans, 1969

WALKER, E. A., *A History of Southern Africa*, Longmans, 1965

WILSON, M. & THOMPSON, L., *Oxford History of South Africa, Vol. 1, South Africa to 1870*, Oxford University Press, 1969

Botswana, B.I.S., 1966

Lesotho, B.I.S., 1966

Swaziland, B.I.S., 1966

Articles

Africa Digest, 1950–1971

AMERY, L. S., 'The South African War', London *Times*, 11 & 12 October 1949

KUPER, H., 'The Indians of South Africa', *The Listener*, 30 August 1956

LEWIN, J., 'White South Africans', *The Listener*, 8 July 1965

LISTOWEL, J., 'Transkei: A State Apart', *The Listener*, 8 July 1965

MINTY, A., 'Apartheid – Threat to Peace', Anti-Apartheid Movement, London, 1975

MOROKA, DR J. S., 'Prisoner's Profile', *British Weekly*, 18 September 1952

OMER-COOPER, J. D., 'Shaka and the Rise of the Zulu', *Tarikh*, **1**, no. 1, Longman, 1965

OMER-COOPER, J. D., 'Moshesh and the Creation of the Basuto Nation, *Tarikh*, **1**, no. 1, Longman, 1965

PATTERSON, S., 'A Tragic Problem in South Africa', *The Listener*, 23 October 1952

SEGAL, R. M., 'South Africa's Coloureds: Disinheritance by Erosion', *Times Educational Supplement*, 31 May 1957

SMITH, N. J., 'South-West Africa', *Weekly News*, 8 January 1965

South Africa Year Books, 1906, 1928, 1941

'The Case of Nelson Langer', *New Statesman*, 16 November 1957

UNITED NATIONS, 'A Trust Betrayed – Namibia', 1974

UNITED NATIONS, 'Decolonisation', Vol. 1, no. 3, Namibia, December 1974

UNITED NATIONS YOUTH & STUDENTS ASSOCIATION, 'The Namibia File, 1974

VIGNE, R. A., 'A Dwelling Place of our Own', International Defence & Aid Fund, 1973

Glossary

The words explained in this glossary are in bold type the first time they appear in the text.

cultures
Ways of living, differences of which can be seen in language, religion, agriculture, settlement and government.

archaeological sites
Places of interest in the study of Early Man; often they are concerned with early settlement patterns and burial grounds.

radio-carbon methods
A method of putting an age to dead plant and animal matter by measuring the amount of carbon fourteen, a radio-active form of carbon, in the dead materials found on archaeological sites.

monopolies
The control by a single person or company of the trade in a particular article.

freemen-settlers
Dutch settlers who were freed from working for the Company and allowed to farm as freemen.

burgher militia
The freemen farmers organised their own defence by enrolling men between sixteen and sixty in armed groups.

puritanical
Being very strict in all matters of religion and behaviour.

dividend
Money paid as part of the profit of the company to people owning shares in that company.

share
A sum of money which forms part of the working capital (money) of a company. The owner of the share is entitled to share in the profits made by that company.

liberty
The enjoyment of certain freedoms such as speech, worship, movement, and the right to vote.

equality
Being on equal terms; often related to an equality of opportunity in education, housing, and employment.

fraternity
Recognition of the brotherhood of man.

Revolutionaries
People attempting to make a great change in the political government of a country. Usually revolution involves the use of violent methods.

upper class
Members of a society who are born of rich and privileged parents. Usually associated with British society.

middle class
The middle band of society (in this case British) made up of professional (doctors, teachers, managers etc.) and office workers.

non-conformists
People who do not agree with widely accepted views and practices of the time. One group of religious non-conformists, the Methodist Church, has become one of the largest Protestant groups of the Christian Church.

evangelical reformers
People who led a religious revival in the Church of England and assisted the movement for social reform in nineteenth century Britain.

aristocratic
Belonging to the privileged, noble class which has been or still is the ruling class.

municipal
Concerned with the local government of a town, often with an elected town council.

apprenticeship
A four year period after the abolition of slavery during which slaves stayed with their previous owners. It was an attempt to prevent the complete breakdown of the farming system after abolition.

contract
An agreement made between people for the supply of goods or labour.

tariff
A customs duty or tax which is paid on goods moving from one country to another.

non-sectarian
Not belonging to one particular religious sect or body.

squatting
Africans living on White property in return for a share of the produce they grow.

Mandate
The power given to a country to govern a people on behalf of an international organisation, i.e. South Africa was given the power to govern South-West Africa (Namibia) on behalf of the League of Nations.

referendum
The making of a decision on a single question by the direct vote of all the voters.

trusteeship
A United Nations arrangement to encourage gradual movement towards independence for previously mandated territories.

Index